FRENCH

A Self-Teaching Guide

Dr. Suzanne Abitbol Hershfield

A Wiley Press Book
JOHN WILEY & SONS, INC.
New York • Chichester • Brisbane • Toronto • Singapore

Publisher: Stephen Kippur
Editor: Susan Gies
Managing Editor: Katherine S. Bolster
Production Service: G&H/SOHO, Ltd.

Library of Congress Cataloging-in-Publication Data

Hershfield, Suzanne Abitbol.
French, a self-teaching guide.

1. French language—Text-books for foreign speakers—English. 2. French language—Self-instruction. 3. French language—Grammar—1950— . I. Title.
PC2129.E5H47 1986 448.2′421 85-32293
ISBN 0-471-83794-6

Printed in the United States of America

20 19 18 17 16 15 14 13 12 11

To My Mother's Memory, S. D. A.

Acknowledgments

Two unique individuals, my agents Michael Larsen and Elizabeth Pomada, have been the guiding light for this book; their unlimited counsel, support, and encouragement will always be remembered. Special accolades go to my fourteen-year-old daughter, Elizabeth, whose help allowed me to submit this book on time. I also wish to thank my daughter Deborah and my son David for their love and support. Special terms of gratitude are in order for the Stark family and Mary Neel, for their friendship and understanding. I also wish to thank my editor, Elizabeth Perry of John Wiley and Sons, for her kindness and encouragement.

S.A.H.

Contents

Preface

French: A Self-Teaching Guide is a simplified and practical beginner's course for anyone who would like to learn French. It is aimed in particular at self-learners, students in adult education courses, and those in a classroom setting of first-year college French.

The book is organized to teach the essentials of the French language in fifteen lessons. Each lesson introduces you to a useful list of words that are transformed into practical expressions, repeated in a French dialog that is then translated into English, and finally practiced in a series of exercises. Material is presented in a clear and interesting manner, inviting you to teach and test yourself every step of the way. Your interest is further reinforced with cultural notes and current information on French trends.

French: A Self-Teaching Guide aims to teach reading, writing, and speaking with an equal emphasis on all three skills. Each of the book's fifteen lessons contains several "grammar boxes" designed to instruct you in the basics of French grammar and usage. The exercises within each lesson provide an opportunity for you to practice and test yourself on the concepts you have learned. There are answers for each exercise on the designated pages of the book. In addition to the lesson exercises, you can evaluate your newly acquired skills by taking the three review tests in this book, one for every five lessons. Check yourself against the answers that are provided immediately following the review questions.

To make the best use of this book, you should follow these steps:

1. At the beginning of each lesson, review the rules on pronunciation and then read each word aloud from the vocabulary list for that particular lesson.

2. Take your time in learning every part of a lesson before moving on to the next. Be sure to test yourself with each exercise; your results are a way of measuring your success in acquiring all the skills you need to learn French.

3. When testing yourself, allow yourself no more than two errors per exercise. If there are more, stay with the lesson until it's mastered.

4. Do your exercises with the vocabulary provided in the book. Do not rush to a French-English dictionary; this will not be helpful until you cover the fourteenth or fifteenth lesson.

5. The review tests are a way of making sure you have mastered each group of five lessons before tackling the next. Be sure to review thoroughly before you take each test.

6. Listen to French records, French movies, or, if you have a short-wave radio, French radio programs. This will accustom your ear to French sounds and inflections. It is not necessary for you to understand all that is said; merely concentrate on the French intonations and try to get a general sense of what is being discussed. You will soon learn how to pronounce a word on sight and to understand sentences as you hear them.

French: A Self-Teaching Guide also includes two unique features found in no other French textbook: a lesson on computers, introducing you to the newest French vocabulary of the subject, and another lesson on cognates, which instructs you on how to enrich your French vocabulary by some 2,000 words, without monotonous memorization.

The methodology and content of this book are based on a course I developed for doctoral students at Indiana University who were majoring in disciplines other than French. These students did not know a word of the language before they started, but became fluent after nine weeks of intensive study, eighty percent of which was self-guided. The same teaching method was then used successfully in subsequent years with undergraduate students enrolled in a first-year course.

French: A Self-Teaching Guide will not turn you into a polished speaker of French overnight. It will not enable you to deal immediately with every French text. But it will provide you with the basic tools to understand, to speak, to read, and to write simple French. It opens the gateway to a very gratifying experience: understanding and appreciating the language and culture of the French-speaking people.

Pronunciation Guide

The secret of proper French pronunciation lies in the distinct articulation of each syllable, word, and word group. In French, all words must be well articulated in a flowing, linking way, with only a slight stress on the last syllable in words of two syllables or more. Examples are: ca*fé,* gar*age,* monu*ment,* évolu*tion.*

English and French have many similar sounds. There are, however, certain English sounds that do not exist in French, while some French sounds, involving vowels and consonants, are different from English sounds with the same vowels or consonants. For example, there is no *h* sound in French, and the *th* English sound is a *t* sound in French. Following are other differences in vowels and consonant sounds.

A. *Vowels.* The vowels *a, e, i, o,* and *u* acquire a nasal sound in French when they are followed by *m* or *n*. There are no exact English equivalents for French nasal sounds, but there are approximations that could be termed "neighbor sounds." There are four French nasal sounds:

	ENGLISH NEIGHBOR SOUNDS	FRENCH WORDS
1. an, em, en	*alm* in balm	ch*an*ter (to sing)
2. om, on	*on* in don't	*on*cle (uncle)
3. in, im, eim, ein	*en* in represent	ce*in*ture (belt)
4. un, um	*am* in amber	*un* (one)

You can practice all four nasal sounds in this phrase: *un bon vin blanc* (a good white wine). The fourth nasal sound is not as frequently encountered as the other three.

B. *Consonants*

1. English and French consonants basically have the same sounds, except for the *th* and *h* in English, and the *r* and *ch* in French:
   - *th* in French has the *t* sound, *théâtre* is pronounced *téâtre*
   - there is no *h* sound in French, as previously stated
   - *r* in French is guttural, and is made in the back of the mouth to resemble a gargling sound
   - *ch* in French has the *sh* sound
2. In French, consonants at the end of words are not pronounced, with the exception of *c, f, l, r,* and *q* (the *r* in *-er* verbs is not pronounced. Examples are: *arc, neuf, naturel, fleur, coq.*
3. *c* + *e, i, y* = *s,* as in *cela, ceci, Cyrano*
4. *ç* + *o, a, u* = *s,* as in *garçon, ça*
5. *c* + *a, o, u* = *k,* as in *café, coq*
6. *g* + *e, i* = *j,* as in gara*ge*
7. *g* + *a, o, u* = *g,* as in *ga*rage
8. *gn* is pronounced *ni,* as in o*ni*on
9. *ph* is pronounced f, as in *philosphie*
10. *ll* preceded by *i* is pronounced *y,* as in *yet*—travai*ller*
11. *qu* is pronounced *k,* as in musi*que*
12. *x* + a consonant is pronounced *ks,* as in e*x*tase (ekstase)
    x + a vowel is pronounced *gz,* as in e*x*aminer (egzaminer)
13. *s* + any vowel is pronounced *z*

C. *The liaison (linking of words).* In French pronunciation, a consonant at the end of a word is generally linked to the vowel at the beginning of the following word. This is called *la liaison* (linking). There are instances where the liaison is imperative, and others where it is absolutely not allowed.

1. The liaison is imperative in the following:
   - personal pronouns + verbs. Example: *ils aiment* (*ilza*iment)
   - verbs + personal pronouns. Example: *aiment-ils* (aimen*t*ils)
   - adjectives + nouns. Example: *vieux arbres* (vieu*za*rbres)
   - short adverbs + adjectives. Example: *très intelligent* (trēzin-telligent)
   - after *sans*. Example: *sans avis* (san*z*avis)
   - after *est*. Example: *c'est intérressant* (c'e*st*intéressant)
2. The liaison is absolutely not allowed in the following cases:
   - after *et*. Example: *il est gentil et intelligent*
   - before a pronounced *h,* as in *Hollande, haricot.* Example: *les haricots* (beans); *les Hollandais* (the Dutch)
3. The following sound changes occur in the liaison:
   - the *s* at the end of a word becomes *z*. Example: *elles aiment*
   - the *x* becomes *z*. Example: *vieux arbres*
   - the *d* becomes *t*. Example: *un grand ami* (gran*t*ami)
   - the *f* becomes *v*. Example: *neuf ans* (neu*v*ans)

Lesson 1

EXPRESSIONS DE BASE (Basic Expressions)

Bonjour, madame.	Good morning, madam.
Comment allez-vous, monsieur?	How are you, sir?
Assez bien, merci, mademoiselle.	Fairly well, thank you, miss.
Comment vous appelez-vous?	What's your name?
Je m'appelle Jacques.	My name is Jack.
Où habitez-vous?	Where do you live?
J'habite à San Francisco.	I live in San Francisco.
Puis-je vous aider?	May I help you?
Oui, s'il vous plaît.	Yes, please (if you please).
Où sont les toilettes?	Where are the restrooms?
Là-bas à gauche.	Over there to the left.
En face du Cinéma.	In front of the Cinema.
Comment dit-on *on the right* en français?	How do you say *on the right* in French?
On dit *à droite*.	We say *à droite*.
À bientôt.	See you soon.
À demain.	See you tomorrow.
Au revoir.	Goodbye.

PRACTICE THE FOLLOWING EXPRESSIONS

(Answers for Lesson 1, pp. 59–60)

1. How do you say *Good morning* in French? Bonjour ______.
2. How do you say *my name is* in French? je máppelle ______.

3. How do you say *Where do you live?* Où habitez-vous.
4. How do you reply to *Comment allez-vous?* assez bien merci.
5. How do you reply to *Où sont les toilettes?* là-bas (à gauche).
6. How do you say *to the left?* à gauche.
7. What is the opposite of *à droite?* à gauche.
8. How do you say *please* in French? S'il vous plaît.
9. *À bientôt* is translated into English by see you soon.
10. How do you say *in front of?* en face.
11. There are two ways of answering to *au revoir:* ~~au revoir~~ demain and à bientôt.
12. *À demain* is translated into English by see you tomorrow.

MOTS NOUVEAUX (New Words)

Try to memorize these words. They will be repeated in exercises and future lessons. Pronounce each word aloud.

après	after	**le jour**	day
l'arbre (masc.)	(the) tree	**la leçon**	lesson
l'arc-en-ciel (masc.)	rainbow	**le livre**	book
		la lumière	light
aujourd'hui	today	**le lundi**	Monday
avant	before	**la maison**	house
la bougie	candle	**le matin**	morning
la chaise	chair	**la mer**	sea
le chat	cat	**la mère**	mother
le chien	dog	**le mot**	word
la couleur	color	**la nuit**	night
le crayon	pencil	**l'oiseau (masc.)**	bird
demain	tomorrow	**le papier**	paper
l'enfant	child	**le parapluie**	umbrella
la famille	family	**le père**	father
la femme	woman	**le soleil**	sun
la fille	girl	**le stylo**	pen
le frère	brother	**le temps**	time; weather
le garçon	boy	**la tête**	head
le goût	taste	**la vérité**	truth
hier	yesterday		
l'homme (masc.)	man		

PRACTICE THE VOCABULARY

Match the two columns by writing the appropriate letters in the spaces provided and adding the correct article.

Example: 1. F l'arbre

1. F arbre	A. pen
2. C chaise	B. head
3. E papier	C. chair
4. A stylo	D. woman
5. G parapluie	E. paper
6. D femme	F. tree
7. B tête	G. umbrella
8. I demain	H. taste
9. K mot	I. tomorrow
10. L matin	J. house
11. H goût	K. word
12. J maison	L. morning
13. O soleil	M. light
14. M lumière	N. rainbow
15. N arc-en-ciel	O. sun
16. Q nuit	P. mother
17. S vérité	Q. night
18. P mère	R. book
19. T hier	S. truth
20. R livre	T. yesterday
21. V père	U. cat
22. X bougie	V. father
23. W homme	W. man
24. U chat	X. candle
25. b crayon	Y. time
26. Z oiseau	Z. bird
27. Y temps	a. dog

(continued on the next page)

28. d garçon b. pencil

29. c fille c. girl

30. a chien d. boy

GRAMMAR I Definite articles. Gender of nouns.

A. The definite article *the* is translated into French by *le, la, les,* and *l'*. We use *le* before masculine singular nouns, *la* with feminine singular nouns, and *les* with the plural nouns, both masculine and feminine. *L'* is the contraction of *le* and *la* when followed by a noun starting with a vowel or a mute *h* as in: *l'homme, l'avion,* and *l'hôtel.*

B. In French, things are either masculine or feminine. There is no neuter gender of nouns as there is in English. Articles in French agree with the nouns, as in: *la table, le garçon, la chaise, la maison, le matin, le stylo, le père,* and *la mère.*

C. Since there is no exact manner in which to recognize the gender of nouns simply by examining them, it is very important to learn the following patterns in order to help distinguish the feminine nouns from the masculine nouns. Be aware, however, that these are patterns only, with numerous exceptions; there are no hard and fast rules. The only sure way to know the gender of each noun is to memorize.

1. Females are always feminine and males masculine.

   EX.: *l'homme* (the man) masc.

   la femme (the woman) fem.

   le garçon (the boy) masc.

   la fille (the girl) fem.

2. Most nouns ending in *on, in, o, ier, al,* and *ot* are masculine, as in: *le bouillon, le matin, le métro, le papier, le cheval* (the horse), and *le gigot* (the leg of lamb).
3. Most nouns ending in *ion, eur, ance, ence, te, ude,* and *ie* are feminine, as in: *l'aviation, la passion, la grandeur, la chance, la présence, la bonté, la biologie, la latitude,* and *la multitude.*

NOTE:

About 2% of the nouns contained in this book do not belong to the preceding categories. The following is a small sample of those nouns: *le livre* (the book), *le soleil* (the sun), *le parapluie* (the umbrella), *l'ordinateur* (masc., the computer), *le chat* (male cat), *la chatte* (female cat), *le chien* (male dog), *la chienne* (female dog).

PRACTICE THE ARTICLES

1. List four translations of *the* ________________.
2. Things in French are either ________________ or ________________.
3. List two masculine definite articles ________________.
4. What does *l'* stand for? ________ and when? ________________
5. What is the definite article for ________ *splendeur* (splendor)? ________ *santé* (the health)?
6. What are two feminine definite articles? ________________.
7. Write the definite articles of ________ *arbre* (the tree) ________, *homme* (the man), ________ *papier* (the paper).
8. Write the definite articles of ________ *location* (rent, rental), ________ *patience* (the patience), ________ *zoologie* (the zoology), ________ *attitude* (the attitude), ________ *longueur* (the length).

EXERCISE

Write the articles *le, la, l'*. Then say each word aloud.

1. ______ matin
2. ______ professeur
3. ______ bonté
4. ______ vérité
5. ______ fille
6. ______ journal
7. ______ femme
8. ______ garçon
9. ______ homme
10. ______ crayon
11. ______ grandeur
12. ______ avion
13. ______ hôtel
14. ______ papier
15. ______ bougie
16. ______ arc-en-ciel
17. ______ parapluie
18. ______ chance

GRAMMAR II Indefinite articles.

A. The indefinite articles in French are *un* for masculine singular nouns, and *une* for feminine singular nouns—for example, *un garçon* (a boy) and *une fille* (a girl). Indefinite articles and definite articles agree with the nouns they precede. These nouns are either masculine or feminine, even when they are objects or things.

B. The neuter gender *it,* used with things and objects in English, does not exist in French.

C. In French, every effort is made to avoid the "hiatus" or the encounter of two consecutive vowels, one at the end of a word followed by another at the beginning of the next word. (A silent *h* is considered a vowel in such a case.) One of the largest exceptions to this rule occurs with *une,* the indefinite feminine article. Thus, there is no problem with saying *une addition, une abréviation, une histoire, une altitude,* etc.

PRACTICE THE INDEFINITE ARTICLES

1. What are the indefinite articles in French? un, une .
2. What is the gender of *un?* masculine .
3. What is the gender of *une?* feminine .
4. What is the gender of *un garçon?* masculin .
5. Which nouns are always masculine? males .
6. Which nouns are always feminine? Females .
7. What is the meaning of "hiatus"? encounter of 2 vowels .
8. Are there neuter nouns in French? NO .
9. Objects in French are either masculine or femine .
10. What is a major exception to the hiatus? une .

EXERCISE

Write the appropriate indefinite article *(un* or *une)* before each noun. Then say each combination aloud.

1. une action
2. un jour
3. un livre
4. un garçon
5. un papier
6. un chien
7. un chat
8. un crayon
9. une couleur
10. un matin
11. un soleil
12. une nuit
13. une tête
14. un oiseau
15. une chaise
16. un goût
17. un mot
18. un parapluie

GRAMMAR III Subject pronouns and the verbs **être** (to be) and **avoir** (to have). The interrogative.

A. Memorize the verbs *être* (to be) and *avoir* (to have):

SUBJECT	ÊTRE	SUBJECT	TO BE
je	**suis**	I	am
tu (sing. familiar)	**es**	you (familiar)	are
il (masc.), elle (fem.), on	**est**	he, she, it, one	is
nous	**sommes**	we	are
vous	**êtes**	you	are
ils (masc. pl.), elles (fem. pl.)	**sont**	they	are

SUBJECT	AVOIR	SUBJECT	TO HAVE
je = j'	**ai**	I	have, am having, do have
tu (familiar)	**as**	you	have
il (masc.), elle (fem.), on	**a**	he, she, it, one	has
nous	**avons**	we	have
vous	**avez**	you	have
ils (masc. pl.), elles (fem. pl.)	**ont**	they	have

B. The interrogative form in French is expressed in two ways. The first is by starting any sentence asking a question with the phrase *est-ce que*.

EX.: *Est-ce que* tu es un garçon? (Are you a boy?)
Est-ce que vous avez des stylos? (Do you have pens?)

The second way is by inverting the pronoun subject and verb as in English, except that French adds a hyphen between the words.

EX.: *Es-tu* un garçon? (Are you a boy?)
Avez-vous des stylos? (Do you have pens?)

Note that French adds the letter *-t-* between two vowels in the interrogative form in order to avoid the "hiatus" (explained on page 6).

EX.: *A-t-il?* Has he?
A-t-elle? Has she?
Mange-t-on? Are we eating? (Does one eat?)
Aide-t-elle? Does she help?
Commande-t-il? Is he ordering?

NOTES:

1. In French, *je* is not capitalized as is the English "I"; *tu* ("you", singular) is used with friends, relatives, and in informal situations.
2. *Vous* (you) is used in formal situations when speaking with one person and in formal and informal situations when speaking with more than one person.
   EX.: Monsieur, vous mangez bien.
   Mesdames et Messieurs, vous mangez bien.
3. *Il* is the masculine singular ("he"), and *elle* is the feminine singular ("she").
4. *Ils* is used for "they" (plural masculine) and *elles* for "they" (plural feminine). *Ils* and *elles* have the same sound as *il* and *elle:* the last consonant ("s") is mute.
   EX.: Ils (les garçons) sont ici.
   Elles (les filles) sont ici.
5. *Ils* refers also to a mixed group of people, people in general, as in *ils sont ici* (les garçons et les filles). *Il* is also used in what is called "impersonal expressions" such as *il fait chaud* (it is warm), *il fait froid* (it is cold). This is the only time we encounter the impersonal equivalent of the English "it." French also has another third-person singular construction which is *on.* This *on* translates the English *one,* as in *on dit* (one says, we say, people say), *on fait* (one does, we do, people do).
6. *Il, elle, ils,* and *elles* also refer to animals and to things that are either masculine or feminine, singular or plural. *Le chat est blanc* (the cat is white), *il est blanc* (he is white), *la table est grande* (the table is big), *elle est grande* (it is big).
7. Note that in French, *j'ai* means "I have," whereas in English it can mean "I have," "I'm having," or "I do have."

PRACTICE THE SUBJECT PRONOUNS

1. Which pronoun is always capitalized in English and not in French? I) j'ai .
2. The pronoun *you* has three equivalents in French. What are they? TU, VOUS, VOUS .

3. The pronoun *tu* is used in informal situations.
4. What is the singular formal equivalent of *tu*? vous.
5. What is the plural formal equivalent of *you*? vous.
6. What are two ways in which *il* is used? he is - it is.
7. What is the feminine form of *il*? elle.
8. What is the plural of *elle*? elles.
9. What are two uses of *ils* (they)? ils son ici / ils fait froid.
10. How do you say *it is cold* in French? il fait froid.
11. When is the impersonal *it* used in French? impersonal expressions.
12. Write the English for *il fait chaud*. it is hot.

EXERCISES

A. Write the French pronouns with the corresponding forms of *être* (to be).

Example: you are - *vous êtes*

1. you (formal) vous êtes
2. you (familiar sing.) tu es
3. I je suis
4. we nous sommes
5. you (pl.) vous etes
6. they (masc. pl.) ils sont
7. they (fem. pl.) elles sont
8. he il est
9. she elle est
10. they (all females) elles sont
11. they (mixed male and female) ils sont
12. they (things in general) ils sont
13. they (people in general) ils sont
14. they (animals in general) ils sont

B. Match the verbs with the correct pronouns.

Example: 1. Je suis (to be) une fille. 2. Nous avons (to have) le temps aujourd'hui.

1. J (e) ai (to have) une maison.
2. Ils sont (to be) deux frères.
3. Je suis (to be) une fille.
4. Elles ont (to have) des crayons.
5. Vous etes (to be) une mère.
6. Ils ont (to have) le temps aujourd'hui.

7. Tu ______ (to be) le père.
8. Vous ______ (to have) des bougies.
9. Elles ______ (to be) des chattes.
10. Tu ______ (to have) des stylos.

C. Write the following in the interrogative form, as in *avez-vous?*

1. vous avez ______
2. il a ______
3. il est ______
4. nous avons ______
5. nous sommes ______
6. vous êtes ______
7. ils sont ______
8. vous étudiez ______
9. elles ont ______
10. nous parlons ______

Lesson 2

AU RESTAURANT
(At the Restaurant)

l'addition (fem.)	(the) bill, check, addition	**la glace**	ice cream
l'agneau (masc.)	lamb	**le homard**	lobster
l'assiette (fem.)	plate, dish	**le jardin**	garden
la caissière	cashier	**la laitue**	lettuce
les côtelettes (fem.)	chops	**la langouste**	crayfish
le couteau	knife	**les légumes (masc.)**	vegetables
la crème	cream	**le plat**	dish
les crevettes (fem.)	shrimp	**le poisson**	fish
le déjeuner	lunch	**le poulet**	chicken
le flan	custard	**le repas**	meal
la fourchette	fork	**la salade**	salad
les frites	fries	**la serviette**	napkin, briefcase
les fruits de mer (masc.)	sea food	**le veau**	veal
		le verre	glass
		la viande	meat
acheter	to buy	**manger**	to eat
avoir	to have	**partir**	to leave
boire	to drink	**préférer**	to prefer
chercher	to look for	**prendre**	to take
commander	to order	**revenir**	to come back
commencer	to start	**savoir**	to know
décider	to decide	**travailler**	to work
demander	to ask	**trouver**	to find
entendre	to hear	**vendre**	to sell
être	to be	**vouloir**	to want

avec	with	**moi aussi**	me too
bien sûr	of course	**peut-être**	maybe
déjà	already	**quelquefois**	sometimes
délicieux	delicious	**souvent**	often
en retard	late	**superbe**	superb
excellent	excellent	**vraiment**	truly
maintenant	now		

PRACTICE THE NEW WORDS

(Answers for Lesson 2, pp. 61–62)

A. Write the proper article *(le, la,* or *l')* in front of the words.

1. le couteau
2. l' assiette
3. le repas
4. le plat
5. la fourchette
6. la viande
7. le veau
8. la salade
9. la glace
10. la crème
11. la langouste
12. le homard
13. le poisson
14. le poulet
15. l' addition
16. la caissière
17. l' assiette
18. le flan

B. Match the two columns below.

1. M repas
2. N maintenant
3. A assiette
4. I déjà
5. L frites
6. J côtelettes
7. H langouste
8. C fruits de mer
9. K caissière
10. F poisson
11. E viande
12. B flan
13. D plat
14. G crevette

A. plate
B. custard
C. sea food
D. dish
E. meat
F. fish
G. shrimp
H. lobster
I. already
J. chops
K. cashier
L. fries
M. meal
N. now

DIALOGUE *Au restaurant Chez Jeannine*

LE GARÇON:	Bonjour, mesdames. Puis-je vous aider?
MME RAYMOND:	Oui merci. Nous voulons une table pour deux personnes, s'il vous plaît.
LE GARÇON:	Bien, mesdames. Suivez-moi.
MME SIMON:	Voilà, c'est parfait en face du jardin. Merci.
LE GARÇON:	Voici la carte, mesdames.
MME RAYMOND:	Ils ont mon plat préféré.
LE GARÇON:	Vous voulez commander maintenant?
MME RAYMOND:	Oui, pour moi la salade de laitue, le plat de fruits de mer, des frites, et du café. Merci.
MME SIMON:	Moi, je préfère les côtelettes d'agneau et les légumes. Merci.
LE GARÇON:	Quelque chose à boire pour commencer?
MME RAYMOND:	Oui. Une bouteille de Perrier avec le repas, s'il vous plaît.
MME SIMON:	C'est vraiment délicieux. Ce restaurant est excellent.
MME RAYMOND:	Je suis d'accord. La cuisine est superbe ici.
MME SIMON:	Garçon, l'addition s'il vous plaît. Nous sommes en retard—nous travaillons cet après-midi.
LE GARÇON:	Voilà. Payez la caissière là-bas s'il vous plaît. Au revoir, à bientôt.

DIALOG *At Jeannine's Restaurant*

WAITER:	Hello, ladies. May I help you?
MRS. RAYMOND:	Yes, thank you. We want a table for two people, please.
WAITER:	O.K. (good), ladies. Follow me.
MRS. SIMON:	There, perfect, in front of the garden. Thank you.
WAITER:	Here's the menu, ladies.
MRS. RAYMOND:	They have my favorite dish.
WAITER:	Do you want to order now?
MRS. RAYMOND:	Yes, I want the lettuce salad, the seafood dish, fries, and coffee. Thank you.
MRS. SIMON:	I prefer the lamb chops and the vegetables. Thank you.
WAITER:	Something to drink for a start (to start)?
MRS. RAYMOND:	Yes, a bottle of Perrier with the meal, please.
MRS. SIMON:	It's truly delicious. This restaurant is excellent.
MRS. RAYMOND:	I agree. The cuisine (cooking) is superb here.
MRS. SIMON:	Waiter, the bill please. We're late—we are working this afternoon.
WAITER:	Here (it is). Pay the cashier over there, please. Goodbye, see you soon.

DIALOG EXERCISES

A. Complete the sentences matching the dialog.

1. Madame Raymond et Madame Simon sont chez ______.
2. Le restaurant est ______ et la cuisine est ______.
3. Madame Raymond veut boire le ______.
4. Madame Simon commande les côtelettes ______.
5. Madame Raymond préfère la salade de ______.
6. Le garçon dit au revoir et ______.
7. Madame Raymond boit du Perrier avec ______.
8. Madame Simon aime les ______ et la viande.
9. Madame Raymond préfère les fruits de mer et les ______.
10. Madame Simon et Madame Raymond sont en ______.
11. Elles travaillent cet ______.
12. Madame Simon et Madame Raymond paient la ______.

B. Select the appropriate word.

1. La cuisine dans le restaurant est ______ (table, fourchette, délicieuse).
2. Madame Simon veut boire ______ (le flan, le homard, le café).
3. Madame Simon préfère ______ (les légumes, le couteau, l'assiette).
4. Madame Raymond paie ______ (le garçon, la caissière, la table).
5. La table de Madame Simon est en face du ______ (poisson, plat, jardin).
6. Madame Simon et Madame Raymond sont ______ (à la maison, à l'hôtel, au restaurant).
7. Madame Simon et Madame Raymond partent du restaurant parce qu'elles ______ (mangent, commandent, travaillent, sont en retard).
8. Les côtelettes d'agneau sont ______ (du poisson, des crevettes, de la viande).
9. Le homard est ______ (un agneau, un veau, un fruit de mer).
10. Les frites sont ______ (des légumes, du flan, de la viande).

GRAMMAR I Regular verbs in the present indicative.

A. There are three groups of regular French verbs:
1. Verbs ending in *-ER* are of the first group: *parler* (to speak).
2. Verbs ending in *-IR* are of the second group: *choisir* (to choose).
3. Verbs ending in *-RE* are of the third group: *attendre* (to wait for).

All the verbs in the above groups have two parts, a *stem* and an *ending*.

EX.: *parler:* stem - *parl;* ending *-er*

NOTE:

Payer (to pay for) and other verbs with *-yer,* such as *employer* (to use), *envoyer* (to send), and *ennuyer* (to bore, to bother) change the *y* into *i* with all pronouns except *nous* and *vous*.

je paie	nous payons
tu paies	vous payez
il, elle paie	ils, elles paient

B. Present indicative of *parler.*

SUBJECT	PARLER	SUBJECT	TO SPEAK
je	**parl e**	I	speak, am speaking, do speak
tu	**parl es**	you (sing. fam.)	speak, are speaking, do speak
il, elle (on)	**parl e**	he, she, it, one	speaks, is speaking, does speak
nous	**parl ons**	we	speak, are speaking, do speak
vous	**parl ez**	you (plural)	speak, are speaking, do speak
ils, elles	**parl ent**	they	speak, are speaking, do speak

NOTES:

1. In French, the present indicative translates three different equivalents in English.

   EX.: *Je parle:* I speak, I am speaking, I do speak

2. The French word *on* is used the same way that "one" is used in English, with the third person singular form of the verb.

PRACTICE THE REGULAR FRENCH VERBS

A. Answer the following questions.

1. How many groups of regular verbs are there in French? 3 ______.
2. What are the infinitive endings of each group? er ir RE ______.
3. Why are these verbs called regular? the stem remains same
4. Write the stem of the verb *parler* (to speak) parl ______.
5. Write the stem of the verb *danser* (to dance) dans ______.
6. Since the present indicative translates an action in progress, what is the French equivalent of *we are speaking*? NOUS - parlons.

B. Complete the following sentences with the correct verb forms.

1. Vous parlez ______ (parler) beaucoup.
2. Charles et Antoinette commandent ______ (commander) le repas.
3. Le garçon travaille ______ (travailler) au Restaurant Parisien.
4. Elles cherchent ______ (chercher) le cinéma Voltaire.
5. Ils voyasent ______ (voyager) toujours.
6. Nous regardons ______ (regarder) la télévision.
7. J(e) j'arme ______ (aimer) la glace au chocolat.
8. J(e) j'etudie ______ (étudier) la leçon.
9. Charles et Antoinette pensent ______ (penser) beaucoup.
10. Nous rentrons ______ (rentrer) tard.

GRAMMAR II The present indicative of regular verbs ending in **-IR** and **-RE**.

A. The present indicative of regular *-IR* verbs, such as *choisir* (to choose).
Verbs in these groups are also divided into stems and endings.
As in the *-ER* verbs, the stems remain the same and the endings change according to tense and subject.

SUBJECT	CHOISIR	SUBJECT	TO CHOOSE
je	**chois is**	I	choose, am choosing, do choose
tu	**chois is**	you	choose, are choosing, do choose
il, elle (on)	**chois it**	he, she, it, one	chooses, is choosing, does choose
nous	**chois issons**	we	choose, are choosing, do choose
vous	**chois issez**	you	choose, are choosing, do choose
ils, elles	**chois issent**	they	choose, are choosing, do choose

NOTE:

The addition of *-iss* in the plural forms is to be observed in all the *-IR* regular verbs. This group includes *finir* (to finish), *agir* (to act), *réussir* (to succeed), and *réfléchir* (to reflect, to consider).

B. Present indicative of regular verbs ending in *-RE,* such as *attendre* (to wait for).
As in the regular verbs ending in *-ER* and *-IR,* the verbs ending in *-RE* follow the same pattern of finding the stems and then attaching the endings according to tense and subject.

SUBJECT	ATTENDRE	SUBJECT	TO WAIT FOR
j'	**attend s**	I	wait for, do wait for, am waiting for
tu	**attend s**	you	wait for, do wait for, are waiting for
il, elle (on)	**attend**	he, she, it, one	waits for, does wait for, is waiting for
nous	**attend ons**	we	wait for, do wait for, are waiting for
vous	**attend ez**	you	wait for, do wait for, are waiting for
ils, elles	**attend ent**	they	wait for, do wait for, are waiting for

NOTE:

Other *-RE* verbs include *vendre* (to sell), *entendre* (to hear), *rendre* (to give back), *perdre* (to lose), and *répondre* (to answer).

C. Recapitulation of endings to be attached to the stems of the regular verbs in *-ER, -IR,* and *-RE:*

PARLER	CHOISIR	ATTENDRE
je **-e**	je **-is**	j'(e) **-s**
tu **-es**	tu **-is**	tu **-s**
il, elle **-e**	il, elle **-it**	il, elle
nous **-ons**	nous **-issons**	nous **-ons**
vous **-ez**	vous **-issez**	vous **-ez**
ils, elles **-ent**	ils, elles **-issent**	ils, elles **-ent**

EXERCISES

A. Complete the sentences with the appropriate verb forms.

1. Charles _repond_ (répondre) à Antoinette.
2. Le monsieur _attend_ (attendre) la dame.
3. Monsieur et Madame _finissent_ (finir) la conversation.
4. Antoinette _réussit_ (réussir) à l'examen.
5. Le garçon _reflechit_ (réfléchir) à l'addition.
6. Nous _rendons_ (rendre) les livres.
7. Vous _choisissez_ (choisir) le restaurant.
8. Elles _agissent_ (agir) rapidement.
9. Charles et Antoinette _repondent_ (répondre) à Juliette.
10. Ils _vendent_ (vendre) des maisons.

B. Say aloud, then write the French equivalent of the following sentences.

1. I am finishing the book. _Je finis le livre_.
2. We do speak French. _Nous parlons_. _Francais_
3. We are looking for the restaurant. _Nous cherchons_. _le resaurant_
4. She is waiting for Charles. _Elle attend Charles_.
5. They do like the cake. _Ils aiment le_. _gateau_

GRAMMAR III The negative form of *être* and *avoir*.

The simplest way to convert an affirmative verb into the negative form is to follow this formula:

SUBJECT +	NE +	VERB +	PAS
Ex.: Je	**ne**	**suis**	**pas.**
Ex.: Je	**ne**	**parle**	**pas.**

A. Study the formation of the negative with the verb *être* (to be).

SUBJECT +	NE +	VERB +	PAS
je	**ne**	**suis**	**pas**
tu	**n'(e)**	**es**	**pas**
il, elle	**n'(e)**	**est**	**pas**
nous	**ne**	**sommes**	**pas**
vous	**n'(e)**	**êtes**	**pas**
ils, elles	**ne**	**sont**	**pas**

B. Study the formation of the negative with the verb *avoir* (to have).

SUBJECT +	NE +	VERB +	PAS
je	**n'(e)**	**ai**	**pas**
tu	**n'(e)**	**as**	**pas**
il, elle	**n'(e)**	**a**	**pas**
nous	**n'(e)**	**avons**	**pas**
vous	**n'(e)**	**avez**	**pas**
ils, elles	**n'(e)**	**ont**	**pas**

PRACTICE THE NEGATIVE FORM

Write the negative of the following.

1. Je ne suis pas une fille.
2. Elle n' a pas le stylo.
3. Nous n' avons pas le menu.
4. Ils ne sont pas au restaurant.

5. Vous __n'__ êtes __pas__ Américain.
6. Vous __n'__ avez __pas__ quelque chose à boire.
7. Ils __ne__ commandent __pas__ le poulet.
8. Charles __ne__ finit __pas__ tard.
9. Antoinette __ne__ travaille __pas__ beaucoup.
10. Ils __n'__ attendent __pas__ l'autobus.
11. Nous __ne__ payons __pas__ l'addition.
12. Ils __ne__ finissent __pas__ le repas.
13. Nous __ne__ cherchons __pas__ le restaurant.
14. Vous __ne__ trouvez __pas__ le parapluie.

Lesson 3

AU GRAND MAGASIN (At the Department Store)

l'achat (masc.)	(the) purchase	**la lampe**	lamp
l'argent (masc.)	money	**le lit**	bed
la boîte	box	**les meubles (masc.)**	furniture
le camion	truck		
le cendrier	ashtray	**le rayon**	aisle
la chambre	room	**la robe**	dress
la chose	thing	**la valeur**	value
le crédit	credit	**le vendeur**	salesman
l'employé (masc.)	employee	**le voisinage**	neighborhood
		la volonté	will
le fauteuil	armchair		

accepter	to accept	**durer**	to last
accompagner	to accompany	**encourager**	to encourage
admirer	to admire	**espérer**	to hope
adorer	to adore	**fêter**	to celebrate
aider	to help	**gaspiller**	to waste
apporter	to bring	**hésiter**	to hesitate
bricoler	to putter around	**marcher**	to walk; to work (a machine, a motor)
comparer	to compare		
compter	to count		
coûter	to cost	**organiser**	to organize
décider	to decide	**porter**	to carry
dépenser	to spend	**ramener**	to bring back
descendre	to get off	**rentrer**	to return home, to come back
désirer	to wish, to desire		
discuter	to discuss		

avec	with	**depuis**	since
c'est	it is	**étroit**	narrow
cher	expensive	**zut! (familiar)**	darn!
déjà	already		
grand	big	**que**	which, whom
large	wide	**satisfait (masc.)**	satisfied
mais	but	**surtout**	mostly, especially
(avec) moi	(with) me		
partout	everywhere	**tout de suit**	immediately
petit (masc.)	small	**utile**	useful
prêt (masc.)	ready	**vrai (masc.)**	true
le prix	cost		

NOTES:

1. *L'achat* means "a purchase." It is derived from *acheter,* to buy.

2. The word *(les) meubles* is always used in the plural form when speaking of the contents of a room or a house and translating the word "furniture." It is used in the singular only to denote a single piece of furniture, as in: *"J'ai un meuble Louis XV.* (I have a Louis XV piece of furniture.)

3. *L'argent* is "money" and *la monnaie* is "change," as in *Avez-vous de la monnaie?* (Do you have any change?)

4. *Cher* (masc.), *chère* (fem.) means "dear," as in "Dear Charles" at the beginning of a letter. It also means expensive, as in *Le meuble Louis XV est cher.* (The Louis XV piece of furniture is expensive.) Other examples are: *c'est cher* (it's expensive) and *ce n'est pas cher* (it's not expensive).

PRACTICE THE NEW WORDS

(Answers for Lesson 3, pp. 62–64)

A. Write the correct definite article before each noun *(le, la, les, l')*.

1. ______ chose
2. ______ argent
3. ______ rayon
4. ______ meubles
5. ______ employé
6. ______ lampes
7. ______ cendrier
8. ______ trottoir
9. ______ achats

B. Complete the sentences with the appropriate words.

1. Charles admire ____________ (les meubles, surtout, depuis).
2. Le camion est ____________ (descendre, petit, la rue).
3. Les fauteuils ne sont pas ____________ (satisfait, grands, déjà).
4. Le magasin n'accepte pas le ____________ (rue, chaise, crédit).

5. Charles compare les ___________ (chambres, miroirs, prix).
6. Antoinette ne compte pas ___________ (la chose, le voisinage, l'argent).
7. La rue est ___________ (chère, étroite, prête).
8. Charles et Antoinette ne marchent pas dans ___________ (le magasin, la robe, la rue).

DIALOGUE *Au grand magasin*

LE VENDEUR: Bonjour, Mademoiselle!
ANTOINETTE: Je cherche une grande lampe et un fauteuil pour ma chambre.
LE VENDEUR: Très bien, Mademoiselle. Suivez-moi.
ANTOINETTE: Ah! Voilà les lampes! Mais je n'aime pas les couleurs. Avez-vous quelque chose en blanc?
LE VENDEUR: Oui, Mademoiselle. Suivez-moi, nous avons des lampes blanches mais elles sont en haut.
ANTOINETTE: Montrez-moi cette lampe à côté du grand lit là-bas.
LE VENDEUR: La voici, Mademoiselle.
ANTOINETTE: C'est combien?
LE VENDEUR: Quarante-cinq francs, mademoiselle.
ANTOINETTE: C'est parfait. Maintentant, j'ai besoin d'un fauteuil; montrez-moi le rayon des meubles, s'il vous plaît.
LE VENDEUR: Le voilà en face de vous.
ANTOINETTE: C'est combien, le fauteuil rouge?
LE VENDEUR: Deux-cent francs.
ANTOINETTE: Oh là là! Comme c'est cher! Mais j'aime le style.
LE VENDEUR: La qualité a de la valeur, Mademoiselle.
ANTOINETTE: Vous avez raison. Voici ma carte de crédit, je prends la lampe et le fauteuil.
LE VENDEUR: Merci, Mademoiselle. Suivez-moi.

DIALOG *At the Department Store*

THE SALESMAN: Good morning, Miss!
ANTOINETTE: I'm looking for a big lamp and an armchair for my room.
THE SALESMAN: Very well, Miss. Follow me.
ANTOINETTE: Ah! Here are the lamps! But I don't like the colors. Do you have something in white?
THE SALESMAN: Yes, Miss. Follow me, we do have white lamps, but they are upstairs.
ANTOINETTE: Show me the lamp next to the big bed over there.
THE SALESMAN: Here it is, Miss.
ANTOINETTE: How much is it?
THE SALESMAN: Forty-five francs, Miss.

ANTOINETTE:	It's perfect. Now I need an armchair; show me the furniture department, please.
THE SALESMAN:	It's over there facing you (in front of you).
ANTOINETTE:	How much is the red armchair?
THE SALESMAN:	Two hundred francs.
ANTOINETTE:	Oh la la! How expensive! But I like the style.
THE SALESMAN:	Quality does have value, Miss.
ANTOINETTE:	You're right. Here's my credit card, I'm taking the lamp and the armchair.
THE SALESMAN:	Thank you, Miss. Follow me.

DIALOG EXERCISES

A. According to the dialog, write the missing words.

1. Antoinette a besoin d'une __________ et d'un __________ pour sa (her) chambre.
2. Antoinette et le vendeur vont __________ (upstairs).
3. Le lampe est __________ (expensive).
4. Le fauteuil est dans le __________ (furniture department).
5. Antoinette n'aime pas les __________ (colors) des lampes.
6. Antoinette donne __________ (the credit card) au vendeur.
7. Le vendeur pense que __________ a de la __________.
8. Antoinette prend la __________ et le __________.
9. Le fauteuil coûte __________ et la lampe coûte __________.
10. Antoinette achète une lampe __________ (white) et un fauteuil __________ (red).

B. Match the two columns by writing the appropriate letters in the spaces provided.

1. ______ Elle dépense beaucoup.	A. She organizes the room.
2. ______ Il aide le vendeur.	B. He looks for the ashtray.
3. ______ Le miroir est petit.	C. She spends too much.
4. ______ Êtes-vous prêt?	D. He helps the salesman.
5. ______ Aimes-tu marcher?	E. Are you ready?
6. ______ Il va partout.	F. I need money.

(continued on the next page)

7. __B__ Il cherche le cendrier.
8. __F__ J'ai besoin d'argent.
9. __A__ Elle organise la chambre.
10. __J__ Il vend les meubles.

G. The mirror is small.
H. Do you like to walk?
I. He goes everywhere.
J. He sells the furniture.

GRAMMAR I Adjective-noun agreement. Descriptive adjectives.

A. An adjective describes a noun, conveying shape, color, quality, size, nationality, etc. The adjective agrees in number and gender with the noun it modifies.

EX.: *un homme intelligent* (masc. sing.)
des hommes intelligents (masc. pl.)
une femme intelligente (fem. sing.)
des femmes intelligentes (fem. pl.)

The feminine singular form is obtained by adding *e* to the masculine form.

EX.: *intéressant* is the masculine form (interesting)
intéressante is the feminine form

B. To form the plural, both nouns and adjectives follow the same rule by adding *s* to the singular form.

EX.: *un homme intelligent*
des hommes intelligents
une femme intelligente
des femmes intelligentes

NOTES:

1. Observe that both nouns and adjectives require *s* in the plural.
2. If the masculine form of an adjective ends with a silent *e*, the ending does not change in the feminine form.
   EX.: un homme sociab*le*
   une femme sociab*le*
3. In French, the final consonants: *t, d, s,* are usually silent, as in *intelligent, anglais,* and *grand.*
4. If the masculine singular form of nouns or adjectives ends with *s, x,* or *z,* the ending does not change in the plural:
   EX.: *Adjectives*
   Le garçon est *français.*
   Les garçons sont *français.*
   Le garçon est *sérieux.*
   Les garçons sont *sérieux.*
   Nouns
   le *cours* (course) les *cours*
   le *nez* (nose) les *nez*
   le *choix* (choice) les *choix*

C. Adjectives with irregular forms:

1. Adjectives ending in *-eux* and *-eur* in the masculine form require *-euse* in the feminine form.

   EX.: un garçon *sérieux*
   une fille *sérieuse*
   un garçon *travailleur*
   une fille *travailleuse*

2. Adjectives ending in *er* require *-ère* in the feminine form:

   EX.: un fauteuil *cher*
   une lampe *chère*

   The *r* in che*r* is pronounced in the singular form, even though there is no vowel after it. The feminine form of *chère* is pronounced exactly like the masculine form. Notice that an accent grave (`) is required on the *e* before the *r* in the feminine of chère.

3. Adjectives ending with *-if* require *-ive* in the feminine form:

   EX.: un garçon *actif*
   une fille *active*

4. Adjectives ending with *il* and *el* in the masculine require *ille* and *elle* in the feminine form:

   EX.: un garçon *gentil*
   une fille *gentille*
   un homme *intellectuel*
   une femme *intellectuelle*

5. Adjectives ending with *-ien* in the masculine require *-ienne* in the feminine form:

   EX.: Jacques est *canadien*
   Juliette est *canadienne*

6. Other adjectives that follow the above rules include: *paresseux* (lazy), *courageux* (courageous), *naif* (naïve), *fier* (proud), *ancien* (old, antique). Please note that adjectives of nationality and place are not capitalized:

   EX.: *Jacques est francais* (Jacques is French)
   un restaurant parisien (A Parisian restaurant)

7. A certain number of adjectives precede the nouns they modify. They often describe physical attributes:

   EX.: *une jolie fille* (a pretty girl)
   un grand garçon (a big boy)

8. Adjectives of color generally follow the nouns they modify:

   EX.: *une robe verte* (a green dress)

NOTES:

1. Nouns ending in *-eau* in the singular require the ending *x* in the plural form.
   EX.: *le tableau* (the board)
   les tableaux (the boards)

2. Nouns ending in *-al* or *-ail* require *aux* in the plural form.
   EX.: *un cheval* (a horse), *des chevaux* (horses)
   le travail (the work), *les travaux* (the works)

3. Where there is a group that includes one or more males, French uses the masculine form.
   EX.: *un Français et neuf Françaises* = *dix* (ten) *Français.*

4. When *t, s, d,* and *n* end a masculine word, they are not pronounced. When they are followed by *e,* they are pronounced.
5. Nouns ending in *-te* have the same ending in the masculine and feminine forms.
   EX.:

le touriste	the tourist (masc.)
la touriste	the tourist (fem.)
le scientiste	the scientist (masc.)
la scientiste	the scientist (fem.)

6. Words ending in *r, f, rs,* and *fs* have these last consonants pronounced even though they are not followed by *e.*
   EX.: voir (to see)
   cher (dear, expensive)
   neuf (new) (masc.)

   Other exceptions that require pronunciation of a consonant ending are: *cinq* (*q* = *k*), *six* (*x* = ss), *dix* (*x* = ss), sept (*pt* = t), *huit* (*t* = *t*), *neuf* (*f* = *f*). Note that *neuf* means "nine," but is also used as an adjective meaning *new.* The feminine of *neuf* is *neuve.*

EXERCISES

A. Practice the grammar.

1. An adjective describes a __________ to convey __________ and __________.
2. What do you add to a masculine adjective to convert it into a feminine one? __________.
3. What is the feminine of *arménien?* __________.
4. What is the masculine of *française?* __________.
5. What is the feminine of *gentil?* __________.
6. What is the feminine of *vif?* __________. (alert, alive)
7. What is the feminine of *joyeux?* __________. (joyful, happy)
8. What is the feminine plural of *sérieux?* __________.

9. What is the masculine plural of *joyeux?* joyeux.
10. What is the masculine plural of *anglais?* anglais.
11. What is the feminine plural of *complet?* complettes. (complete)
12. What is the masculine of *lumineuse?* lumineux. (luminous)
13. What is the masculine plural of *heureuses?* heureaux. (happy)
14. What is the feminine plural of *chanteur?* chanteuses. (singer)
15. What is the feminine singular of *fier?* fière. (proud)

B. Write, then say aloud, the plural forms of the following.

Example: le grand chien <u>les grands chiens</u>.

1. le petit chalet les Petites chalets.
2. la grande chambre les grandeschambres.
3. l'arbre vert l'arbres verts. X
4. l'homme sportif les hommes sportifs. (atheletic)
5. le chien noir les chiens noirs. (black)
6. le meuble anglais les meubles anglais.
7. l'étudiant sérieux les étudiant sérieux.

GRAMMAR II The partitive constructions: **du, de la, des,** and **de l'.** Numbers.

A. The *partitive* means part of a whole, conveying the idea of *some,* or *any.* Sometimes some and any are only implied in English, while in French they must be expressed. For example, "There is wine in the bottle" implies there is *some* wine in the bottle. In French, the partitive is expressed by *de* + the definite article.

EX.: *Il a de la bière.* (He has [some] beer.)
J'ai du vin. (I have [some] wine.)
Ils ont des fleurs. (They have [some] flowers.)

B. The definite articles *le* and *les* are contracted in the following manner: *de* + *le* becomes *du,*

EX.: *Il a du vin.*

and *de* + *les* becomes *des.*

EX.: *Il a des stylos.*

Note that *la* and *l'* do not change.

EX.: *J'ai de l'argent.* (I have [some] money.)
Il a de la bière. (He has [some] beer.)

C. In general, the partitive is expressed by *de* or *d'* alone in a negative sentence.

EX.: *Je n'ai pas d'argent.* (I don't have [any] money.)
Il ne commande pas de vin. (He does not order [any] wine.)
Nous ne cherchons pas de restaurant. (We are not looking for [any] restaurant.)
Il n'a pas de courage. (He does not have [any] courage.)

D. Memorize the following numbers in French

1. un	5. cinq	9. neuf	13. treize	17. dix-sept
2. deux	6. six	10. dix	14. quatorze	18. dix-huit
3. trois	7. sept	11. onze	15. quinze	19. dix-neuf
4. quatre	8. huit	12. douze	16. seize	20. vingt

EXERCISES

A. Complete the sentences with *du, de la, des, de l'*.

1. Avez-vous ___a de la___ bière? √
2. Nous avons besoin ___de l'___ argent. X
3. Nous n'avons pas ___du___ poulet. X
4. Vous avez ___du___ vin blanc.
5. Ils n'ont pas ___de la___ patience. (fem.) X
6. Charles a ___du___ courage. (masc.)
7. Voulez-vous ___de la___ viande?
8. Les roses ont ___des___ pétales.
9. Antoinette a ___du___ talent. (masc.)
10. Charles a ___de la___ chance. (fem.)

Note: avoir de la chance = to be lucky, to have (some) luck

B. Practice the numbers 1-12 by memorizing this short nursery rhyme.

Un, deux, trois = One, two, three

nous allons au bois = we go to the woods

quatre, cinq, six = four, five, six

ramasser des cerises = to gather cherries

sept, huit, neuf = seven, eight, nine

dans mon panier neuf = in my new basket

dix, onze, douze = ten, eleven, twelve

elles sont toutes rouges. = they are all red.

C. Practice the partitives *de, du, de la, des, de l'*.

1. What is a partitive? Part of a whole
2. How is the idea of *some* and *any* rendered in French?
   de, ~~des~~ plus definate article.
3. Are *some* and *any* ever omitted in French? yes X.
4. How is the partitive always expressed in a negative sentence?
   De D' alone. Y
5. What is the partitive equivalent of *de* + *les?* des.
6. What is the partitive equivalent of *de* + *le?* du.
7. What are the two definite articles that are not affected by contractions?
   de la, d l'. X

D. Match the French partitives with their English equivalents.

1. J'ai de jolies robes (dresses). G
2. Avez-vous du vin blanc? H
3. Nous avons des cendriers. E
4. Ont-ils des fauteuils anciens? D
5. Elle ne mange pas de viande. F
6. Nous ne commandons pas de dessert. A
7. Ils n'ont pas de livres français. B
8. Tu n'as pas d'argent. C

A. We're not ordering any dessert.
B. They don't have any French books.
C. You don't have any money.
D. Do they have any antique armchairs?
E. We have (some) ashtrays.
F. She does not eat any meat.
G. I have some pretty dresses.
H. Do you have any white wine?

GRAMMAR III Present indicative of **aller** (to go). Question words.

A. The verb *aller* (to go) is an irregular verb, as are *être* (to be) and *avoir* (to have). These three verbs are very important and should be memorized because all three are used to form other tenses and verb constructions.

SUBJECT	ALLER	SUBJECT	TO GO
je	**vais**	I	go, am going, do go
tu	**vas**	you	go, are going, do go
il, elle, on	**va**	he, she, it	goes, is going, does go
nous	**allons**	we	go, are going, do go
vous	**allez**	you	go, are going, do go
ils, elles	**vont**	they	go, are going, do go

NOTE:

"To go to" is *aller à*. The contraction of à and *la* or *le* is handled as follows: *à* + *la* = *à la; à* + *le* = *au,* as in *Je vais au cinéma.*

B. Question words are always followed by the interrogative accent and invert verb and pronoun subject.

EX.: *Comment allez-vous?* (How are you?)

The verb precedes the subject. Other question words are:

quand, as in *Quand étudiez-vous?* When do you study?
où, as in *Où étudiez-vous?* Where do you study?
comment, as in *Comment étudiez-vous?* How do you study?
pourquoi, as in *Pourquoi étudiez-vous?* Why do you study?
combien, as in *Combien?* How much?

NOTES:

1. *Combien c'est?* How much is it?
2. *Combien de?* How many? as in *Combien de garçons?* How many boys?

C. The other question words are the English equivalents of "who," "whom," and "what." They are: *qui* (who), *quoi* (what), and *que* (which, whom). "To whom," "of whom," "what," "about what," "whom" translate the following French question expressions:

> *à qui?* to whom, as in *À qui parlez-vous?* To whom are you speaking?
> *de qui?* of whom, as in *De qui parlez-vous?* Of whom are you speaking?
> *à quoi?* to what, about what, as in *À quoi pensez-vous?* What are you thinking about?
> *de quoi?* of what, about what, as in *De quoi parlez-vous?* What are you talking about?

EXERCISES

A. Practice the verb *aller* (to go).

1. Charles __va__ (goes) au cinéma avec Antoinette.
2. Charles et Antoinette __vont__ (are going) à la maison.
3. Les étudiants (students) __vont__ (do go) au théâtre.

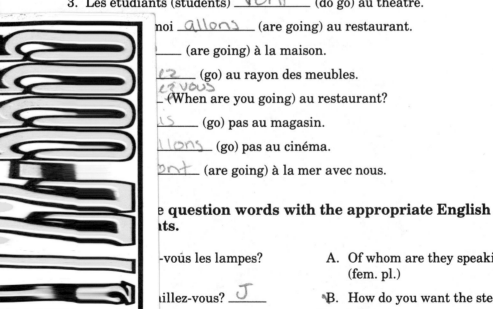

...moi __allons__ (are going) au restaurant.

...__ (are going) à la maison.

...ez__ (go) au rayon des meubles.

...ez vous __ (When are you going) au restaurant?

...is__ (go) pas au magasin.

...llons__ (go) pas au cinéma.

...ont__ (are going) à la mer avec nous.

...e question words with the appropriate English ...ts.

...-vous les lampes?

...illez-vous? __J__

...ous aimez l'argent?

4. À qui téléphonez-vous aujourd'hui? __I__
5. De quoi discutez-vous? __H__

A. Of whom are they speaking? (fem. pl.)
B. How do you want the steak?
C. Where do you look for the lamps?
D. How many armchairs do you have?
E. What are you thinking about?

(continued on the next page)

6. Comment voulez-vous le biftek? B
7. Combien de fauteuils avez-vous? D
8. À quoi penses-tu? E
9. De qui parlent-elles? A
10. Pourquoi fumez-vous? G

F. Do you like money?
G. Why do you smoke?
H. What are you discussing?
I. Whom are you calling today?
J. When do you work?

Lesson 4

À L'AÉROPORT
(At the Airport)

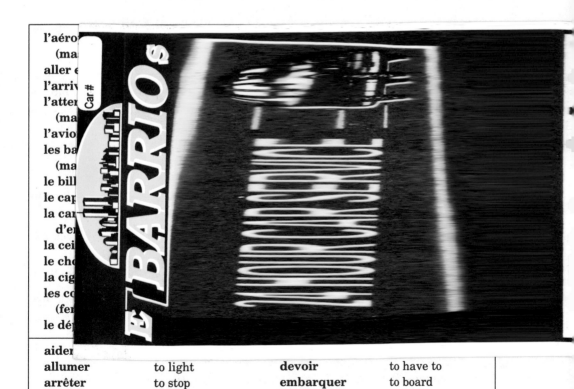

l'aéro
(ma
aller e
l'arriv
l'atter
(ma
l'avio
les ba
(ma
le bill
le cap
la car
d'e
la cei
le ch
la cig
les co
(fe
le dé

aider			
allumer	to light	**devoir**	to have to
arrêter	to stop	**embarquer**	to board
arriver	to arrive, to happen	**faire escale**	to stop over
		faire la queue	to stay in line
atterrir	to land	**fumer**	to smoke
décoller	to take off	**inspecter**	to inspect
descendre	to go down	**monter**	to go up

montrer	to show	**sortir**	to go out
partir	to leave	**voler**	to fly, to steal
pouvoir	to be able to	**vouloir**	to want
recevoir	to receive		
à l'heure	on time	**fabuleux**	fabulous
aussi	also	**heureusement**	happily
car	for, therefore	**loin de**	far from
court	short	**lourd**	heavy
devant	before, in front of	**poli**	polite
		tout à fait	quite

PRACTICE THE NEW WORDS

(Answers for Lesson 4, pp. 64–66)

A. Choose the word that fits in the sentence.

1. Les passagers arrivent à la ____________________. (bagages, douane, parachute)
2. L'hôtesse de l'air ____________________. (arrête, fume, aide)
3. Nous ne ____________________ (achetons, partons, fumons) pas dans la cabine.
4. Nous achetons les ____________________ (billets, bagages, pilote) à l'aéroport.
5. L'avion ____________________ (dépense, décolle, la queue) à temps.
6. Nous ____________________ (partons, dépensons, attachons) les ceintures de sécurité.
7. Le douanier inspecte ____________________. (les commandes, les bagages, les cigarettes)
8. L'hôtesse de l'air est ____________________. (le pilote, passager, polie)
9. Le voyage de New York à Paris n'est pas ____________________. (lourd, court, poli)

B. Write the appropriate words and read the sentences aloud.

1. Les bagages sont ____________________. (gentils, lourds, polis)
2. L'hôtesse est ____________________. (à l'heure, aussi, polie)
3. Les passagers attachent ____________________. (les bagages, les valises, les ceintures)
4. L'avion décolle ____________________. (lourd, fenêtre, à l'heure)

5. Le douanier inspecte ______________________. (l'avion, le voyageur, les bagages)
6. L'avion atterrit ______________________. (à l'hôtel, à la fenêtre, à l'aéroport)

DIALOGUE *À l'aéroport*

Charles arrive à l'aéroport pour acheter deux billets, aller et retour New York-Paris. Antoinette attend au café.

L'EMPLOYÉ: Bonjour Monsieur, vous désirez?
CHARLES: Oui, j'ai besoin de deux billets aller et retour New York-Paris.
L'EMPLOYÉ: Nous avons deux vols, le vol 620 décolle à quatorze heures et le vol 412 décolle à dix-huit heures trente.
CHARLES: Je voudrais deux billets pour le vol 412.
L'EMPLOYÉ: Très bien Monsieur. Voilà vos billets. Pour le choix des sièges, allez à la porte douze pour obtenir la carte d'embarquement.
ANTOINETTE: Dans une heure, l'avion décolle et dans quelques heures nous allons atterrir à Paris.
CHARLES: Mais avant cela, il faut obtenir les cartes d'embarquement. C'est à la porte numéro douze. Tiens, voilà, demande à l'hôtesse de l'air.
ANTOINETTE: Pardon Mademoiselle. Où doit-on obtenir les cartes d'embarquement?
L'HÔTESSE: Ici, Madame—devant vous.
CHARLES: Antoinette, c'est ici. Il faut faire la queue.
ANTOINETTE: Dans quelques heures nous allons atterrir à Paris . . . quelle chance!
CHARLES: Oui, nous avons de la chance!
L'EMPLOYÉ: Voilà, Monsieur, deux sièges dans la section pour non-fumeurs. Bon voyage!
CHARLES: Merci beaucoup, Monsieur.

DIALOG *At the Airport*

Charles arrives at the airport to buy two New York–Paris round trip tickets. Antoinette is waiting at the coffee shop.

EMPLOYEE: Good morning, sir, you wish? (what do you wish?)
CHARLES: Yes. I need two round trip tickets, New York–Paris.
EMPLOYEE: We have two flights, flight 620 departing at 2:00 P.M. and flight 412 at 6:30 P.M.

CHARLES:	I would like two tickets for flight 412.
EMPLOYEE:	Very well, sir. Here are your tickets. For the choice of seats, go to gate 12 to get the boarding pass.
ANTOINETTE:	In one hour the plane takes off and in a few hours we will land in Paris.
CHARLES:	But before that we have to get the boarding passes. It's at gate twelve. Well, here, ask the stewardess.
ANTOINETTE:	Pardon me, miss, where do you get the boarding passes?
THE STEWARDESS:	Here, madam, in front of you.
CHARLES:	Antoinette, it's here. We have to stand in line.
ANTOINETTE:	How lucky! In a few hours we will land in Paris.
CHARLES:	Yes, we are lucky!
EMPLOYEE:	Here, sir, two seats in the non-smoking section. Have a good trip.
CHARLES:	Thank you very much, sir.

DIALOG EXERCISES

A. Match the two columns according to the dialog.

1. L'avion ____________ dans une heure.	A. aide
2. Charles achète ____________.	B. au café
3. Antoinette attend ____________.	C. à Paris
4. L'hôtesse ____________ Antoinette.	D. les billets
5. Antoinette est ____________.	E. ne fument pas
6. Il faut faire la queue ____________.	F. décolle
7. Ils sont devant ____________.	G. heureuse
8. Charles et Antoinette ____________.	H. pour la carte d'embarquement
9. L'avion atterrit ____________.	I. de la chance
10. Antoinette et Charles ont ____________.	J. l'employé

B. Complete the sentences according to the dialog.

1. Charles arrive à ______________________________ pour ______________ deux billets ______________ New York–Paris.
2. Où Antoinette attend-elle? ____________.

3. De quoi Charles a-t-il besoin? ______________________.
4. Charles choisit le vol ______________________.
5. Où va Charles après? ______________________.
6. Qu'est-ce que Charles veut (wants) à la porte douze? ______________________
______________________.
7. Pourquoi Charles et Antoinette font la queue? ______________________.
8. Pourquoi ont-ils de la chance? ______________________.
9. Où Charles et Antoinette vont-ils atterrir? ______________________.
10. Les sièges de Charles et Antoinette sont dans la section ______________________
______________________.

GRAMMAR I Present indicative of **faire** (to do, to make).

A. Memorize the following chart.

SUBJECT	VERB	SUBJECT	VERB
je	**fais**	I	do
tu	**fais**	you	do
il, elle (on)	**fait**	he, she, it, one	does
nous	**faisons**	we	do
vous	**faîtes**	you	do
ils, elles	**font**	they	do

B. *Il fait,* the third-person singular, is used in describing the weather. In French, as in English, *il* (it) replaces *le temps* (the weather). Thus we have the following expressions which should be memorized:

il fait beau (temps)	it is beautiful (weather)
il fait mauvais (temps)	it is bad (weather)
il fait chaud	it is warm
il fait froid	it is cold
il fait du vent (wind)	it is windy
il fait du soleil	it is sunny

C. Other useful expressions with *faire* are:

faire des courses	to go shopping, to run errands
faire une promenade	to take a walk
faire la cuisine	to cook
faire le ménage	to do housework
faire un voyage	to take a trip
faire partie de	to belong to
faire la vaisselle	to do the dishes
faire le marché	to do the (grocery) shopping

EXERCISES

A. Read aloud and answer the following questions.

Example: Est-ce qu'il joue au football?
Oui, il joue au football.

1. Est-ce qu'il fait chaud? ______________.
2. Est-ce qu'elles font du ski? ______________.
3. Est-ce que vous faîtes des courses? ______________.
4. Est-ce qu'il fait du soleil? ______________.
5. Est-ce qu'il fait beau? ______________.
6. Est-ce qu'il fait mauvais? ______________.
7. Est-ce qu'il fait froid? ______________.
8. Est-ce qu'il fait du vent? ______________.
9. Est-ce que vous faîtes la vaisselle? ______________.
10. Est-ce qu'elles font du sport? ______________.
11. Est-ce que vous faîtes une promenade? ______________.
12. Est-ce qu'elle fait le ménage? ______________.

B. Write in French the following sentences, using the verb *faire.*

1. ______________. I'm (studying) skiing, I'm a skier.
2. ______________. She's going shopping.
3. ______________. He plays music.
4. ______________. They do housework.

5. ______________________. The weather is beautiful.
6. ______________________. I'm going skiing.
7. ______________________. We're taking a walk.
8. ______________________. She does the cooking.
9. ______________________. They study French.
10. ______________________. We're doing the dishes.

GRAMMAR II **Quelle heure est-il?** (What time is it?) More numbers.

A. Memorize the following chart and related expressions.
The answer to *Quelle heure est-il?* is *Il est,* followed by the hour and minutes. The chart below gives the pattern to learn for telling time.

1. Exact hour: *(l'heure exacte)*	**Il est une heure.**	It's one o'clock.
	Il est quatre heures.	It's four o'clock.
	Il est six heures.	It's six o'clock.
2. After the hour: *(après l'heure)*	**Il est une heure dix.**	It's 1:10.
	Il est quatre heures vingt.	It's 4:20.
	Il est six heures quinze.	It's 6:15.
3. Before the hour: *(avant l'heure)*	**Il est une heure moins dix.**	It's 12:50.
	Il est quatre heures moins vingt.	It's 3:40.
	Il est six heures moins quinze.	It's 5:45.

NOTES:

1. To tell time with the half hour and the quarter hour, we say for half past: *il est six heures et demie,* or *il est six heures trente;* for quarter past we say: *il est six heures et quart,* or *il est six heures quinze.*
2. We translate time before the hour by *moins* (minus), as in *il est six heures moins quinze.* Note that we add the article *le* when we use *moins* with *quart,* as in *moins le quart.*

    EX.: *Il est une heure moins le quart.* (It's a quarter to one.)
    Il est sept heures moins le quart. (It's a quarter to seven.)

    This is the only time we use *le* to tell time.
3. French avoids the confusion between P.M. and A.M. by simply adding *du matin* for the A.M. hours and *de l'après midi* for the P.M. hours. Also used is the expression *du soir* for the evening hours.

    EX.: *Je prends mon café au lait à huit heures du matin.*
    (I take my coffee with milk at eight A.M.)
    Je fais des courses à deux heures de l'après-midi.
    (I go shopping at two P.M.)
    Je dîne au restaurant à sept heures du soir.
    (I have dinner at the restaurant at seven P.M.)

4. To translate the English "sharp," as in "it is twelve noon, sharp," French uses the word *pile,* as in *il est midi pile.* To translate "about," as in "it's about noon," French uses *vers* or *environ,* as in *il est environ midi,* or *je rentre vers midi.* (I return home around noon.)

B. Memorize the numbers 20–1,000.

20.	vingt, vingt et un, vingt-deux, etc.	20, 21, 22, etc.
30.	trente, trente et un, trente-deux, etc.	30, 31, 32, etc.
40.	quarante, quarante et un, quarante-deux, etc.	40, 41, 42, etc.
50.	cinquante, cinquante et un, cinquante-deux, etc.	50, 51, 52, etc.
60.	soixante, soixante et un, soixante-deux, etc.	60, 61, 62, etc.
70.	soixante-dix, soixante et onze, soixante-douze, etc.	70, 71, 72, etc.
80.	quatre-vingts, quatre-vingt-un, quatre-vingt-deux, etc.	80, 81, 82, etc.
90.	quatre-vingt-dix, quatre-vingt-onze, quatre-vingt-douze, etc.	90, 91, 92, etc.
100.	cent, cent un, cent deux, etc.	100, 101, 102, etc.
200.	deux cents, deux cent un, deux cent deux, etc.	200, 201, 202, etc.
1,000.	mille, deux milles, trois milles, etc.	1,000, 2,000, 3,000, etc.

NOTES:

1. From 21 to 71, French adds *et un* and uses *onze* with 60 and with 80: *soixante et onze, quatre-vingt-onze.*
2. The numbers between 2 and 9 are added directly after 21, 31, 41, etc., up to 69: *soixante-neuf.* Then the structure changes to *soixante-dix* and continues counting after ten, as in *soixante-douze, soixante-treize, soixante-quatorze,* etc. this pattern continues up to 99: *quatre-vingt-dix-neuf.* Then comes *cent* (100). After *cent,* counting in French follows the English pattern, as in *cent* (100), *deux cents* (200), *trois cents* (300), and so on up to *neuf cents* (900).

EXERCISES

A. Answer the following questions.

1. Write the answer to: Quelle heure est-il? ____________________.
2. What are the two ways for fifteen minutes past the hour, as in, *il est une heure* ____________________ and ____________________.
3. In telling time, half past is expressed in two ways: *il est une heure* ____________________ and ____________________.
4. To indicate the minutes before the hour, we use the word ____________________.
5. What does French use to indicate A.M.? ____________________.

6. What are the two ways of specifying P.M. in French?
   ____________________ and ____________________.
7. Write the two French words that translate "about":
   ____________________.
8. How do you say "it is one o'clock sharp"? *Il est une heure*
   ____________________.
9. Write the French for "What time is it?" ____________________?
10. What is required to translate into French, "a quarter to"?
    ____________________.

B. Translate the following time expressions.

1. It's 4:20 P.M. ____________________.
2. It's 10:10 A.M. ____________________.
3. It's 9:15 P.M. ____________________.
4. It's 2:05 A.M. ____________________.
5. It's 6:30 P.M. ____________________.
6. It's 8:15 A.M. ____________________.
7. It's 7:08 P.M. ____________________.
8. It's 3:05 P.M. ____________________.
9. It's 1:10 A.M. ____________________.
10. It's 2:00 P.M. sharp ____________________.

C. Practice the numbers.

1. French uses *et* after *un* in __________, __________, __________, __________, and __________.
2. What happens after *soixante-dix* and *quatre-vingt-dix?*
   ____________________.
3. At what number between *20* and *90,* do the French not use *et* with *un?*
   ____________________.
4. Write the following numbers in letters:
   81 ____________________.
   91 ____________________.
   97 ____________________.
   75 ____________________.
   61 ____________________.
   71 ____________________.

GRAMMAR III Present indicative of irregular verbs: **pouvoir** (to be able to) and **vouloir** (to want).

A. Memorize these two verbs.

SUBJECT	POUVOIR (to be able to)	VOULOIR (to want)
je	**peux**	**veux**
tu	**peux**	**veux**
il, elle, on	**peut**	**veut**
nous	**pouvons**	**voulons**
vous	**pouvez**	**voulez**
ils, elles	**peuvent**	**veulent**

B. Observe the changes in the above verbs: the stem vowels in *pou*voir and *vou*loir alternate between *eu* and *ou*. We have the *eu* vowel in all the forms of the verbs except with *nous* and *vous*.

C. *Vouloir* (to want) and *pouvoir* (to be able to) are used with direct objects.

EX.: *Je veux de la salade.* (I want some salad.)
Nous voulons du vin. (We want some wine.)
Je peux comprendre le menu. (I can understand the menu.)

However, *vouloir* is also used with the direct infinitive, and as such *vouloir* translates "to wish to" + infinitive.

EX.: *Je veux écrire une lettre.* (I wish to write a letter.)
Nous voulons regarder le film. (We wish to see the movie.)
Il veut comprendre la leçon. (He wants to understand the lesson.)

NOTE:

The general rule in French is that when two verbs follow each other, the second verb is always in the infinitive.

EX.: *J'aime danser.* (I like to dance.)

They are also called direct independent infinitives, as in *je veux manger, je peux manger.* French uses no prepositions to denote an infinitive, except with some verbs which require *à* or *de* and which we will discuss in Lesson 6.

EXERCISES

A. Practice the verb *vouloir* (to want).

1. They want the books. ____________________.
2. He does want to eat. ____________________.
3. We wish to understand. ____________________.
4. Do you want to travel? ____________________.
5. You do wish to help. ____________________.
6. The customs officer wants the luggage. ____________________.
7. She wishes to smoke. ____________________.
8. You do want to finish the lesson. ____________________.
9. We wish to speak French. ____________________.
10. They want to stop over in Paris. ____________________.

B. Practice the verb *pouvoir* (to be able to).

1. L'avion __________ faire escale à Paris.
2. Charles et Antoinette __________ aider le douanier.
3. Le capitaine __________ comprendre les voyageurs.
4. Est-ce que Charles __________ fumer dans l'avion?
5. L'hôtesse et le capitaine __________ parler.
6. Les passagers ne __________ pas toucher les commandes.
7. L'avion __________ décoller à l'heure.
8. Vous ne __________pas aider le capitaine.
9. Nous __________acheter les billets.
10. Les passagers __________ montrer les cartes d'embarquement.

Lesson 5

LA FAMILLE (The Family)

l'ami (masc.)	friend	**la maison**	house
le bain	bath	**la salle de bains**	bathroom
le balcon	balcony	**la salle à manger**	dining room
les bijoux (masc.)	jewels	**la salle de séjour**	living room
le couloir	hallway	**la télévision**	television
la cour	yard	**la vaisselle**	dishes
la douche	shower	**le voisin (masc.)**	neighbor
la fleur	flower		
le jardin	garden		
la machine (à laver)	washing machine		

le beau-fils	son-in-law	**les époux**	spouses
le beau-frère	brother-in-law	**la femme**	wife, woman
les beaux-parents	parents-in-law	**le fiancé**	fiancé
le beau-père	father-in-law	**le fils**	son
la belle-fille	daughter-in-law	**le frère**	brother
la belle-mère	mother-in-law	**la grand-mère**	grandmother
la belle-soeur	sister-in-law	**les grands-parents**	grandparents
le cousin (masc.)	cousin	**le grand-père**	grandfather
la cousine (fem.)	cousin	**le mari**	husband
l'enfant	child	**la mère**	mother
l'épouse (fem.)	spouse (wife)	**le neveu**	nephew
		la nièce	niece
		l'oncle (masc.)	uncle

les parents	parents	**le petit-fils**	grandson
le père	father	**la soeur**	sister
la petite-fille	granddaughter	**la tante**	aunt
accompagner	to accompany	**envoyer**	to send
appeler	to call	**essayer**	to try
apporter	to bring	**faire la table**	to set the table
apprécier	to appreciate	**habiter**	to live in, inhabit
baigner (se)	to bathe (oneself)		
conduire	to drive	**inviter**	to invite
connaître	to know	**laver (se laver)**	to wash (oneself)
croire	to believe	**préparer**	to prepare
devoir	to have to	**rester**	to stay, to remain
dormir	to sleep		
écouter	to listen	**savoir**	to know
entendre	to hear	**venir**	to come
aujourd'hui	today	**hier**	yesterday
aussi	also	**jeune**	young
célibataire	single	**jolie (fem.)**	pretty
chez moi	at my home	**maintenant**	now
demain	tomorrow	**mon, ma, mes**	my
dès que	as soon as	**plein (masc.)**	full
enchanté	pleased (enchanted)	**souvent**	often
		tôt	early
gentil	kind	**vrai (masc.)**	true
heureux	happy, glad	**vraiment**	truly

NOTES:

1. The adjectives *beau* (beautiful), *nouveau* (new) and *vieux* (old) are always placed before the nouns they modify. They also are irregular. Please note the following examples:

   beau *un beau garçon,* but *un bel homme* (a handsome man)
   nouveau *un nouveau livre,* but *un nouvel ami* (a new friend, masc.)
   vieux *un vieux livre,* but *un vieil homme* (an old man)

   These irregular forms occur only in the masculine and only when the nouns start with a vowel or a mute "h."

2. The feminine forms of the above adjectives are:

   belle *une belle femme, des belles femmes*
   nouvelle *une nouvelle maison, des nouvelles maisons*
   vieille *une vieille table, des vieilles tables*

3. Note also that *beau* and *belle* used with a hyphen and with members of a family always translate to *in-law,* as in *belle-soeur* (sister-in-law).

4. *Laver* (to wash) + direct object, as in *laver la vaisselle* (to wash the dishes), and *baigner* (to bathe), as in *baigner l'enfant* (to bathe the child). These verbs are also

used with *se,* the reflexive pronoun. Thus, *se laver* translates into "to wash oneself," and *se baigner* is "to bathe oneself." We will study these constructions in Lesson 9.

5. *Mon, ma,* and *mes* are possessive adjectives for "my". *Mon* is used with masculine singular nouns and feminine singular nouns beginning with a vowel, *ma* with feminine singular nouns, and *mes* is used with plural of either or both genders. We will study these adjectives in Lesson 6.

PRACTICE THE VOCABULARY

(Answers for Lesson 5, pp. 67–69)

A. Write *un* or *une* in front of the following nouns, as appropriate.

1. _____ couloir	7. _____ oncle
2. _____ cousine	8. _____ mère
3. _____ fils	9. _____ tante
4. _____ père	10. _____ balcon
5. _____ fleur	11. _____ machine
6. _____ douche	12. _____ voisine

B. Complete the following sentences.

1. Le frère de ma mère est mon __________.
2. La sœur de mon père est ma __________.
3. Le mari de ma mère est mon __________.
4. La femme de mon père est ma __________.
5. Les enfants de ma tante sont mes __________.
6. Mes grands-parents sont les __________ de mon __________.
7. Le père de mon mari est mon __________.
8. Le frère de ma femme est mon __________.
9. La fille de ma mère est ma __________.
10. Le fils de mon père est mon __________.
11. Les parents de mon mari sont mes __________.
12. La sœur de ma femme est ma __________.

C. Match the two columns.

1. Mon père lit le journal ____________.
2. Ma mère prépare le dîner ____________.
3. Nous regardons la télévision ____________.
4. Mon jardin est joli ____________.
5. Je fais la vaisselle ____________.
6. Ils sont gentils, ____________.
7. Ma soeur fait la table ____________.
8. Nous faisons une promenade ____________.
9. Ils sont vieux, ____________.
10. Elle est grande et belle, ____________.

A. après le dîner
B. la maison
C. avant le dîner
D. mes parents
E. dans la salle à manger
F. avec des arbres et des fleurs
G. mes grands-parents
H. avec nos voisins
I. dans la salle de séjour
J. dans la cuisine

D. Underline the words that fit.

1. La cuisine est dans (le jardin, la salle de bains, la maison).
2. La douche est dans (la chambre, le balcon, la salle de bains).
3. Se baigner est aussi (dormir, appeller, se laver).
4. Les parents aident (l'avion, la cour, les enfants).
5. Ma belle-mère est (la nièce, l'oncle, gentille).
6. Nous apportons (la télévision, le jardin, les fleurs).
7. Nous bricolons (dans le camion, la chambre, la cuisine).
8. Les fauteuils sont (heureux, calmes, chers).
9. Nous passons le weekend (avec des fleurs, avec des amis, avec la lampe).
10. J'admire et j'aime les (couloirs, bijoux, balcons) de ma mère.
11. Le fauteuil et la lampe sont dans (la cuisine, le salon, le bain).
12. Mes beaux-parents sont les parents de (mon oncle, mon frère, mon mari).

E. Translate the following phrases into French and write them in the spaces provided.

1. A handsome man ____________________.
2. A beautiful woman ____________________.

3. A new tree ______________________.
4. An old hotel ______________________.
5. An old boyfriend ______________________.
6. My sister-in-law is beautiful ______________________.
7. My lamp is old ______________________.
8. My garden is new ______________________.
9. My parents are kind ______________________.
10. My husband does the dishes ______________________.

DIALOGUE *La fiancée de Charles*

CHARLES: Demain ma fiancée arrive de Boston.
ANTOINE: C'est vrai? À quelle heure?
CHARLES: L'avion atterrit à quatre heures de l'après-midi, plus ou moins.
ANTOINE: As-tu besoin de ma voiture?
CHARLES: Non, merci, mes parents vont conduire à l'aéroport. Ma sœur et ma tante vont venir avec nous.
ANTOINE: Tu m'invites pour faire la connaisance de mademoiselle!
CHARLES: Bien sûr, cher ami!

(arrivée à la maison)

CHARLES: Chérie, voilà ta chambre. Elle est à côté de la petite salle de bains.
JULIETTE: Oh! C'est charmant. Elle donne sur le jardin. Je suis vraiment heureuse d'être ici!
CHARLES: Et moi aussi, je suis très heureux de t'avoir avec nous.
JULIETTE: Nous sortons demain?
CHARLES: Oui, si tu veux. Aussi, mon ami Antoine veut faire ta connaissance.
JULIETTE: Ah, c'est vrai, tu parles toujours d'Antoine dans tes lettres.
CHARLES: Tu sais, ma sœur et ma tante veulent aller faire des courses demain. Peut-être que nous pouvons aller ensemble dans la voiture d'Antoine.
JULIETTE: Il est déjà cinq heures du soir. Je dois ranger mes affaires et aider ma future belle-mère à préparer le dîner.
CHARLES: Ah! Une fiancée parfaite! Et la belle-fille idéale.

DIALOG *Charles' Fiancée*

CHARLES: Tomorrow my fiancée arrives from Boston.
ANTOINE: Is it true? At what time?
CHARLES: The plane lands at four P.M., more or less.
ANTOINE: Do you need my car?
CHARLES: No, thanks, my parents are going to drive to the airport. My sister and my aunt are going to come with us.
ANTOINE: Will you invite me to (make acquaintance of) meet the Miss?
CHARLES: Of course, dear friend!

(arrival at home)

CHARLES: Darling, here's your room. It's next to the small bathroom.
JULIETTE: Oh! It's charming. It overlooks the garden. I'm truly happy to be here!
CHARLES: And me too, I'm very happy to have you with us.
JULIETTE: Are we going out tomorrow?
CHARLES: Yes, if you like. Also, my friend Antoine wants to meet you.
JULIETTE: Ah! It's true, you're always talking about Antoine in your letters.
CHARLES: You know, my sister and aunt want to go shopping tomorrow. Maybe we'll all go together in Antoine's car.
JULIETTE: Can you imagine, it's already five in the evening. I have to put away my things (effects) and help my future mother-in-law prepare dinner.
CHARLES: Ah! The perfect fiancée and the ideal daughter-in-law.

DIALOG EXERCISE

Match the English with the French.

1. Ma future belle-sœur s'appelle Juliette.
2. Mes parents aiment ma future femme.
3. Mon ami veut toujours m'aider.
4. Je connais bien mes futurs beaux-parents.
5. Ma sœur apprécie mes amis.
6. Mémé reste à la maison.

A. I know my future in-laws well.
B. My boyfriend is always willing to help.
C. My future sister-in-law's name is Juliette.
D. My parents like my future wife.
E. My girlfriend likes being single.
F. My fiancée is happy at my home.

(continued on the next page)

7. Mon ami veut m'accompagner à l'aéroport.
8. Ma fiancée est heureuse chez moi.
9. Mon amie aime être célibataire.
10. Je préfère être marié(e).

G. My sister appreciates my friend.
H. Grandma stays at home.
I. I prefer being married.
J. My boyfriend wants to accompany me to the airport.

GRAMMAR I Present indicative of stem-changing verbs **manger** (to eat), **commencer** (to start), **acheter** (to buy), and **payer** (to pay for).

A. Memorize the stem-changing verbs below.

SUBJECT	MANGER	COMMENCER	ACHETER	PAYER
je	**mange**	**commence**	**j'achète**	**paie**
tu	**manges**	**commences**	**achètes**	**paies**
il, elle, on	**mange**	**commence**	**achète**	**paie**
nous	**mangeons**	**commençons**	**achetons**	**payons**
vous	**mangez**	**commencez**	**achetez**	**payez**
ils, elles	**mangent**	**commencent**	**achètent**	**paient**

B. Please note the following rules:

1. In French, *g* and *c* have the hard sounds of *g* and *k* before *a, o, oi, ou;* and soft sounds of *j (g)* and *s (c)* before *e* and *i*. The consonant *c* has another feature. It converts to a soft sound when a cedilla is added under the *c,* as in *garçon.*
2. With the verbs *manger, changer,* and others ending in *-ger,* an *e* is added to the *-ons* ending to keep the soft sound throughout the conjugation, as in nous mang*e*ons, nous chang*e*ons. The remaining forms follow the regular ending of the *-ER* verbs.
3. With the verbs ending in *-cer,* such as *commencer,* the soft sound is kept throughout the conjugation by adding a cedilla to the *c* of the *-ons* ending, as in *nous commençons.*
4. With a few verbs like *acheter,* the *e* of the stem (aché) is not pronounced in the infinitive nor in the *nous achétons* and *vous achétez* forms; but the *e* in all other forms is pronounced, thanks to an "accent grave," as in *j'achète* etc.

5. With *payer* and other verbs ending in *-yer,* the *y* of the stem *(pay)* becomes *i* in all forms except with *nous* and *vous,* as in *nous payons, vous payez,* but *je paie, tu paies,* etc.

C. Below is a chart containing some of the verbs included in these four categories of stem-changing verbs.

MANGER	COMMENCER	ACHETER	PAYER
changer (de) (to change)	**dénoncer** (to denounce)	**achever** (to complete)	**employer** (to hire, to employ)
engager (to engage; to engage in)	**menacer** (to threaten)	**amener** (to bring)	**essayer (de)** (to try)
juger (to judge)	**prononcer** (to pronounce)	**lever (se)** (to rise)	
nager (to swim)	**remplacer** (to replace)	**promener (se)** (to take a walk)	
partager (to share)	**tracer** (to lay out)		
voyager (to travel)			

PRACTICE THE STEM-CHANGING VERBS

1. The consonants *g* and *c* are hard sounding before ____________ and ____________.

2. The consonants *g* and *c* become soft with ____________ and ____________.

3. What is added to *c* to convert it to an *s* sound before the vowels *o* and *u?* ____________.

4. The verbs ending in *-ger* are kept soft throughout the conjugation thanks to ____________.

5. The verb *tracer* (to trace) has a *nous* form of ____________; name two more verbs requiring the same forms: ____________ and ____________.

6. The verb *achever* (to complete) is among a small number of verbs that require an accent grave. Give all the forms where this happens: ____________, ____________, ____________, ____________.

7. *Essayer* (to try) is among a few verbs that change *y* into *i*. Name two other verbs: ____________ and ____________.

8. Name the two forms of *employer* (to employ) where the *y* remains: ______________________ and ______________________.
9. Say and write in French: *We pronounce well.* ______________________.
10. Say and write in French: *We travel a lot.* ______________________.

EXERCISE

Write the appropriate form of the following verbs.

1. Nous ______________________ (to denounce) la méchanceté.
2. Tu ______________________ (to buy) les beaux meubles.
3. Pourquoi ______________________ (do you change) d'hôtel?
4. Vous ne ______________________ (to pay) pas bien les employés.
5. Nous ______________________ (to try) d'acheter une maison.
6. Comment ______________________ (do you buy) un avion?
7. Il ______________________ (to bring) sa sœur.
8. Nous ne ______________________ (to travel) pas assez.
9. Nous ______________________ (to pronounce) bien.
10. Nous ne ______________________ (to judge) pas nos voisins.

GRAMMAR II Present indicative of **connaître** (to know) and **savoir** (to know). The difference between **connaître** and **savoir.**

Memorize the conjugation below:

SUBJECT	CONNAÎTRE	SAVOIR
je	**connais**	**sais**
tu	**connais**	**sais**
il, elle, on	**connaît**	**sait**
nous	**connaissons**	**savons**
vous	**connaissez**	**savez**
ils, elles	**connaissent**	**savent**

NOTES:

Notice the following facts about the verb *connaître* (to know):

1. The verb *connaître* translates the English "to be familiar with" or "to be acquainted with." "To be familiar with" is always used with persons, animals, and places:

   EX.: *Je connais Antoinette.* I know Antoinette.
   Je connais cette maison. I know this house.
   Elle connaît mon chien. She knows my dog.

   Note that in *connaître,* the accent circonflexe (ˆ) on the *i* always appears before a *t (connaître, connaît).*

2. The verb *savoir,* on the other hand, translates something we know for certain. It never involves human beings, animals, or places:

   EX.: *Je sais très bien la leçon.* I know the lesson very well.
   Elle sait mon âge. She knows my age.
   Nous savons notre problème. We know our problem.

3. *Savoir* followed by an infinitive translates the English *to know how to do* (something) although the English also uses *can* or *to be able to.*

   EX.: *Je sais danser.* I know how to dance. I can dance.
   Savez-vous nager? Do you know how to swim? Can you swim?

PRACTICE *CONNAÎTRE* AND *SAVOIR*

1. *Connaître* is used with direct objects denoting ____________,
   ____________, and ____________.
2. *Savoir* is never used with ____________,
   ____________, and ____________.
3. *Connaître* is the French equivalent of ____________ and
   ____________.
4. *Savoir* followed by an infinitive is the French equivalent of
   ____________, ____________, and
   ____________.

EXERCISE

Complete the following sentences with *connaître* or *savoir.*

1. Est-ce que Jacques ____________ ses parents?
2. Je ____________ que Jacques est gentil.
3. Nous ____________ le théâtre Sarah Bernhard.
4. Vous ____________ la question et la réponse.
5. Ils ____________ la Maison Blanche.

6. Elle ______________________ pourquoi le restaurant est plein.
7. Vous ______________________ mon petit chat.
8. Je ______________________ que le restaurant ferme (closes) à onze heures du soir.
9. Ils ______________________ ma tante et mon oncle.
10. Je ______________________ quand l'avion décolle.
11. Il ne ______________________ pas la réponse.
12. Nous ne ______________________ pas l'hôtesse.
13. Jeannine et Charles ______________________ parler français.
14. Je ne ______________________ pas les voisins.
15. Il ne ______________________ pas faire du ski.

GRAMMAR III Negative constructions.

Memorize the negative constructions in the chart below.

Ne + verb + jamais	never
ne + verb + plus	no more, no longer
ne + verb + personne	no one
ne + verb + ni	neither, nor
ne + verb + que	only
ne + verb + rien	nothing
ne + verb + pas encore	not yet

NOTES:

Note the following facts of the above negations:

1. The most important part of the negation *ne + verb + pas* is the word *pas*. It is so important that in negative answers it can stand on its own.

   EX.: *Voulez-vous du vin?* Do you want some wine?
   Negative answer: *Pas moi, merci.* Not me, thanks.
   Other examples:
   pas ici not here
   pas encore not yet
   pas nous not us
   pas elle not her

2. The negation *ne* + *verb* + *pas* is always kept in this order: *ne* + *verb* + *pas*. In using the other negative forms, *pas* is replaced by *plus* in *ne* + *verb* + *plus*, or *pas* is replaced by *jamais* in *ne* + *verb* + *jamais*. Study the following examples:

   EX.: *Je ne danse pas.* I don't dance.
   Je ne danse jamais. I never dance.
   Je ne danse plus. I no longer dance.
   Je ne mange rien à midi. I eat nothing at noon.
   Il ne connaît personne. He knows no one.

3. In the negative forms, the indefinite article and the partitive article become *de* and *d'*, except with *ni . . . ni*, where the article and the partitive are not used at all.

   EX.: *Je n'ai pas d'argent.* I don't have any money.
   Je n'ai plus d'argent. I have no more money.
   Je n'ai jamais d'argent. I never have any money.
   Je n'ai ni argent, ni cigarettes. I have neither money nor cigarettes.
   Je n'achète ni vin, ni bière. I buy neither wine nor beer.

4. The negative interrogative expression *n'est-ce pas* is used as in English—at the end of a sentence, as a confirmation of a suggested fact or statement.

   EX.: *Vous fumez, n'est-ce pas?* You smoke, don't you?
   Il est gentil, n'est-ce pas? He's kind, isn't he?
   Vous êtes français, n'est-ce pas? You're French, aren't you?

5. *Jamais, rien, personne,* and *pas* may be used without *ne* in answering questions.

   EX.: *Que cherchez-vous?* What are you looking for?
   Rien. Nothing.
   Qui est à la maison? Who is in the house?
   Personne. No one.

6. *Jamais,* on the other hand, when used in the affirmative without *ne,* translates *ever,* as in:

   Peut-il jamais danser. Can he ever dance!

7. *Rien* and *personne* can be used as subjects in a sentence, as in:

   Personne *ne* fume. No one smokes.
   Rien *ne* change. Nothing changes.

   Note that in these constructions *ne* is directly after *rien* and *personne*.

PRACTICE THE NEGATIVE CONSTRUCTIONS

1. All the negative forms use a two-word negation. Name the standard one. ____________.
2. Which part of these two words has more importance? ____________ ____________.
3. Which part of the negation remains constant? ____________.

4. What happens to the indefinite and partitive articles in negative expressions? ____________.
5. What is unusual about the negative construction *ni + verb + ni* regarding all articles? ____________.
6. What is the English equivalent of *jamais* used alone in an affirmative sentence? ____________.
7. When *rien* and *personne* are used as subjects of a sentence, what happens to *ne?* ____________.
8. What is the usual place of *ne* in negative constructions? ____________ ____________.
9. Name the four negation words that are used without *ne* in answers to questions. ____________, ____________, ____________, ____________.
10. Name the French equivalents of: neither ____________, nor ____________, nor ____________.

EXERCISES

A. Match the two columns.

1. Il n'a plus de confiance.
2. Nous ne savons jamais l'heure du départ.
3. Elle ne cherche rien ici.
4. Vous n'allez jamais au balcon.
5. Ils ne connaissent personne ici.
6. Rien n'est facile à faire.
7. Personne n'admire les méchants.
8. Est-il jamais à l'heure?

A. No one admires mean people.
B. He does not have any more confidence.
C. Is he ever on time?
D. She's not looking for anything here.
E. Nothing is easy to do.
F. They don't know anyone here.
G. You never go to the balcony.
H. We never know the time of departure.

B. Say and then write in French:

1. Not yet ____________
2. Not I ____________
3. Not you ____________
4. Not at the airport ____________
5. Not with me ____________
6. Not with us ____________
7. Not now ____________
8. Not tomorrow ____________

ANSWERS FOR LESSONS 1-5

Lesson 1

Basic Expressions

1. Bonjour
2. Je m'appelle . . .
3. Où habitez-vous?
4. Je vais bien, merci
5. En face du Cinéma *or* Là-bas à gauche.
6. À gauche
7. À gauche
8. S'il vous plaît
9. See you soon
10. En face de . . .
11. a. Au revoir b. À bientôt
12. See you tomorrow

Vocabulary

1. F	6. D	11. H	16. Q	21. V	26. Z
2. C	7. B	12. J	17. S	22. X	27. Y
3. E	8. I	13. O	18. P	23. W	28. d
4. A	9. K	14. M	19. T	24. U	29. c
5. G	10. L	15. N	20. R	25. b	30. a

Grammar I

Practice

1. le, la, les, l'
2. masculine or feminine
3. le, les
4. le, la with words starting with a vowel or silent *h*
5. la, la
6. la, les
7. l', l', le
8. la, la, la, l', la

Exercise

1. le	7. la	13. l'
2. le	8. le	14. le
3. la	9. l'	15. la
4. la	10. le	16. l'
5. la	11. la	17. le
6. le	12. l'	18. la

Grammar II

Practice

1. *un, une*
2. masculine
3. feminine
4. masculine
5. male nouns
6. female nouns
7. encounter of two vowels from two consecutive words
8. no
9. masculine/feminine
10. *une*

Exercise

1. une	7. un	13. une
2. un	8. un	14. un
3. un	9. une	15. une
4. un	10. un	16. un
5. un	11. un	17. un
6. un	12. une	18. un

Grammar III

Practice

1. I
2. *tu* (familiar), *vous* (formal sing.), *vous* (pl.)
3. informal situations
4. *vous*
5. *vous*
6. personal (he), impersonal (it)
7. *elle*
8. *elles*
9. Masc. pl./mixed
10. *il fait froid*
11. in impersonal expressions
12. it's warm (hot)

Exercises

A.

1. vous êtes	6. ils sont	11. ils sont
2. tu es	7. elles sont	12. ils sont
3. je suis	8. il est	13. ils sont
4. nous sommes	9. elle est	14. ils sont
5. vous êtes	10. elles sont	

B.

1. j'ai	6. ils ont
2. ils sont	7. tu es
3. je suis	8. vous avez
4. elles ont	9. elles sont
5. vous êtes	10. tu as

C.

1. avez-vous?	6. êtes-vous?
2. a-t-il?	7. sont-ils?
3. est-il?	8. étudiez-vous?
4. avons-nous?	9. ont-elles?
5. sommes-nous?	10. parlons-nous?

Lesson 2

Vocabulary

Practice

A.

1. le	7. le	13. le
2. l'	8. la	14. le
3. le	9. la	15. l'
4. le	10. la	16. la
5. la	11. la	17. l'
6. la	12. le	18. le

B.

1. M	8. C
2. N	9. K
3. A	10. F
4. I	11. E
5. L	12. B
6. J	13. D
7. H	14. G

Dialog Exercises

A.

1. chez Jeannine
2. excellent, délicieuse
3. Perrier
4. d'agneau
5. laitue
6. à bientôt
7. le repas
8. légumes
9. frites
10. retard
11. après-midi
12. caissière

B.

1. délicieuse
2. le café
3. les légumes
4. la caissière
5. jardin
6. au restaurant
7. travaillent
8. de la viande
9. un fruit de mer
10. des légumes

Grammar I

Practice

A.

1. three
2. *er, ir,* and *re*
3. Because the stem remains the same throughout the conjugation.
4. *parl-*
5. *dans-*
6. *nous parlons*

B.

1. parlez
2. commandent
3. travaille
4. cherchent
5. voyagent
6. regardons
7. j'aime
8. j'étudie
9. pensent
10. rentrons

Grammar II

Exercises

A.
1. répond
2. attend
3. finissent
4. réussit
5. réfléchit
6. rendons
7. choisissez
8. agissent
9. répondent
10. vendent

B.
1. Je finis le livre.
2. Nous parlons français.
3. Nous cherchons le restaurant.
4. Elle attend Charles.
5. Ils, elles aiment le gâteau.

Grammar III

Practice

A.
1. Je ne suis pas . . .
2. Elle n'a pas . . .
3. Nous n'avons pas . . .
4. Ils ne sont pas . . .
5. Vous n'êtes pas . . .
6. Vous n'avez pas . . .
7. Ils ne commandment pas . . .
8. Charles ne finit pas . . .
9. Antoinette ne travaille pas . . .
10. Ils n'attendent pas . . .
11. Nous ne payons pas . . .
12. Ils ne finissent pas . . .
13. Nous ne cherchons pas . . .
14. Vous ne trouvez pas . . .

Lesson 3

Vocabulary

Practice

A.
1. la
2. l'
3. le
4. les
5. l'
6. les
7. le
8. le
9. les

B.
1. les meubles
2. petit
3. grands
4. crédit
5. prix
6. l'argent
7. étroite
8. la rue

Dialog Exercises

A.
1. lampe, fauteuil
2. en haut
3. chère
4. rayon des meubles
5. couleurs
6. . . . la carte de crédit
7. . . . la qualité, valeur
8. lampe, fauteuil
9. deux cents francs, quarante-cinq
10. blanche, rouge

B.
1. C
2. D
3. G
4. E
5. H
6. I
7. B
8. F
9. A
10. J

Grammar I

Exercises A.
1. a noun, shape, quality
2. *e*
3. arménienne
4. français
5. gentille
6. vive
7. joyeuse
8. sérieuses
9. joyeux
10. anglais
11. complètes
12. lumineux
13. heureux
14. chanteuses
15. fière

B.
1. les petits chalets
2. les grandes chambres
3. les arbres verts
4. les hommes sportifs
5. les chiens noirs
6. les meubles anglais
7. les étudiants sérieux

Grammar II

Exercises A.
1. de la
2. d'
3. de
4. du
5. de
6. du
7. de la
8. des
9. du
10. de la

B. Nursery rhyme: Recite it without looking at the words.

C.
1. part of a whole, some, any
2. de, du, de la, des, de l'
3. no
4. pas de . . .
5. des
6. du
7. la and l'

D.
1. G
2. H
3. E
4. D
5. F
6. A
7. B
8. C

Grammar III

Exercises A.
1. va
2. vont
3. vont
4. allons
5. vas
6. vous allez
7. Quand allez-vous? (or) Quand vas-tu?
8. vais
9. allons
10. vont pas . . .

B.
1. C
2. J
3. F
4. I
5. H
6. B
7. D
8. E
9. A
10. G

Lesson 4

Vocabulary

Practice A.
1. douane
2. aide
3. fumons
4. billets
5. décolle
6. attachons
7. les bagages
8. polie
9. court

B.
1. lourds
2. polie
3. les ceintures
4. à l'heure
5. les bagages
6. à l'aéroport

Dialog Exercises

A.
1. F
2. D
3. B
4. A
5. G
6. H
7. J.
8. E
9. C
10. I

B.
1. l'aéroport, acheter, aller et retour
2. au café
3. . . . de deux billets
4. 412
5. à la porte numéro douze (12)
6. les cartes d'embarquement
7. pour obtenir les cartes
8. Parce que dans quelque heures ils vont atterrir.
9. à Paris
10. pour non-fumeurs

Grammar I

Exercises A.
1. Oui, il fait chaud.
2. Oui, elles font du ski.
3. Oui, vous faîtes des courses.
4. Oui, il fait du soleil.
5. Oui, il fait beau.
6. Oui, il fait mauvais.
7. Oui, il fait froid.
8. Oui, il fait du vent.
9. Oui, vous faîtes la vaisselle.
10. Oui, elles font du sport.
11. Oui, vous faîtes une promenade.
12. Oui, elle fait le ménage.

B.
1. Je fais du ski.
2. Elle fait des courses.
3. Il fait de la musique.
4. Ils, elles font le ménage.
5. Il fait beau.
6. Je vais faire du ski.
7. Nous faisons une promenade.
8. Elle fait la cuisine.
9. Ils, elles font du français.
10. Nous faisons la vaisselle.

Grammar II

Exercises A.
1. Il est une heure trente. (or any time you wish)
2. Il est une heure quinze (and) il est une heure et quart.
3. Il est une heure trente (and) il est une heure et demie.
4. moins
5. du matin
6. de l'après-midi (and) du soir
7. environ, vers
8. pile
9. Quelle heure est-il?
10. *le* as in "il est midi moins *le* quart"

B.
1. Il est quatre heures vingt de l'après-midi.
2. Il est dix heures dix du matin.
3. Il est neuf heures quinze du soir.
4. Il est deux heures cinq du matin.
5. Il est six heures et demie de l'après-midi.
6. Il est huit heures et quart du matin.
7. Il est sept heures huit du soir.
8. Il est trois heures cinq de l'après-midi.
9. Il est une heure dix du matin.
10. Il est deux heures de l'après-midi, pile.

C.
1. In 21, vingt et un, in 31, trente et un, in 41, quarante et un, in 51, cinquante et un, and in 61, soixante et un
2. After *soixante-dix* and *quatre-vingt-dix, onze, douze,* etc. are used.
3. quatre-vingt-un
4. quatre-vingt-un (81)
   quatre-vingt-onze (91)
   quatre-vingt-dix-sept (97)
   soixante-quinze (75)
   soixante et un (61)
   soixante et onze (71)

Grammar III

Exercises

A.
1. Ils veulent les livres.
2. Il veut manger.
3. Nous voulons comprendre.
4. Voulez-vous voyager?
5. Vous voulez aider.
6. Le douanier veut les bagages.
7. Elle veut fumer.
8. Vous voulez finir la leçon.
9. Nous voulons parler français.
10. Ils, elles veulent faire escale à Paris.

B.
1. peut
2. peuvent
3. peut
4. peut
5. peuvent
6. peuvent
7. peut
8. pouvez
9. pouvons
10. peuvent

Lesson 5

Vocabulary

Practice

A.
1. un
2. une
3. un
4. un
5. une
6. une
7. un
8. une
9. une
10. un
11. une
12. une

B.
1. oncle
2. tante
3. père
4. mère
5. cousins
6. parents, père
7. beau-père
8. beau-frère
9. sœur
10. frère
11. beaux-parents
12. belle-sœur

C.
1. C
2. J
3. I
4. F
5. A
6. D
7. E
8. H
9. G
10. B

D.
1. la maison
2. la salle de bains
3. se laver
4. les enfants
5. gentille
6. les fleurs
7. la cuisine
8. chers
9. avec des amis
10. bijoux
11. le salon
12. mon mari

E.
1. un bel homme
2. une belle femme
3. un nouvel arbre
4. un vieil hôtel
5. un vieil ami
6. Ma belle-soeur est belle.
7. Ma lampe est vieille.
8. Mon jardin est nouveau.
9. Mes parents sont gentils.
10. Mon mari fait la vaisselle.

Dialog Exercise

1. C
2. D
3. B
4. A
5. G
6. H
7. J
8. F
9. E
10. I

Grammar I

Practice

1. *a, o, oi,* and *ou*
2. *e* and *i*
3. a cedilla
4. vowel *e*
5. nous traçons, nous plaçons, nous commençons
6. j'achève, tu achèves, il, elle achève, ils, elles achèvent
7. payer, employer
8. nous employons, vous employez
9. Nous prononçons bien.
10. Nous voyageons beaucoup.

Exercise

1. denonçons
2. achètes
3. . . . changez-vous
4. . . . payez
5. essayons
6. acheter
7. amène
8. voyageons
9. prononçons
10. jugeons

Grammar II

Practice

1. people, places, animals
2. people, places, animals
3. to be acquainted with, to be familiar with
4. to know how to do, to be able to, can

Exercise

1. connaît
2. sais
3. connaissons
4. savez
5. connaissent
6. sait
7. connaissez
8. sais
9. connaissent
10. sais
11. sait
12. connaissons
13. savent
14. connais
15. sait

Grammar III

Practice

1. ne . . . pas
2. pas
3. ne
4. they become *de* and *d'*
5. no articles and no partitives are used
6. ever
7. *ne* is directly after rien
8. after the subject and before the verb
9. jamais, rien, personne, pas
10. ne . . . ni . . . ni

Exercises A.

1. B
2. H
3. D
4. G
5. F
6. E
7. A
8. C

B.

1. Pas encore.
2. Pas moi.
3. Pas vous.
4. Pas à l'aéroport.
5. Pas avec moi.
6. Pas avec nous.
7. Pas maintenant.
8. Pas demain.

REVIEW EXAM FOR LESSONS 1–5

(Answers, p. 73)

COMPREHENSION: VOCABULARY

Read the following text aloud, once, to get a general idea, then a second time for detailed understanding.

Juliette et Charles sont de bons amis; ils sont aussi des voisins. Aujourd'hui ils décident d'aller faire des courses ensemble (together). Juliette a besoin d'acheter une robe pour le mariage de sa sœur, et Charles veut une lampe pour sa salle de séjour. Après les courses, Charles a faim et demande à Juliette de l'accompagner au restaurant. Juliette n'a jamais faim mais elle accepte l'invitation de Charles. Au restaurant Charles commande une bière et un plat de fruits de mer; Juliette, une glace et un morceau (piece) de gâteau au chocolat. Les deux amis commencent à parler de leurs (their) familles. Charles pense que son père travaille beaucoup, mais n'a jamais le temps de partir en vacances. Juliette refuse de croire que sa sœur va devenir l'épouse du Docteur Godard, le grand médecin (doctor) de la ville. Charles et Juliette finissent le repas et retournent à la maison à quatre heures moins le quart, satisfaits de leurs achats et de leur après-midi ensemble.

In French, answer the following questions according to the facts of the text. Write in complete sentences.

1. Qui sont Juliette et Charles? ____________________.
2. Que décident-ils de faire? ____________________.
3. Quand vont-ils faire des achats? ____________________.
4. Est-ce que Juliette et Charles sont célibataires?
   ____________________.
5. Que veut acheter Juliette? ____________________.
6. Que pense Charles de son père? ____________________.
7. Le Docteur Godard est-il le futur beau-frère de Juliette? ____________________
   ____________________.
8. Qui est le Docteur Godard? ____________________.
9. Que commande Juliette au restaurant? ____________________.
10. Pourquoi Charles commande-t-il un repas? ____________________.

11. Que font Charles et Juliette après le repas? ______________________.

12. À quelle heure retournent-ils à la maison? ______________________.

NOTE:

Whenever a question starts with *pourquoi* (why?), always start the answer with *parce que* (because).

EX.: Pourquoi Charles commande-t-il un repas?
Parce qu'il a faim.

GRAMMAR EXERCISES

A. Complete the sentences with the correct form of the present indicative

1. Pourquoi ____________ tu (to have) les billets?
2. Les enfants ne ____________ (to be) à la maison.
3. Ils ____________ (wish, want) acheter des fauteuils.
4. Mémé ne ____________ (never + can, be able to) distinguer les couleurs.
5. Quand l'avion ____________ (land)?
6. Nous ne ____________ (to know) la ville.
7. Elles n' ____________ (to buy) rien.
8. Vous n' ____________ (to like) plus les cigarettes.
9. Le douanier ne ____________ (to know) mon adresse.
10. Est-ce que le capitaine ____________ (is looking for) l'hôtesse?
11. Nous ____________ (to share) le repas avec nos voisins.
12. Après le repas nous ____________ (to pay) la caissière.
13. Le vol de Paris à New York ____________ (to start) bien.
14. À quelle heure ____________ (to eat) -vous?
15. Pourquoi ____________ (to finish) -ils tard?
16. Comment ____________ (to go) les petites-filles?
17. Nous ____________ (to buy) toujours du vin blanc.
18. Que ____________ (to wish) -ils commander?
19. Aujourd'hui ma sœur ____________ (to do) la vaisselle.
20. Mon frère n' ____________ (to be) jamais en retard.

B. Write the appropriate indefinite article before each noun.

1. ______ avion
2. ______ maison
3. ______ billet
4. ______ valise
5. ______ homard
6. ______ flan
7. ______ glace
8. ______ attitude
9. ______ ferveur
10. ______ gigot
11. ______ métro
12. ______ lampe
13. ______ valeur
14. ______ miroir
15. ______ robe
16. ______ meuble
17. ______ chose
18. ______ couloir
19. ______ choix
20. ______ époux

C. Complete the following sentences with the appropriate adjective.

1. Ma belle-sœur est ____________ (beautiful).
2. Ma grand-mère est ____________ (old).
3. Le restaurant est ____________ (near, next to) de l'aéroport.
4. Ils sont toujours ____________ (kind).
5. Le rayon des meubles est ____________ (big).
6. L'hôtesse est ____________ (ready) à aider les passagers.
7. Le douanier n'est pas ____________ (polite).
8. Mémé est ____________ (happy) d'habiter chez nous.
9. Ma sœur est ____________ (sociable).
10. Les femmes sont toujours ____________ (curious).
11. Les hommes sont souvent ____________ (serious).

REVIEW EXAM: ANSWERS

Lessons 1-5

Comprehension

1. Ils sont de bons amis.
2. Ils décident d'aller faire des courses.
3. Ils vont faire des achats aujourd'hui.
4. Oui, ils sont célibataires.
5. Juliette veut acheter une robe.
6. Il pense que son père travaille beaucoup.
7. Le docteur Godard est le futur beau-frère de Juliette.
8. Le docteur Godard est le grand medecin de la ville.
9. Juliette commande une glace et un morceau de gâteau.
10. Parce qu'il a faim.
11. Ils parlent de leurs familles.
12. Ils retournent à quatre heures moins le quart.

Grammar

A.
1. as-tu
2. ne sont pas
3. ils veulent
4. ne peut jamais distinguer
5. atterrit-il
6. nous ne connaissons pas
7. elles n'achètent rien
8. vous n'aimez plus
9. ne connaît pas
10. cherche
11. nous partageons
12. nous payons
13. commence
14. mangez-vous
15. finissent-ils
16. vont
17. nous achetons
18. veulent-ils
19. fait
20. n'est jamais

B.
1. un
2. une
3. un
4. une
5. un
6. un
7. une
8. une
9. une
10. un
11. un
12. une
13. une
14. un
15. une
16. un
17. une
18. un
19. un
20. un

C.
1. belle
2. vieille
3. à côté
4. gentils
5. grand
6. prête
7. poli
8. heureuse
9. sociable
10. curieuses
11. sérieux

Lesson 6

À L'HÔTEL (At the Hotel)

l'armoire (fem.)	wardrobe (furniture)	**le matelas**	mattress
l'ascenseur (masc.)	elevator	**le mer**	sea
la bibliothèque	library	**la montagne**	mountain
la chambre	room	**l'oreiller (masc.)**	pillow
la chance	luck	**le paysage**	scenery
la clef	key	**la plage**	beach
la commode	dresser	**le porteur**	porter
la couverture	blanket	**le prix**	price
le drap (de lit)	sheet	**le propriétaire**	owner
l'eau (fem.)	water	**la réception**	front desk
l'évasion (fem.)	escape	**le rez-de-chaussée**	ground floor
la femme de chambre	maid	**le savon**	soap
le lavabo	washbasin	**la serviette**	towel
le lit	bed	**le soleil**	sun
le lit à une place	single bed	**la taie d'oreiller**	pillowcase
les loisirs (masc.)	activities	**le tapis**	rug
le loyer	rent	**les vêtements (masc.)**	clothing
s'amuser	to have fun	**dire**	to say
composer	to compose, to dial	**dormir**	to sleep
devenir	to become	**quitter**	to leave, to quit
		taquiner	to tease

à part	separate	**par hasard**	per chance
disponible	available	**passé(e)**	past
étroit(e)	narrow	**prochain(e)**	next
mauvais(e)	mean, bad	**tapageur (masc.)**	noisy
meublé (masc.)	furnished		
nuageux (masc.)	cloudy		

PRACTICE THE VOCABULARY

(Answers for Lesson 6, p. 139–140)

A. Write in the appropriate word.

1. Le paysage est ____________ (armoire, nuageux, beau).
2. Elle ____________ (arrange, compose, choisit) le numéro de téléphone.
3. Nous aimons les ____________ (montagnes, savons, loisirs).
4. La chambre n'est pas ____________ (loisirs, loyer, disponible).
5. Le propriétaire est vraiment ____________ (chambre, lavabo, aimable).
6. L'armoire est à côté de ____________ (la chance, l'ascenseur, la commode).
7. Nous cherchons la ____________ (lit, plage, clef).
8. Les voisins ne sont pas ____________ (tapageurs, disponibles, meubles).

B. Match the two columns.

1. Nous désirons une chambre ____________.
2. Mon époux veut ____________ au tennis.
3. Nous aimons beaucoup les ____________ de l'hôtel.
4. Nous devons (have to) ____________ le propriétaire aujourd'hui.
5. La chambre est ____________ et petite.
6. Nous voulons passer deux jours à ____________.
7. La femme de chambre ____________ l'hôtel.
8. Nous prenons ____________ pour le sixième.
9. L'hôtel est près de la plage, ____________!
10. Il ne fait jamais ____________ temps ici.

A. étroite
B. avertir
C. quitte
D. l'ascenseur
E. quelle chance!
F. mauvais
G. loisirs
H. jouer
I. à part
J. la plage

DIALOGUE *À l'Hôtel Rivoli*

Jacques et Odette sont devant la réception de l'Hôtel Rivoli à Nice.

JACQUES:	Bonjour Madame, mon amie et moi avons besoin d'une chambre.
LA CONCIERGE:	Très bien Monsieur, j'ai une très belle chambre au sixième étage. Elle donne sur la plage.
ODETTE:	Oh! C'est magnifique! J'adore la mer.
LA CONCIERGE:	Suivez-moi à l'ascenseur et laissez vos valises en bas pour l'instant.
JACQUES:	D'accord. Cet hôtel est vraiment beau. Combien de chambres a-t-il?
LA CONCIERGE:	Dans ce quartier les hôtels n'ont pas plus de cinquante chambres. Le nôtre a trente-huit chambres.
JACQUES:	Oh! la chambre a l'air d'être parfaite pour nous!
ODETTE:	Oui, tu as raison, c'est une chambre magnifique. Regarde ce lit et cette commode-là, et ces grandes fenêtres!
JACQUES:	Nous la prenons. Vous avez la clef?
LA CONCIERGE:	Oui, voici deux clefs. Celle-ci est pour la chambre et celle-là est pour l'armoire. On ne sait jamais, surtout si vous avez des bijoux.
JACQUES:	Merci, mais je n'ai pas de bijoux.
ODETTE:	C'est pour les miens, Jacques!
JACQUES:	Très bien, cette clef est pour toi et tes bijoux!
ODETTE:	Ta gentillesse n'a pas de limites, Jacques.
JACQUES:	Et ton sarcasme n'arrête jamais!
LA CONCIERGE:	Bon, je vous laisse à vos amours, mes pigeons! Vous êtes les bienvenus au Rivoli!
JACQUES:	Merci, Madame. Au revoir!

DIALOG *At the Rivoli Hotel*

Jacques and Odette are at the front desk of the Rivoli Hotel in Nice.

JACQUES:	Good morning, Madam. My friend and I need a room.
THE CARETAKER:	Very good, sir, I have a very beautiful room on the sixth floor, overlooking the beach.
ODETTE:	Oh! That's wonderful (magnificent)! I adore the sea.

THE CARETAKER:	Follow me to the elevator and leave your suitcases downstairs for now.
JACQUES:	All right. This hotel is truly beautiful. How many rooms does it have?
THE CARETAKER:	In this section (of town) the hotels don't have more than fifty rooms. Ours has thirty-eight rooms.
JACQUES:	Oh! This room looks like it is perfect for us!
ODETTE:	Yes, you are right, it's a magnificent room. Look at this bed and that dresser, and those big windows!
JACQUES:	We are taking it. Do you have the key?
THE CARETAKER:	Yes, here are two keys. This one is for the room and that one is for the wardrobe. One never knows, especially if you have jewels.
JACQUES:	Thank you, but I don't have any jewels.
ODETTE:	It's for mine, Jacques!
JACQUES:	Very well, this key is for you and your jewels!
ODETTE:	Your kindness has no limits, Jacques.
JACQUES:	And your sarcasm never ends!
THE CARETAKER:	I leave you love birds with your loving talk! You are welcome (you are the welcome ones) at the Rivoli.
JACQUES:	Thank you, Madam. Good-bye!

DIALOG EXERCISES

A. Answer the questions according to the dialog, with complete sentences.

Example: Qui est Odette? <u>Odette est l'amie de Jacques.</u>

1. Où sont Jacques et Odette? ______________________.
2. À qui parle Jacques à la réception? ______________________.
3. Dans quelle ville est l'Hôtel Rivoli? ______________________.
4. Que veulent Jacques et Odette? ______________________.
5. Qui est Odette? ______________________.
6. Comment Jacques trouve la chambre? ______________________.
7. À quel étage est la chambre? ______________________.
8. Sur quoi donne la chambre? ______________________.

B. Complete the sentences with the most appropriate word or words.

1. Jacques aime la chambre parce qu'elle est __________ (grande, belle, parfaite).

2. Jacques n'accepte pas les deux clefs parce qu'il n'a pas de __________ (argent, patience, bijoux).

3. La concierge taquine Jacques et Odette parce qu'ils sont __________ (américains, amis, sarcastiques).

4. L'Hôtel Rivoli est magnifique parce qu'il __________ (est grand, est beau, donne sur la plage).

5. Odette veut avoir une clef pour protéger ses __________ (meubles, robes, bijoux).

GRAMMAR I Idiomatic expressions with *avoir*.

A. Most of the ideas expressed in English by *to be* are translated by *avoir* in French. Below are some of the most commonly used expressions:

avoir besoin de	to be in need of (to need)
avoir chaud	to be hot
avoir de la chance	to be lucky
avoir envie de	to feel like
avoir faim	to be hungry
avoir froid	to be cold
avoir l'air de	to look like
avoir l'intention de	to intend to
avoir peur de	to be afraid of
avoir raison	to be right
avoir sommeil	to be sleepy
avoir tort	to be wrong

B. Some verbs in French are followed directly by an infinitive, as in *il aime manger* (he likes to eat), *il veut danser* (he wishes to dance).

C. However, many other verbs require either *de* or *à* before the infinitive. In the expressions with *avoir besoin de, avoir peur de* and the like, *de* is always used before a noun or a verb.

EX.: *J'ai besoin de mon stylo.* I need my pen.
J'ai besoin de travailler. I need to work.

The same is true with the verbs that require the preposition *à* before the infinitive.

EX.: *Je commence à comprendre.* I am beginning to understand.

Verbs that require *à* or *de* before infinitives are always designated with these prepositions in dictionaries. There are no set rules to facilitate the task.

GRAMMAR II Verbs used with *à* and *de*.

The following chart lists the most commonly used verbs in the three verb categories:

1. Verbs that are used with a direct infinitive.
2. Verbs using the preposition *de*.
3. Verbs using the preposition *à*.

VERBS + INFINITIVE		VERBS + DE + INFINITIVE		VERBS + À + INFINITIVE	
aimer	to like, to love	**accepter de**	to accept	**aider à**	to hope
aller	to go	**cesser de**	to stop	**apprendre à**	to learn
détester	to dislike	**conseiller de**	to advise	**commencer à**	to begin
devoir	to have to	**décider de**	to decide	**encourager à**	to encourage
espérer	to hope	**essayer de**	to try	**inviter à**	to invite
oser	to dare	**demander de**	to ask	**hésiter à**	to hesitate
pouvoir	to be able to	**oublier de**	to forget	**réussir à**	to succeed
préférer	to prefer	**regretter de**	to regret	**tenir à**	to be eager, to insist
vouloir	to wish, to want	**suggérer de**	to suggest		

NOTES:

1. The verbs *conseiller de, demander de,* and *suggérer de* require *à* before a person and *de* before an infinitive.

   EX.: *Je conseille à Jacques de partir.* I advise Jacques to leave.

   So we have: verb + *à* + person + *de* + infinitive.

2. Other verbs following this pattern include: *dire* + *à* + person + *de* + infinitive.
   EX.: *Je dis à Odette de sortir.* I tell Odette to go out.

   demander + *à* + person + *de* + infinitive
   défendre + *à* + person + *de* + infinitive
   ordonner + *à* + person + *de* + infinitive
   EX.: *Il demande à Marie de danser.* He asks Marie to dance.
   Il défend à Marie de danser. He forbids Marie to dance.
   Il ordonne à Marie de danser. He orders Marie to dance.

3. Any verb that is not followed with *de* or *à* (after checking a dictionary) belongs to the general category of verbs using a direct infinitive (without any preposition).

PRACTICE

A. Practice the expressions with *avoir* and the three verb categories.

1. The verb *avoir* translates to __________ in many English expressions.
2. Name two French verbs with a direct infinitive: __________ et __________.
3. *Avoir peur de* and *avoir envie de* always use *de* with __________ and __________.
4. What is the best way to be sure that a verb takes *à* or *de?* __________.
5. There are three categories of verbs using infinitives: __________, __________, and __________.
6. Some of the verbs requiring *de* also require *à*. Which verbs are these? __________, __________, __________, __________, and __________.
7. Are there any set rules for these verb categories? __________.

B. Say and then write the following expressions in French.

1. "We are hungry today." __________.
2. "Odette is afraid of Jacques." __________.
3. "I feel like dancing." __________.
4. "The *concierge* seems nice." __________.
5. "I am thirsty when I am here." __________.
6. "I need to go shopping (to do errands)." __________.
7. "I intend to succeed." __________.
8. "We are lucky to be here." __________.

GRAMMAR III Demonstrative adjectives and pronouns.

A. The demonstrative adjectives are *ce, cette, ces,* and *cet* (used with masculine nouns starting with a vowel or mute "h"). Memorize the following chart of demonstrative adjectives.

DISTANCE	MASCULINE	FEMININE	PLURAL	ENGLISH
	ce garçon	cette fille	ces (garçons, filles)	this boy, this girl; these (boys, girls)
Near speaker	ce garçon-ci	cette fille-ci	ces garçons-ci ces filles-ci	this boy, this girl; these boys, these girls
Far speaker	ce garçon-là	cette fille-là	ces garçons-là ces filles-là	that boy, that girl, those boys, those girls

1. Demonstrative adjectives precede the nouns they modify and agree with them in number and gender. Demonstrative adjectives translate the English, *this, that, these, those* and are used to designate a specific place, idea, object, or person.
   EX.: *J'aime ce livre parce qu'il est intéressant.*
   Il aime cette ville parce qu'elle est belle.
   Nous aimons cette solution parce qu'elle est parfaite.
   Vous aimez cette femme parce qu'elle est intelligente.

2. Remember how French avoids the "hiatus" by adding a *t* in *a-t-il?* Well, with demonstrative adjectives, *ce* becomes *cet* before any masculine noun starting with a vowel or a silent *h*.
   EX.: *cet homme* this, that man
   cet arbre this, that tree
   cet escargot this, that snail

3. Distance to the speaker is translated in French by adding a hyphen and *-ci* to demonstrate closeness to the speaker and distance from the listener; a hyphen and *là* as in *-là* demonstrate distance from the speaker and closeness to the listener.
   EX.: *cette table-ci* this table (close to me)
   cette table-là that table (far from me)

B. The demonstrative pronouns are *celui, celle, ceux,* and *celles.* Memorize the following chart of demonstrative pronouns.

DISTANCE	MASCULINE	FEMININE	PLURAL	ENGLISH
	celui	celle	ceux (masc.)	this one, these ones
Near spaker	celui-ci	celle-ci	ceux-ci (masc.) celles-ci (fem.)	this one, these ones
Far speaker	celui-là	celle-là	ceux-là (masc.) celles-là (fem.)	that one, those ones

1. Demonstrative pronouns refer to something or someone previously mentioned. Demonstrative pronouns translate the English "this one," "that one," "the one," and their plurals. Demonstrative pronouns agree in number and gender with the nouns they replace.

   EX.: *J'ai deux clefs, celle qui ouvre* (opens) *l'armoire et celle qui ouvre la chambre.*
   I have two keys, the one which opens the wardrobe and the one which opens the room.

2. Closeness and distance are translated in the same way as they are with demonstrative adjectives, a hyphen and *-ci (celui-ci)* for closeness and a hyphen and *-là (celui-là)* for distance.

   EX.: *Celle-ci est pour l'armoire, celle-là est pour la chambre.*
   This one is for the wardrobe and that one is for the room.

3. There are three demonstrative pronouns that do not follow any of the preceding rules and that show neither gender nor number. They refer to indefinite things or ideas, and they are: *ceci* (this), *cela* (that), and *ça* (abbreviation of *cela,* and more commonly used).

   EX.: *Ça ne fait rien = Cela ne fait rien.*
   That does not matter. (That does nothing.)

4. Demonstrative pronouns do not stand by themselves; they need either one of the following:
   a. A suffix *-ci* or *-là,* as in *J'ai deux clefs, mais je n'ai besoin ni de celle-ci, ni de celle-là.* (I have two keys, but I need neither this one nor that one.)
   b. A relative clause, as in *Nous avons besoin de beaucoup de vendeuses* (salesladies), *celles qui travaillent la nuit et celles qui travaillent le jour.* (We need many salesladies, those who work at night and those who work during the day.)

PRACTICE THE DEMONSTRATIVE ADJECTIVES

A. Rewrite the following sentences using the demonstrative adjectives: *ce, cet, cette,* and *ces.*

Example: L'homme est intéressant. Cet homme est intéressant.

1. L'avion est immense. ______________________.
2. Les repas sont délicieux. ______________________.
3. J'aime la maison. ______________________.
4. J'achète des escargots. ______________________.
5. L'armoire n'est pas grande. ______________________.
6. La fille à la robe verte est ma voisine. ______________________.
7. Les croissants sont bien chauds. ______________________.
8. Le lit et le matelas sont neufs (new). ______________________.

B. Following the model given, write a full sentence using the same question, *voulez-vous* (do you want), but with the appropriate demonstrative adjective.

Example: Voulez-vous ce livre-ci ou celui-là? (Do you want this book or that book?)

1. Une salade. ______________________ ou ______________________
2. Un arbre. ______________________ ou ______________________
3. Une taie d'oreiller. ______________________ ou ______________________
4. Un lavabo. ______________________ ou ______________________
5. Des escargots. ______________________ ou ______________________
6. Un gâteau. ______________________ ou ______________________
7. Un fauteuil. ______________________ ou ______________________
8. Une commode. ______________________ ou ______________________
9. Une pizza. ______________________ ou ______________________
10. Des bijoux. ______________________ ou ______________________

C. Match the two columns.

1. Ça va toujours bien ici.
2. Ce Monsieur est mon frère.
3. Je préfère ce poisson à celui-là.
4. Ceci n'est pas à propos.
5. De ces deux films, celui que j'aime est long.
6. Mes enfants sont ceux qui parlent.
7. Que voulez-vous? Cette lampe-ci ou celle-là?
8. Ils ne pensent ni à ceci ni à cela.
9. Ce livre est long, mais celui que je veux est court.
10. Cette pizza-là est délicieuse, mais celle que je mange n'a pas de goût.

A. This book is long, the one I want is short.

B. Which do you want? This lamp or that one?

C. They think neither of this nor of that.

D. That pizza is delicious, but the one I'm eating has no taste.

E. It's always nice here (goes well).

F. This gentlemen is my brother.

G. I prefer this fish to that one.

H. Of these two movies, the one I like is long.

I. This is not the subject (purpose).

J. My children are the ones who are speaking.

Lesson 7

UNE FÊTE D'ANNIVERSAIRE (A Birthday Party)

les amuse-gueules	appetizers	**juillet (masc.)**	July
l'anniversaire (masc.)	birthday	**lundi (masc.)**	Monday
les ballons (masc.)	balloons	**mardi (masc.)**	Tuesday
le bavardage	gossip, chatting	**le matin**	morning
le champagne	champagne	**le mélange**	mix
le dimanche	Sunday	**à la mode**	fashionable
la fête	party	**le passe-temps**	pastimes
le frigo	refrigerator	**le progrès**	progress
le fromage	cheese	**le régime**	diet
les glaçons (masc.)	ice cubes	**les renseignements (masc.)**	information
la grève	strike	**le rythme**	rhythm
l'honneur (masc.)	honor	**le sentiment**	feeling
la joie	joy	**le trésor**	treasure
		le visage	face
		la voiture	car
		la volonté	will
arriver	to arrive	**fêter**	to celebrate
bavarder	to chat	**gagner**	to win, earn
danser	to dance	**inviter**	to invite
décorer	to decorate	**manquer**	to miss, to lack
deviner	to guess	**organiser**	to organize

remercier	to thank	**terminer**	to end
ressembler	to look like	**unir**	to unite
rêver	to dream	**vouloir bien**	to be willing
rire	to laugh		
avec plaisir	with pleasure	**quelque chose**	something
bavard	talkative	**qui**	who, that, which (subject)
décontracté	relaxed		
dehors	outside	**salut!**	hi!
drôle	funny	**sauvage**	wild
encore	again	**semblable**	similar
fragile	fragile	**triste**	sad
mutuellement	mutually	**vive!**	long live!
occupé	busy	**voyant(e)**	fortune teller
passionnant	exciting	**zut!**	darn it!
prochain	next		
que	whom, which, that (object)		

PRACTICE THE VOCABULARY

(Answers for Lesson 7, pp. 140–142)

Write the appropriate word to complete the sentences.

1. Lundi matin ma sœur __________ (vouloir, bien, organiser) une fête d'anniversaire.
2. Les amis arrivent dans une petite __________. (renseignement, régime, voiture)
3. Avant la fête, ma sœur __________ (attendre, manger, décorer) la maison.
4. La musique et la danse sont des __________. (boisson, trésor, passe-temps)
5. Quand je compose ton numéro de téléphone, la ligne (line) est toujours __________. (complète, passée, occupée)
6. Mardi __________ (meuble, nuageux, prochain) je fête mon anniversaire.
7. Quand les travailleurs ne sont pas satisfaits ils __________. (faire des courses, faire le ménage, faire la grève)
8. Les invités sont sophistiqués, ils ne sont pas __________. (semblables, passionants, sauvages)
9. On mange les __________ (fruits, glaces, amuse-gueules) avant les repas.
10. Le contraire de joyeux est __________. (heure, triste, gentil)

11. Say "long live" la musique. __________.
12. La voyante devine __________. (les glaçons, la musique, le futur)
13. Say "darn it" in French. __________.
14. La réception donne les __________. (tables, fruits, renseignements)

DIALOGUE *Juliette a vingt et un ans!*

ROBERT: Allo? Pierre est là, s'il vous plaît? Oui, attendez une minute, je vous le passe.
PIERRE: Bonjour Robert. Quoi de neuf?
ROBERT: Quelque chose de spécial. Je t'invite à l'anniversaire de ma sœur Juliette.
PIERRE: Je te remercie. J'accepte si je suis disponible. C'est quand?
ROBERT: La fête est fixée pour samedi prochain, le douze mars, à quatre heures de l'après-midi.
PIERRE: J'accepte avec grand plaisir, parce que je ne travaille plus le samedi. Veux-tu que j'apporte quelque chose?
ROBERT: Oui. Attends une minute, je cherche ton nom sur la liste. Voilà. Toi, tu apportes des ballons et des glaçons.
PIERRE: D'accord. À samedi prochain alors?
ROBERT: Attends une minute. Tu sais qu'on va danser et que Jacqueline, ta voisine, va jouer de la guitare, et plus tard, la voyante Madame Soleil va lire notre futur.
PIERRE: Ceci a l'air d'une grande fête. Peut-on danser avec Madame Soleil?
ROBERT: Bien sûr. C'est un anniversaire spécial, vingt-et-un ans. C'est l'age officiel de la majorité où tout est permis!
PIERRE: Écoute, je n'ai pas le temps de faire de la philosophie. Tu sais très bien que cette question d'âge est plutôt psychologique. Je dois partir, mon vieux—à bientôt.
ROBERT: Au revoir, Pierre. A samedi prochain, quatre heures pile! Je compte sur toi!

DIALOG *Juliette Is Twenty-one Years Old!*

ROBERT: Hello, is Pierre there?—No, wait a minute, I'll get him for you (pass him to you).
PIERRE: Good morning, Robert. What's new?
ROBERT: Something special. I'm inviting you to my sister Juliette's birthday.
PIERRE: I thank you. I accept, if I'm available. When is it?
ROBERT: The party is scheduled for Saturday, March twelfth, at four P.M.

PIERRE: I accept with great pleasure, because I no longer work on Saturdays. Do you want me to bring anything?

ROBERT: Yes. Wait a minute, I'm looking for your name on the list. Here. You, you're bringing balloons and ice cubes.

PIERRE: See you next Saturday, then?

ROBERT: Wait a minute. You know, we're going to dance and Jacqueline, your neighbor, is going to play the guitar, and later the fortune teller, Madame Soleil (Mrs. Sun) is going to read our future.

PIERRE: This looks like a big party! May one dance with Mrs. Sun?

ROBERT: Of course (surely). Twenty-one is a special birthday. It's the official age of majority, where everything is permissible.

PIERRE: Listen, I don't have time to talk philosophy. You know very well that this age question is rather psychological. I must leave you, my friend—see you soon.

ROBERT: Goodbye, Pierre. (see you) Next Saturday, four o'clock sharp! I'm counting on you.

NOTES:

1. *Quoi de neuf?* is always "What's new?" It never changes in any way regardless of what comes before or after.

2. *Faire de la philosophie, faire de la psychologie, faire de la morale,* etc. These expressions with *faire* have a sarcastic implication, meaning the *doer* is not knowledgeable enough in the subject, so *faire de la philosophie* would translate *to play at* talking philosophy. You can construct your own expressions with this implication (to play at) any time the subject warrants it.

3. The present participles *passionnant* and *voyant* follow the same rules as adjectives.

   EX.: *Un livre passionnant.*
   Une musique passionnante.

   These participles can also be used as nouns if they are preceded by articles.

   EX.: *Un voyant* fortune teller (male)
   Une voyante fortune teller (female)

4. Note that when *le* precedes a day of the week it is translated by *every,* as in: *le lundi* (every Monday), *le dimanche* (every Sunday). French always uses the articles, *le, la, les,* and *l'* before the times of the day, to translate *in the.*

   EX.: *Le matin je lis le journal.* I read the paper in the morning.
   L'après-midi je fais la sieste. I take a nap in the afternoon.
   Le soir je téléphone à mes amis. I telephone my friends in the evening.

5. *Le matin, l'après midi,* etc., can be placed either at the beginning of a sentence or at the end.

DIALOG EXERCISES

A. Answer the following questions according to the dialog, with complete sentences.

1. Comment Robert commence-t-il la conversation au téléphone?
______________________.
2. Comment Pierre répond-il? ______________________.
3. Pourquoi Robert téléphone-t-il à Pierre? ______________________.
4. Est-ce que Pierre accepte l'invitation tout de suite? ______________________
______________________.
5. Pourquoi Pierre accepte-t-il l'invitation? ______________________.
6. Que doit apporter Pierre? ______________________.
7. Qui va jouer de la guitare? ______________________.
8. Qui va lire le futur? ______________________.
9. Quelle est la date de la fête? ______________________.
10. Quel est l'âge officiel de la majorité? ______________________.
11. Est-ce que la question d'âge est importante? ______________________.
12. Que pense Pierre de cette question d'âge? ______________________.
13. Qui veut danser avec Madame Soleil? ______________________.
14. Pourquoi cette fête d'anniversaire est-elle spéciale? ______________________.

B. In studying the new vocabulary and the dialog you will find many words that derive from other known words. Try to find the verbs that derive from the following nouns.

Example: le sentiment—*sentir*
le mélange—*mélanger*

1. la décoration. ______________________
2. la fête. ______________________
3. l'occupation. ______________________
4. le bavardage. ______________________
5. le progrès. ______________________
6. l'union. ______________________
7. la volonté. ______________________
8. le rêve. ______________________
9. l'invitation. ______________________
10. l'organisation. ______________________

GRAMMAR I Possessive adjectives.

The chart below lists the possessive adjectives corresponding to the subject pronouns, *je, tu,* etc.

SUBJECT PRONOUNS	MASCULINE SINGULAR	FEMININE SINGULAR	PLURAL	ENGLISH
je	**mon**	**ma**	**mes**	my
tu	**ton**	**ta**	**tes**	your
il, elle, on	**son**	**sa**	**ses**	his, her, its
nous	**notre**	**notre**	**nos**	our
vous	**votre**	**votre**	**vos**	your
ils, elles	**leur**	**leur**	**leurs**	their

NOTES:

1. The possessive adjectives in French agree with not only the possessor, but also with the nouns they modify—with the possessed.
   EX.: *ma soeur* my sister
   mes soeurs my sisters
   mon frère my brother
   mes frères my brothers

2. The possessive adjectives, *mon, ton,* and *son* are masculine. However, when a noun starts with a vowel or a silent *h,* French uses the above adjectives with feminine as well.
   EX.: *mon ami* my friend (boy)
   mon amie my friend (girl)
   mon auto my automobile (fem.)
   ton histoire your (*tu*) story (fem.)

3. Notice that *mes, tes, ses, nos, vos,* and *leurs* plural forms are the same for the masculine plural and feminine plural.
   EX.: *mes soeurs* my sisters (fem.)
   mes frères my brothers (masc.)

PRACTICE THE POSSESSIVE ADJECTIVES

Complete the sentences with the appropriate possessive adjective.

Example: Je cherche mon (my) stylo.

1. Où est ____________ (your) maison?
2. J'organize ____________ (our) livres.
3. Nous achetons ____________ (his) automobile.
4. Tu ne finis jamais ____________ (your) histoire.
5. ____________ (my) grand-mère est passionnante.
6. ____________ (my) parents sont sévères.
7. ____________ (their) maison est loin d'ici.
8. Vous aimez ____________ (your) voisins.
9. Ils veulent garder ____________ (their) argent.
10. Nous aimons bien ____________ (our) chiens.

EXERCISES

A. Replace each subject by *il* or *elle* and each definite article by a possessive adjective, *son, sa,* or *ses.*

Example: Marie aime le chat. Elle aime son chat.

1. Juliette décore la maison. ________________________.
2. Robert téléphone à l'ami. ________________________.
3. Les enfants attendent la mère. ________________________.
4. Pierre cherche la voiture. ________________________.
5. La dame veut l'argent. ________________________.
6. La mère adore les enfants. ________________________.
7. La femme change les armoires de place. ________________________.

8. Le chat mange les biscuits. ______________________.
9. Madame vend les bijoux. ______________________.
10. Pierre apporte les ballons. ______________________.

B. Answer the following questions using the appropriate possessive adjective.

Example: Est-ce que c'est l'argent de Jean? Oui, c'est son argent.

1. Est-ce que c'est le chien du voisin? ______________________.
2. Est-ce que ce sont les amis de Jacques? ______________________.
3. Est-ce que ce sont les fauteuils de Charles? ______________________.
4. Est-ce que c'est l'amie de Juliette? ______________________.
5. Est-ce que c'est le cousin de Pierre? ______________________.
6. Est-ce que ce sont les sœurs de Renée? ______________________.
7. Est-ce que c'est le mari de la voisine? ______________________.
8. Est-ce que ce sont les employés des voisins? ______________________.
9. Est-ce que c'est le chat des amis? ______________________.
10. Est-ce que c'est l'armoire des parents? ______________________.

GRAMMAR II Possessive pronouns.

Study the chart of the possessive pronouns.

MASCULINE SINGULAR	FEMININE SINGULAR	MASCULINE PLURAL	FEMININE PLURAL	ENGLISH
le mien	**la mienne**	**les miens**	**les miennes**	mine
le tien	**la tienne**	**les tiens**	**les tiennes**	yours (*tu* form)
le sien	**la sienne**	**les siens**	**les siennes**	his, hers, its
le nôtre	**la nôtre**	**les nôtres**	**les nôtres**	ours
le vôtre	**la vôtre**	**les vôtres**	**les vôtres**	yours
le leur	**la leur**	**les leurs**	**les leurs**	theirs

NOTES:

1. In English and French, a possessive pronoun replaces a noun modified by a possessive adjective.
   EX.: *C'est mon livre. C'est le mien.*
   It's my book. It's mine.

   However, French always uses the definite article, *le, la,* and *les* with possessive pronouns.
2. In French, possessive pronouns agree in number and gender with the nouns they replace, and not with the possessor as they do in English.
   EX.: *L'argent de Paul—son argent—le sien.*
   La sœur de Pierre—sa sœur—la sienne.
   Les bagages des voisins—leurs (adjective) *bagages—les leurs* (pronouns)
3. Make sure to check the gender of the replaced word before replacing it with the possessive pronoun. It is advisable to base your possessive pronouns on the possessive adjectives, as demonstrated in the above examples. Study the following:
   Le frère de Jacques—son frère—le sien
   ton livre—le tien
   notre maison—la nôtre
4. Notice the accent circonflexe (ˆ) on the *o*'s of *le nôtre, les nôtres, le vôtre,* and *les vôtres.*
5. Make sure to remember the definite article contractions of *de* + *le* = *du, de* + *les* = *des*. They apply to *de* + *mes* = *des miens, de* + *tes* = *des tiens,* and to *de* + *ton* = *du tien,* etc.
   EX.: *le stylo de mon frère* becomes *le stylo du mien*

   This rule applies only when *de* is used before the possessive adjective and when you want to replace it with a possessive pronoun.

PRACTICE THE POSSESSIVE PRONOUNS

A. Replace the possessive adjectives in italic with the appropriate possessive pronouns. Pay close attention to the gender and number of the nouns.

Example: Ce sont *mes enfants.* Ce sont les miens.

1. Ce sont *tes bagages.* ______________________.
2. C'est *ta guitare*? ______________________.
3. Voici *mes billets.* ______________________.
4. Pourquoi fumez-vous *leurs cigarettes*? ______________________.
5. Avez-vous *vos bijoux*? ______________________.
6. Nous avons *nos valises.* ______________________.
7. Elles cherchent *leurs chambres.* ______________________.

8. Ce sont *ses amis*. ______________________.
9. Ce n'est pas *son argent*. ______________________.
10. Ce ne sont pas *tes sœurs*. ______________________.
11. Tu as *son adresse*. ______________________.
12. Cherches-tu *ton hôtel*? ______________________.
13. Où sont *leurs journaux*? ______________________.
14. Veux-tu raconter *ton histoire*? ______________________.
15. Nous ne trouvons pas *notre armoire*. ______________________.
16. Pourquoi cherchez-vous *votre clef*? ______________________.
17. Ils ont peur de *leurs parents*. ______________________.
18. Tu invites *ses amies*. ______________________.
19. *Ta maison* est à côté de *mon hôtel*. ______________________.
20. Nous avons peur de *vos chiens*. ______________________.

B. Complete the following sentences with the appropriate possessive pronouns in French.

1. Nous achetons nos billets mais pas (yours) ______________________.
2. Ils trouvent leur chambre mais pas (yours) ______________________.
3. Tu manges ton repas mais pas (mine) ______________________.
4. Il arrange son armoire mais pas (hers) ______________________.
5. Elle décore notre maison mais pas (theirs) ______________________.
6. Elle aide son frère mais pas (ours) ______________________.
7. Elle termine ses études (studies) mais pas (mine) ______________________.
8. Il aime son chat mais pas (ours) ______________________.
9. Vous inspectez leurs valises mais pas (ours) ______________________.
10. Vous fumez ses cigarettes mais pas (yours) ______________________.

GRAMMAR III Direct object nouns and pronouns.

A. Direct object nouns answer the question "what"? or "whom"? In the sentence "Jacques finds the key," *key* is a direct object.

B. A direct object pronoun replaces a direct object noun, as in "Jacques finds *the key*" "Jacques finds *it*." Direct object pronouns replace designated persons, places, objects, or occurrences.

EX.: *Je trouve l'adresse. Je la trouve.*

C. All the direct object nouns are preceded by the definite articles, *le, la, les, l'*.
EX.: Je cherche *le livre*. Je *le* cherche.

D. Direct object nouns can also be used with a demonstrative adjective, or a possessive adjective or proper nouns. Study the following examples:
Je trouve ma mère. Je la trouve.
Je cherche cette adresse. Je la cherche.
J'aime Robert. Je l'aime.

E. It is important to note that in French, as in English, nouns preceded by an indefinite article *(un, une, des)* or a partitive article *(de la, du, des, d') cannot* be replaced with direct pronouns.

F. In French, direct object pronouns are often placed before the verb, and they agree in number and gender with the words they replace.
EX.: *Je cherche la clef. Je la cherche.*
Je cherche les clefs. Je les cherche.

G. The following chart lists the direct pronouns:

MASCULINE & FEMININE SINGULAR	ENGLISH	MASCULINE & FEMININE PLURAL	ENGLISH
me (m')	me	**nous**	us
te (t')	you	**vous**	you
le (l')	him, it	**les**	them
la (l')	her, it		

H. The following examples refer to the chart above:
EX.: Robert *me* cherche. (Robert is looking for *me*.)
La Concierge *te* demande. (The caretaker is asking for *you*.)
Robert *la* cherche (clef). (Robert is looking for *it*. [key])
Ses parents *l'*aiment. (Her parents like *her, him*.)
Il *nous* invite. (He invites *us*.)
Elle *vous* invite. (She invites *you*.)
Ils *les* invitent. (They invite *them*.)

I. Notice how *me, te, le,* and *la,* lose their last vowel when they precede a word starting with another vowel.
EX.: *Ils l'aiment.* They like *her, him.*
Ils l'honorent. They honor *her, him.*

PRACTICE THE DIRECT NOUNS AND PRONOUNS

Replace the italicized direct noun with the appropriate direct pronoun. Write the complete sentence.

1. Jacques adore *Josette.* ______________________.
2. Le propriétaire appelle *le garçon.* ______________________.
3. Je regarde *le paysage.* ______________________.
4. Il achète *les glaçons.* ______________________.
5. Jacques n'a pas *l'argent.* ______________________.
6. Vous refusez *les conseils* (advice). ______________________.
7. Nous organisons *nos armoires.* ______________________.
8. Veux-tu manger *cette viande?* ______________________.
9. Tu fêtes *ton anniversaire* demain. ______________________.
10. Ils aiment bien *la publicité.* ______________________.
11. Elle achète *mes livres.* ______________________.
12. Je décore *ta maison.* ______________________.
13. Je loue *l'appartement.* ______________________.
14. J'invite *vos amis.* ______________________.

NOTE:

Memorize the following ready-made expressions:

me voici	here I am
te voilà	there you are (tu)
la voilà	there she is
le voilà	there he is
les voilà	there they are
nous voilà	there we are
vous voilà	there you are

GRAMMAR IV The imperative form of *être* and *avoir*, and general rules for known verbs.

A. The imperative form is used to command, instruct, and give direction. In French, there are three ways in which to command or give instructions:

1. The *tu* form:	*mange*	eat *(tu)*
2. The *nous* form:	*mangeons*	let's eat *(nous)*
3. The *vous* form:	*mangez*	eat *(vous)*

B. The *tu* form is the familiar form we learned in other conjugations. The *nous* form includes the speaker.

C. The imperative form is the conjugated verb form from which the subject pronouns *tu, vous,* and *nous* have been removed. Thus, in the case of a regular verb of the *-ER* group like *parler,* the imperative will be:

(tu) *parle* (note the *s* from the second person is dropped)
(nous) *parlons*
(vous) *parlez*

All regular verb conjugations follow this pattern: Remove *tu, vous,* and *nous* from the present indicative of a conjugated verb, and you get the imperative. Let's take the verb *finir:*

finis (tu) finish
finissons (nous) let's finish
finissez (vous) finish

D. The same rule applies with the irregular verbs we have studied. Thus, *aller* will be:

va (tu) go
allons (nous) let's go
allez (vous) go

Note that the *s* of *tu manges* and of *tu vas* is dropped in the imperative form.

E. However, the verbs *être* and *avoir* have irregular imperative forms. These forms are constructed on the present subjunctive (which we will study later).

F. Memorize the chart below.

ÊTRE	TO BE	AVOIR	TO HAVE
sois (tu)	be	**aie** (tu)	have
soyons (nous)	let's be	**ayons** (nous)	let's have
soyez (vous)	be	**ayez** (vous)	have

G. Study the examples constructed with the imperative forms of *être* and *avoir:*

sois aimable be pleasant
soyons aimables let's be pleasant
soyez aimable(s) be pleasant
aie du courage have courage
ayons du courage let's have courage
ayez du courage have courage

H. The imperative form in the negative follows the same rule as the present indicative: *subject + ne + verb + pas*
Since the subject is dropped in the imperative we have: *ne + verb + pas,* as in:

ne parle pas	don't speak
ne fumons pas	let's not smoke
ne soyons pas méchant(e)s	let's not be mean

PRACTICE THE IMPERATIVE

A. Rewrite the following sentences in the imperative form.

1. Nous cherchons Jeanette. ____________.
2. Vous ne fumez jamais. ____________.
3. Tu es gentille avec moi. ____________.
4. Nous avons beaucoup d'argent. ____________.
5. Tu n'as pas peur. ____________.
6. Vous n'êtes pas triste. ____________.
7. Vous faîtes vos courses le matin. ____________.
8. Tu ne vas pas au cinéma aujourd'hui. ____________.
9. Vous me racontez une histoire. ____________.
10. Vous attendez votre père. ____________.
11. Nous choisissons le fauteuil rouge. ____________.
12. Tu fais le ménage le lundi. ____________.

B. All the verbs in this exercise are in the infinitive form. Rewrite the sentences in the imperative according to the example:

Example: (nous) marcher vite. Marchons vite.

1. (tu) être patient. ____________.
2. (nous) attendre l'avion. ____________.
3. (vous) acheter les meubles. ____________.
4. (tu) aller à la plage. ____________.
5. (vous) ne pas regarder la télévision. ____________.

6. (vous) ne pas faire la sieste. ______________________.
7. (nous) avoir de la chance maintenant. ______________________.
8. (vous) ne pas jouer au football. ______________________.
9. (tu) finir la conversation. ______________________.
10. (tu) faire attention. ______________________.

Lesson 8

L'ÉPICERIE DU COIN (The Corner Grocery Store)

l'agneau (masc.)	lamb	**les haricots verts (masc.)**	green beans
l'ail (masc.)	garlic	**l'huile (fem.)**	oil
l'assiette (fem.)	dish, plate	**le jus d'orange**	orange juice
la banane	banana	**le lait**	milk
le beurre	butter	**le marchand**	storekeeper
le biftek	steak	**le melon**	melon
le bœuf	beef	**l'œuf (masc.)**	egg
la bouteille	bottle	**l'oignon (masc.)**	onion
le client	customer	**l'orange (fem.)**	orange
la dinde	turkey	**le pain**	bread
l'eau minérale (fem.)	mineral water	**les petits pois (masc.)**	(fresh) peas
les épices (fem.)	spices	**la poire**	pear
la farine	flour	**le poivre**	pepper
les fraises (fem.)	strawberries	**le sel**	salt
		le sucre	sugar
le fromage	cheese	**le vinaigre**	vinegar
le gérant	manager		
s'arrêter	to stop (oneself)	**perdre son temps**	to waste time
bouillir	to boil		
cuire	to cook	**plaisanter**	to joke
fréquenter	to patronize	**rendre la monnaie**	to give back change
gérer	to manage		
livrer	to deliver	**servir**	to serve

supprimer	to suppress	**vérifier**	to verify, to check
tromper	to cheat		
vendre	to sell	**voler**	to steal, to fly
à votre service	you're welcome	**vendeur (masc.), vendeuse (fem.)**	salesclerk
creux, creuse	deep, hollow		
rapé (masc.)	grated		
soudainement	suddenly		
sous	under, below	**week-end (masc.)**	weekend
souvent	often		
utile	useful		

NOTES:

1. In France, the corner grocery store (l'épicerie) and the bakery (la boulangerie) are still the main grocery shopping sites for French homemakers. Both stores are usually located within walking distance of the residential areas and are always crowded before the lunch and dinner hours. Even with supermarkets slowly taking over, the épicerie is still a favorite place to joke with the "épicier," to meet regulars, and to purchase goods between bits of joviality.

2. The verb *prendre* is a very useful verb and, as we have seen with *aller* and *faire,* lends itself to several constructions. Study the following:

prendre son temps	to take time (sarcastically used, it means "taking one's own sweet time!")
prendre un verre	to have a drink
prendre soin de	to take care of
prendre la correspondance	to transfer (airplane, bus, subway)
prendre la retraite	to retire
prendre le soleil	to sunbathe

PRACTICE THE VOCABULARY

(Answers for Lesson 8, pp. 142–144)

A. Without looking at the list, write the article *le, la, les, l'* as appropriate.

1. ______ sel	6. ______ sucre	11. ______ vendeur
2. ______ client	7. ______ petits pois	12. ______ maison
3. ______ eau	8. ______ pain	13. ______ beurre
4. ______ dinde	9. ______ farine	14. ______ gérante
5. ______ melon	10. ______ cliente	15. ______ commerçants

B. Translate into French:

1. Children are having fun at the grocery store. ________________.
2. The storekeeper and the salesclerk work for the manager. ________________.
3. When I go to the supermarket, I like to take my time. ________________.
4. To make a cake, I need oil, eggs, flour, and sugar. ________________.
5. The salesclerk gives me back the change. ________________.
6. I often patronize the corner grocery store. ________________.
7. My sister can't boil water! ________________.
8. When I'm thirsty I like to have a drink with friends. ________________.

DIALOGUE *À l'épicerie du coin*

L'ÉPICIER: Bonjour, Madame Simon. Qu'est-ce qu'on désire aujourd'hui?

MADAME SIMON: Un peu de tout. J'ai des invités ce soir. J'ai besoin d'un joli rôti d'agneau, mais alors quelque chose d'extra.

L'ÉPICIER: Chez nous, Madame Simon, tout ce que vous voyez est extra, inclus le vendeur!

MADAME SIMON: Vous avez toujours le cœur à rire, Monsieur. Cela fait plaisir. Bon, j'ai besoin d'un kilo de haricots verts, d'une livre de fromage rapé, et d'une livre de ces belles fraises.

L'ÉPICIER: Je viens de les recevoir. Ces fraises-là sentent encore l'odeur des champs. Tenez, sentez l'arôme. L'épicerie en est parfumée.

MADAME SIMON: Vous m'avez toujours dit que c'est mon parfum qui vous redonne votre sens de l'humour. Vous voyez, vous m'avez menti, c'est l'arôme de vos fraises qui vous a mis de bonne humeur. Ah! les hommes sont tous pareils.

L'ÉPICIER: Madame Simon, c'est votre parfum qui a aiguisé mon sens olfactif, et c'est à cause de votre parfum que j'ai pu sentir l'arôme délicat des fraises!

MADAME SIMON: D'accord. Je vous pardonne cette fois-ci. Écoutez, ne me faites pas oublier le sucre et un pot de crème fraîche.

L'ÉPICIER: Je m'exuse, Madame Simon, mais je n'ai pas reçu de crème fraiche. Je l'ai commandée hier, et je n'ai pas encore eu de livraison.

MADAME SIMON:	Je ne peux pas perdre de temps alors. Servez-moi vite s'il vous plaît, je dois courir à la laiterie.
L'ÉPICIER:	Voilà, Mme Simon, c'est cent-dix francs au total.
MADAME SIMON:	Voici cent-cinquante francs.
L'ÉPICIER:	Je vous rends quarante francs de monnaie, merci, et surtout amusez-vous bien ce soir.
MADAME SIMON:	Avec tout le travail à faire? Vous plaisantez! Au revoir.

DIALOG *At the Corner Grocery Store*

STOREKEEPER:	Good morning, Mrs. Simon. What do we wish today?
MRS. SIMON:	A little of everything. I'm having guests this evening. I need a pretty lamb roast, but then something special (extraordinary).
STOREKEEPER:	At our place, Mrs. Simon, everything you see is special, including the salesman!
MRS. SIMON:	You're always happy. That's a pleasure. Well, I need one kilo of green beans, one pound of grated cheese, and one pound of these beautiful strawberries.
STOREKEEPER:	I just received those beautiful strawberries. These strawberries still smell like the fields. Here, smell the aroma. The store is perfumed by it.
MRS. SIMON:	You've always told me that it is my perfume that gives you back your sense of humor. You see, you lied to me, it's the aroma of your strawberries that puts you in a good mood. Ah! men, they're all alike.
STOREKEEPER:	Mrs. Simon, it's your perfume that sharpened my olfactory sense, and it's because of your perfume that I could smell the delicate aroma of the strawberries.
MRS. SIMON:	O.K. I forgive you, this time. Listen, don't make me forget sugar and a jar of fresh cream.
STOREKEEPER:	I'm sorry, Mrs. Simon, but I did not receive any fresh cream. I ordered it yesterday, and I have not yet had a delivery.
MRS. SIMON:	I can't waste any time then. Please serve me quickly, I must run to the dairy.
STOREKEEPER:	Here, Mrs. Simon, it is a total of one hundred and ten francs.
MRS. SIMON:	Here is one hundred and fifty.
STOREKEEPER:	I'm going to give you back forty francs in change, thank you, and have a good time this evening.
MRS. SIMON:	With all the work I have to do? You must be joking! Goodbye.

NOTES:

être de bonne humeur	to be in a good mood
être de mauvaise humeur	to be in a bad mood
avoir le sens de l'humour	to have a good sense of humor
ne pas avoir le sens de l'humour	to have a bad sense of humor (to be without a sense of humor)

The above constructions are to be added to your repertoire of expressions with *être* and *avoir*.

DIALOG EXERCISES

A. Answer the questions with complete sentences, according to the dialog.

1. Pourquoi Madame Simon fait-elle le marché? ____________.
2. Que veut acheter Madame Simon? ____________.
3. Comment elle décrit (describes) le rôti d'agneau?
____________.
4. Qu'est-ce que Madame Simon ne trouve pas à l'épicerie?
____________.
5. Où va Madame Simon après l'épicerie? Pourquoi?
____________.
6. Que dit l'épicier au sujet des (about) fraises? ____________.
7. Pourquoi Madame Simon pense-t-elle que l'épicier a menti?
____________.
8. Qu'est-ce que l'épicier dit au sujet du parfum de Madame Simon?
____________.
9. Est-ce que l'épicier plaisante avec Madame Simon?
____________.
10. Croyez-vous (do you believe) que Madame Simon fréquente souvent l'épicerie? Pourquoi? ____________.

B. Match the sentences according to the vocabulary and the dialog.

1. On a toujours besoin de faire le marché.	A. Onion, garlic, salt, and pepper are spices.
2. Les clients et le gérant comptent la monnaie.	B. The woman is vain and the man is like all men.
3. L'oignon, l'ail, le sel, et le poivre sont des épices.	C. One always needs to go shopping.

4. L'épicier est amusant mais il n'a pas une bonne mémoire (memory).
5. La dame est vaine; le monsieur est comme tous les hommes.

D. The customers and the manager count the change.

E. The grocer is funny, but he does not have a good memory.

GRAMMAR I *Passé composé* of regular and irregular verbs with *avoir.*

A. Study the *passé composé* of *parler,* as shown in the chart below.

SUBJECT	AVOIR +	PARLER	TO SPEAK
j' (e)	**ai**	**parlé**	I spoke, have spoken, did speak
tu	**as**	**parlé**	you spoke, have spoken, did speak
il, elle, on	**a**	**parlé**	he, she, it, one, spoke (etc.)
nous	**avons**	**parlé**	we spoke (etc.)
vous	**avez**	**parlé**	you spoke (etc.)
ils, elles	**ont**	**parlé**	they spoke (etc.)

B. In French, as in English, there are several ways to express the past. The *passé composé,* the compound past, is the most commonly used past tense in French. The *passé composé* translates several forms of the past tense in English.

EX.: *J'ai parlé* means "I spoke," "I have spoken," and "I did speak."

The *passé composé* is called that because it is "composed" of the main verb and another verb used as an auxiliary. This auxiliary may be either *être* or *avoir.* The *passé composé* is obtained by conjugating the verb *être* or *avoir* and adding the past participle of the verb you wish to use. The past participles of the regular verbs in *-er, -ir,* and *-re* are as follows:

1. With regular verbs in *-er* and *-ir,* the *r* is dropped from the infinitive and an acute accent is added to the *e* of the *-er* verbs.

   EX.: *parler + avoir + j'ai parlé*
   finir + avoir + j'ai fini

2. With regular verbs in *-re,* the *-re* is dropped and *u* replaces it.

   EX.: *rendre + avoir = j'ai rendu*

C. Since there are many verbs that require irregular past participles, let's list here the past participles of some verbs that you have learned:

avoir	*j'ai eu*	*pouvoir*	*j'ai pu*
boire	*j'ai bu*	*savoir*	*j'ai su*
croire	*j'ai cru*	*voir*	*j'ai vu*
lire	*j'ai lu*	*vouloir*	*j'ai voulu*

D. The above examples are of irregular verbs used with the auxiliary *avoir.* Most French verbs in the *passé composé* are formed with *avoir.* However, there are other verbs that require the auxiliary *être.* Those verbs are discussed below.

GRAMMAR II *Passé composé* of regular and irregular verbs with *être.*

A. Study the chart below.

SUBJECT	ÊTRE	PARTIR	TO LEAVE
je	**suis**	**parti(e)**	I left, have left, did leave
tu	**es**	**parti(e)**	you left, have left, did leave
il, elle, on	**est**	**parti(e)**	he, she, it, one left, has left, did leave
nous	**sommes**	**parti(e)s**	we left, have left, did leave
vous	**êtes**	**parti(e)s**	you left, have left, did leave
ils, elles	**sont**	**parti(e)s**	they left, have left, did leave

B. There are two important facts to remember about the French verbs that require *être* in the *passé composé:*

1. They are usually verbs of movement and motion:
   EX.: *marcher, monter, descendre, passer,* etc.

2. Their past participles *always* agree in number and gender with the subject.

EX.:	*le garçon est parti*	the boy left
	la fille est partie	the girl left
	ils sont partis	they left (boys)
	elles sont parties	they left (girls)

C. Below are additional verbs that require *être* in the *passé composé.*

aller	*je suis allé(e)*
arriver	*elle est arrivée*
partir	*ils sont partis*
sortir	*elles sont sorties*
entrer	*il est entré*
venir	*elle est venue*

D. Note that the past participles used with *être* and regular verbs are formed in the same manner as those using *avoir* with regular verbs in *-er, -ir,* and *-re.*

EX.:	*j'ai parlé*	*(parler + avoir)*
	je suis arrivé(e)	*(arriver + être)*
	j'ai fini	*(finir + avoir)*
	je suis sorti(e)	*(sortir + être)*
	j'ai rendu	*(rendre + avoir)*
	je suis descendu(e)	*(descendre + être)*

E. Some irregular verbs that we have learned have the following participles with *être:*

venir	*je suis venu(e)*
devenir (to become)	*je suis devenu(e)*
tenir (to hold)	*je suis tenu(e)*

F. The verbs below form their past participles in *-it:*

écrire	*j'ai écrit*	I wrote, have written, did write
décrire	*j'ai décrit*	I described (etc.)
faire	*j'ai fait*	I did (etc.)
dire	*j'ai dit*	I said (etc.)

G. The following verbs form their past participles with *-is:*

apprendre	*j'ai appris*
mettre (to put, to wear)	*j'ai mis*
comprendre	*j'ai compris*

H. Please note *especially* the following:

1. The past participle of *être* is "j'ai *été*."
2. Negation occurs in the auxiliary *only.*

EX.:	*J'ai parlé.*	*Je n'ai pas parlé.*
	Je suis sorti(e).	*Je ne suis pas sorti(e).*

PRACTICE THE *PASSÉ COMPOSÉ* WITH *AVOIR*

A. Rewrite, in the *passé composé,* the following sentences using the auxiliary *avoir.*

1. J'achète mes meubles au grand magasin. ________________.
2. L'arôme des fraises parfume la cuisine. ________________.
3. Charles voyage avec sa fiancée. ________________.
4. Le douanier peut nous aider. ________________.
5. Nous choisissons la lampe rouge. ________________.
6. La vendeuse nous rend la monnaie. ________________.
7. Juliette veut organiser un pique-nique (picnic). ________________.
8. Vous avez soif quand il fait chaud. ________________.
9. Qu'est ce que Jacques fait quand il boit? ________________.
10. Pourquoi Juliette est triste? ________________.

B. Rewrite, in the *passé composé,* the following sentences, using the auxiliary *être.*

1. Mes parents reviennent (come back) du restaurant. ________________.
2. Il va à New York et elle arrive à Boston. ________________.
3. Nous montons au cinquième étage. ________________.
4. Vous devenez (devenir) ma belle-soeur. ________________.
5. Elle sort (sortir) avec son mari. ________________.
6. Juliette arrive pour l'anniversaire de son frère. ________________.
7. Elles restent (rester) avec leur tante. ________________.
8. Les feuilles (leaves) tombent de l'arbre. ________________.

C. Say, then write the following sentences in French, using the *passé composé* with *avoir* and *être.*

1. I came to see you before leaving. ________________.
2. I had money, but I spent it. ________________.
3. I have been invited to dinner. ________________.
4. You came down to have a drink. ________________.

5. I wanted a jar of fresh cream. ______________________.
6. They left without saying "thank you." ______________________.
7. We did not lose our keys. ______________________.
8. They did not drink any wine. ______________________.
9. He came back with flowers. ______________________.
10. She liked the music. ______________________.

GRAMMAR III Idiomatic expressions with *avoir, falloir* (to require), and *valoir* (to be worth).

A. Study the chart listing the impersonal expressions of *avoir, falloir,* and *valoir.*

AVOIR	ENGLISH	FALLOIR	ENGLISH	VALOIR	ENGLISH
il y a	there is	**il faut**	one must	**il vaut**	it is worth
il y a	there are	**il ne faut pas**	one must not	**il ne vaut pas**	it is not worth
il n'y a pas	there is not, there are not				

B. *Il y a* and *il n'y a pas* are usually followed by nouns with indefinite articles.

EX.: *Il y a des fruits dans le frigo.* There is fruit in the fridge.
Il y a du vin sur la table. There is wine on the table.

Il y a remains the same whether it is used with singular, plural, masculine, or feminine nouns.

C. *Il y a* is always conjugated as the third person singular of the verb *avoir.* Thus, the passé composé of *il y a* is *"Il y a eu."* (There has been.)

EX.: *Il y a eu des fraises.*	There have been strawberries.
Il n'y a pas eu de fraises.	There have not been any strawberries.
Il y a eu du vin.	There has been some wine.
Il n'y a pas eu de vin.	There has not been any wine.

D. When we study other tenses of *avoir,* the expression *il y a* will be pointed out at the third person singular of those tenses.

E. When the expression *il faut* is used with infinitives, it translates the English "It is necessary to."

EX.:	*Il faut être patient.*	It is necessary to be patient. (One must be patient.)
	Il faut prendre l'avion.	One must take the plane.

The impersonal pronoun *il* may also be translated "we" or "they," depending on the context.

EX.: *Nous sommes en retard, il faut courir.*
We're late, we must run. (One must run.)

Even when *il faut* is used in the negative form, *il ne faut pas,* the expression still strongly implies the necessity *not to do something.*

EX.: *Il ne faut pas fumer.* One must not smoke.

F. *Il vaut* is always used with a qualifying word or phrase such as *la peine de.* Thus we have two ready-made expressions, one using *mieux* and the other using *la peine.* As long as one adds the qualifying words, many useful expressions can be formed by adding the necessary infinitive.

EX.: *Il vaut mieux partir.* It's better to leave.
Ça vaut la peine. It's worth the trouble.
Ça vaut la peine d'étudier le français. It's worth the trouble to study French.

The negative of the above expression is: *Ça ne vaut pas la peine* + infinitive.

EX.: *Ça ne vaut pas la peine de rester.* It is not worth the trouble to stay.

G. The impersonal constructions *il faut* and *il vaut* are the third-person singular of *falloir* and *valoir,* and as with *il y a,* they will always be conjugated in the third-person singular in other tenses. Thus, in the passé composé we have:

il a fallu	it was necessary
il a valu	it was worth (it)

When we learn other tenses, the expressions *il faut* and *il vaut* will be pointed out.

PRACTICE THE IMPERSONAL EXPRESSION *IL Y A*

Write, then say, in French:

1. There is much wine in the refrigerator. ______________________.
2. There is a table, but there are no chairs. ______________________.
3. There is a manager, but there are no salesclerks. ______________________.
4. There is no meat with this meal. ______________________.
5. There is a key for the room, but there is no key for the dresser. __________ ____.
6. There are fruit and vegetables at the grocery store. ______________________ ____.
7. There has been a birthday party here. ______________________.

EXERCISE

Using *il faut* + infinitive, *il ne faut pas,* or *il a fallu,* rewrite the following sentences.

Example: Nous ne regardons pas la télé. <u>Il ne faut pas regarder la télé</u>.

1. Nous ne regardons pas la télé. ______________________.
2. Vous trouvez les clefs pour l'armoire. ______________________.
3. Pourquoi avons-nous changé d'avion? ______________________.
4. Vous organisez le voyage. ______________________.
5. Nous atterrisons à "Bagdad by the Bay." ______________________.
6. Il ne perd pas son temps à fumer. ______________________.
7. On mange quand on a faim. ______________________.

Lesson 9

À LA BANQUE (At the Bank)

l'action (fem.)	stock	**l'emprunt (masc.)**	loan
l'actionnaire (masc.)	stock holder	**l'épargne (fem.)**	saving(s)
l'affaire (fem.)	business	**les fonds (masc.)**	capital
l'agent de change (masc.)	broker	**le guichet**	teller window
le banquier	banker	**l'hypothèque (fem.)**	mortgage
le carnet de chèques	check book	**l'impôt (masc.)**	tax
la caisse	cashier's office	**l'intérêt (masc.)**	interest
le caissier (la caissière)	teller	**le mandat**	money order
le coffre	safe deposit box	**le mois**	month
le comptant	cash	**le montant**	amount
le crédit	credit	**le placement**	investment
les devises (fem.)	foreign money	**le salaire**	wages
l'échange (masc.)	the exchange	**la semaine**	week
		la succursale	branch
		le taux	percentage
		la valeur	value
		le versement	payment
augmenter	to raise, to increase	**emprunter**	to borrow
baisser	to lower	**épargner**	to put aside, to spare
découvrir	to discover	**être à sec**	to be broke
déposer	to deposit	**gagner**	to win, earn
économiser	to save	**laisser**	to leave

payer comptant	to pay cash	**plaire**	to please
		prêter	to lend
placer	to invest	**tirer**	to withdraw
se plaindre	to complain	**valoir**	to be worth
annuel	yearly	**luxueux(-euse)**	luxurious
bas (basse)	low	**mensuel(-uelle)**	monthly
faible	weak	**reconnaissant(e)**	grateful
fort(e)	strong	**satisfaisant(e)**	satisfactory
hebdomadaire	weekly	**sérieux(-euse)**	serious
à la fin	at the end	**selon**	according to
à propos	by the way	**surtout**	above all
de nouveau	again	**vers**	towards, about
pour cent	per hundred		

NOTES:

1. *Les actions* means "stocks." The French equivalent of the Stock Exchange is *La Bourse (de Paris).*

2. *La caisse d'épargne* is the savings bank. The verb *épargner* means "to put aside" when speaking of finances, but *épargner quelqu'un,* when speaking of people, means "to spare someone," as in *épargnez-moi le bavardage,* (spare me the chit-chat). *Bavardage* is related to *bavarder* (to chat), *bavard,* masc. (talkative).

3. *Satisfaire* means "to satisfy." From this verb are derived *satisfait* (adjective meaning "satisfied"); *il est satisfait; satisfaisant* (present participle meaning "satisfactory").

4. The verb *plaire* (to please) gives us: *le plaisir* (pleasure) and *plaisanter* (to joke). Such derivatives can greatly enhance your vocabulary. See how many nouns, adjectives, or verbs you can form from vocabulary that you have already learned.

5. *L'année* (year), *l'an* (year), *annuel* (masc.) (yearly) are all related; *l'année* (fem.) denotes a specific year, as in *l'année 1950. L'an* denotes a year in general, as in *Elle a dix ans.* (She's ten years old.)

PRACTICE THE VOCABULARY

(Answers for Lesson 9, pp. 145–147)

A. Give the feminine of the following adjectives.

1. fort ______
2. satisfait ______
3. reconnaissant ______
4. sérieux ______
5. mensuel ______
6. annuel ______
7. luxueux ______
8. gagnant ______
9. gentil ______
10. patient ______

11. prudent ______
12. courageux ______
13. vieux ______
14. sportif ______
15. naïf ______

B. Write the word or words that belong to the same family as the following words. Your words may be nouns, adjectives, adverbs, verbs, etc.

1. l'emprunt ______
2. valoir ______
3. l'action ______
4. l'année ______
5. bavarder ______
6. satisfaire ______
7. placer ______
8. plaire ______
9. vrai ______
10. fin ______

C. Complete the following sentences using the correct verb tense, and translating into French all English words or expressions. (All verbs are given in the infinitive form.)

1. La banque ___________ (fermer) à quatre heures de l'après-midi.
2. La ___________ (teller) me ___________ (donner) deux cartes ___________. (to fill out)
3. Le ___________ (rate) dans cette banque est très ___________. (low)
4. Il faut payer les ___________ (taxes) d'échange à ce guichet.
5. Le ___________ (teller window) des ___________ (investments) est fermé.
6. À la fin du mois, je ___________. (être à sec)
7. Quand j'achète une voiture, je ___________. (payer à crédit)
8. À l'épicerie il faut ___________. (to pay cash)
9. J'ai deux cent dollars à mon compte à ___________. (savings bank)
10. La valeur des ___________ (foreign currency, money) baisse, ou ___________ (rises) selon la Bourse.

DIALOGUE *Une visite à la banque*

JACQUES:	Bonjour, Madame. Je voudrais ouvrir un compte dans votre banque.
LA CAISSIÈRE:	Il faut aller au guichet numéro seize, Monsieur.
JACQUES:	Bonjour, Mademoiselle. Je voudrais ouvrir un compte ordinaire.

LA CAISSIÈRE:	Monsieur, pour ouvrir un compte, vous avez besoin de remplir ces deux cartes, et n'oubliez pas de signer aux endroits indiqués.
JACQUES:	Merci, Mademoiselle. Je dois aussi toucher ce chèque de cinquante dollars. Puis-je faire cela ici?
LA CAISSIÈRE:	Oui, c'est possible, mais remplissez les cartes d'abord.
JACQUES:	Voici les cartes, signées bien sûr!
LA CAISSIÈRE:	Combien voulez-vous déposer à votre compte? Notre minimum est de vingt-cinq dollars.
JACQUES:	J'ai un chèque de cent dollars à déposer dans le nouveau compte.
LA CAISSIÈRE:	Pourquoi ne déposez-vous pas vingt-cinq dollars au compte ordinaire et soixante-quinze dollars à un compte de caisse d'épargne? Vous pouvez commencer un compte de caisse d'épargne tout de suite. Les comptes ordinaires ne gagnent pas d'intérêt dans cette banque.
JACQUES:	Très bien, c'est une bonne idée! Quel est le taux d'interêt dans votre banque?
LA CAISSIÈRE:	Cinq et demi pour cent, Monsieur. Voici une troisième carte à remplir! Aussi il faut endosser les deux chèques, celui de cent dollars à déposer à vos comptes, et celui de cinquante dollars que vous voulez toucher.
JACQUES:	J'ai déjà endossé celui de cent dollars. Le voici. Celui de cinquante dollars n'est pas à mon nom, mais il a été endossé à mon compte.
LA CAISSIÈRE:	Dans ce cas, il faut vérifier votre identité et votre signature.
JACQUES:	Voici ma carte d'identité et mon permis de conduire.
LA CAISSIÈRE:	C'est tout, c'est fait. Voici votre livret de banque et vos chèques provisoires. Dans quinze jours, il faut revenir à la banque pour les chèques imprimés à votre nom.
JACQUES:	Au revoir, Mademoiselle et merci. Si jamais j'ai besoin d'un emprunt, c'est ici que je vais le faire.
LA CAISSIÈRE:	Merci Monsieur, vous êtes bien gentil.

DIALOG *A Visit to the Bank*

JACQUES:	Good morning, Madam. I would like to open a checking account in your bank.
THE TELLER:	You must go to window number sixteen, sir.
JACQUES:	Good morning, Miss. I would like to open a checking account.
THE TELLER:	Sir, for a checking account, you need to fill out these two cards, and don't forget to sign at the designated places.

JACQUES:	Thanks, Miss. I must also cash this fifty dollar check. Can I do that here?
THE TELLER:	Yes, it is possible, but fill out the cards first.
JACQUES:	Here are the cards, signed of course!
THE TELLER:	How much do you want to deposit in your checking account? Our minimum is twenty-five dollars.
JACQUES:	I have a one-hundred-dollar check to deposit in the new account.
THE TELLER:	Why don't you deposit twenty-five dollars in the checking account and seventy-five dollars in a savings account? You can start a savings account right away. In this bank, the checking accounts don't earn any interest.
JACQUES:	Very well, it's a good idea! What is the interest rate in your bank?
THE TELLER:	Five and a half percent, sir. Here's a third card to fill out! Also you must endorse the two checks, the one-hundred-dollar one for deposit in your accounts, and the fifty-dollar one that you wish to cash.
JACQUES:	I already endorsed the one-hundred-dollar one. Here it is. The fifty-dollar one is not in my name, but it has been endorsed to my account.
THE TELLER:	In that case, I must verify your identity and your signature.
JACQUES:	Here are my identity card and my driver's license.
THE TELLER:	That's all, it's done. Here is your bank book and your temporary checks. In fifteen days, you must come back to the bank for the checks printed with your name.
JACQUES:	Goodbye, miss, and thank you. If I ever need a loan, it's here that I will do it (come).
THE TELLER:	Thank you, sir, you are so kind!

DIALOG EXERCISES

A. Answer the questions according to the dialog, with short complete sentences.

1. Qu'est-ce que Jacques veut commencer? ____________________
2. Combien de chèques Jacques apporte-t-il à la banque? ____________________
____
3. Que fait Jacques avec le chèque de cinquante dollars? ____________________
____

4. Où Jacques a-t-il déposé le chèque de cent dollars? ______________________
____

5. Que doit faire Jacques avant de déposer un chèque? ______________________
____

6. Pourquoi la caissière veut-elle vérifier l'identité de Jacques? __________
____

7. Quel genre (what kind) de chèques la caissière donne-t-elle à Jacques?
____

8. Pourquoi Jacques doit-il revenir à la banque? ______________________

9. Combien d'argent Jacques dépose-t-il à la Caisse d'Épargne? __________
____

10. Combien d'argent Jacques dépose-t-il à son compte de chèques? ________
____

B. Match the two columns.

1. Le guichet est fermé.
2. La gérante est occupée maintenant.
3. J'ai perdu mon carnet de banque.
4. Il ouvre un compte de chèques.
5. La banque a baissé le taux d'intérêt.
6. Je suis toujours à sec!
7. Le versement mensuel est de vingt dollars.
8. Le bureau d'échange n'a pas d'agent.
9. Il faut endosser le chèque.
10. Elle veut toucher le chèque de son salaire.

A. He opens a checking account.
B. The bank lowered its interest rate.
C. She wants to cash her paycheck.
D. One must endorse a check.
E. The monthly payment is twenty dollars.
F. The window is closed.
G. The manager is busy now.
H. I lost my bank book.
I. I am always broke.
J. The exchange office has no broker (agent).

GRAMMAR I Indirect object nouns and pronouns.

A. We have seen in Lesson 7 that direct object nouns and pronouns respond to the questions "what" and "whom"; the indirect object nouns and pronouns answer the questions "to what," "for what," "by what," "by whom," "by whose," etc.

EX.: *J'ai parlé à la caissière. Caissière* is the indirect object noun. When you replace *caissière* by *lui,* as in *Je lui ai parlé* (I spoke to her), *lui* is the indirect object pronoun.

B. Indirect object pronouns replace indirect object nouns. They are exactly the same as the direct object pronouns studied in Lesson 7, except for the third person singular and plural, which are *lui* and *leur.*

C. Study the chart and compare the direct and indirect object pronouns.

SUBJECT	DIRECT	INDIRECT	ENGLISH
je	**me**	**me**	me, to me, for me
tu	**te**	**te**	you, to you, for you
nous	**nous**	**nous**	us, to us, for us
vous	**vous**	**vous**	you, to you, for you
il	**le, l'**	**lui**	him, her, to him or her, for him or her
elle	**la, l'**	**lui**	him, her, to him or her, for him or her
ils	**les**	**leur**	them, to them, for them
elles	**les**	**leur**	them, to them, for them

NOTES:

1. In French, all indirect object nouns require the preposition *à*. With this fact in mind, it will be easy to replace indirect object pronouns.

EX.: *J'ai parlé à Jacques.* I spoke to Jacques.
Je lui ai parlé. I spoke to him.

2. An important similarity with direct object pronouns is that indirect object pronouns also immediately precede the verb they modify, whether it is conjugated or in the infinitive:
   EX.: *Elle m'a donné le chèque.* She gave *me* the check.
   Elle nous a donné le chèque. She gave *us* the check.
   Je ne veux pas leur donner le chèque. I don't wish to give *them* the check.

EXERCISES

A. Answer the following questions about indirect object nouns and pronouns.

1. What does an indirect object pronoun replace? ____________________
2. What is the difference between the direct object pronouns and indirect object pronouns? ____________________
3. What are the third persons singular and plural of the indirect object pronouns? ____________________
4. What is always required by a French indirect object noun? __________ ______________________________
5. Name one important similarity between the direct object pronouns and the indirect object pronouns. ____________________

B. Complete the sentences with the appropriate French verb tense and the indirect object pronoun.

Example: Je (give her) lui donne la clef.

1. Jacques (asks them) __________ des renseignements.
2. Elle (telephoned me) __________ hier soir.
3. Nous (spoke with him) __________ au restaurant.
4. Il (gives us back) __________ la monnaie.
5. La cliente (asks me) __________ de l'aider.
6. Je (telephoned you) __________ ce matin.
7. Il (showed us) __________ son carnet de chèques.

8. Il (looks like her) ____________ en tout.
9. Elle veut (to speak to them) ____________ avant de les voir.
10. Il faut (to write to her) ____________.

NOTE:

Remember to distinguish between *leur* (them) and *leur, leurs* (their); *leur* (them) always precedes a noun.

EX.: *Ils cherchent leur valise.* They're looking for *their* suitcase.
but: *Ils leur donnent leur valise.* They're giving them their suitcase.

GRAMMAR II Reflexive constructions.

A. Reflexive means that the action of the verb reflects on the subject, as in *Je me lave.* (I wash myself). Reflexive constructions are rather rare in English, but they are common in French.

B. In reflexive constructions there is always a pronoun that refers to the subject.

EX.: I hurt *myself.*
She dresses *herself.*
He sings to *himself.*
The pronouns, myself, herself, and himself, are reflexive pronouns. They can be direct pronouns, as in, "I hurt myself." Or indirect as in "He sings to himself."

C. In French, the reflexive pronouns are *me, te, se, nous, vous,* and *se.*

D. Study the following chart with *se laver* (to wash oneself).

SUBJECT	PRONOUN	SE LAVER	ENGLISH
je	**me**	**lave**	I wash myself
tu	**te**	**laves**	you wash yourself
il, elle, on	**se**	**lave**	he, she washes himself, herself
nous	**nous**	**lavons**	we wash ourselves
vous	**vous**	**lavez**	you wash yourself, yourselves
ils, elles	**se**	**lavent**	they wash themselves

1. In reflexive constructions, the pronoun subject (*je, tu,* etc.) and the pronoun object both precede the verb.
   EX.: *Je me lave.* I wash myself.
2. But in negative forms, *ne* is placed right after the subject and *pas* is placed after the verb, as usual.
   EX.: *Je ne me lave pas.* I don't wash myself.
3. In reflexive constructions, the reflexive verb always has a reflexive pronoun that agrees in number and gender with the subject.
   EX.: *Nous nous lavons.* We wash ourselves.
4. The reflexive pronoun for the third person singular and the third person plural is *se,* as in
   Il se lave. He washes himself.
   Ils se lavent. They wash themselves.

PRACTICE THE REFLEXIVE CONSTRUCTIONS

A. Answer the questions.

1. What is a reflexive construction? ______________________.
2. What is always required in a reflexive construction? ________________ ____.
3. How are the pronoun subject and the pronoun object placed in a reflexive construction? ______________________.
4. Give the negative form of *nous nous amusons.* ________________ ____.
5. What kind of reflexive pronoun is in the following construction? *Il se parle.* ______________________.
6. The reflexive pronoun *se* appears in three reflexive constructions. Name them in the phrase "to wash oneself." ______________________.
7. Say, and then write, in French, "I am having a good time." ____________ ____.
8. Give the first person plural of the reflexive French verb *s'arrêter.* ______________________.
9. Give the reflexive construction of "They (masc.) are having a good time." ______________________.
10. Give the reflexive construction of "You *(tu)* speak to yourself." ______________________.

B. Using the appropriate reflexive construction, rewrite the following sentences

1. ma petite sœur/se lever/tôt le matin ______________________.
2. pendant que je/se laver/elle mange ______________________.
3. quand j'ai besoin de/se regarder/dans le miroir, elle m'appelle ______________________.
4. je/se brosser/les dents après le petit déjeûner ______________________.
5. ma petite soeur et moi/s'habiller/en même temps ______________________.
6. dès que je finis je/se préparer/pour sortir ______________________.
7. ma soeur et ma voisine/se promener/après mon départ ______________________.
8. j'ai besoin de/se coucher/de bonne heure ce soir ______________________.
9. mes parents/se réveiller/souvent plus tôt que moi ______________________.
10. mon ami Mark/se marier/la semaine prochaine ______________________.

GRAMMAR III Reflexive verbs.

A. Below is a partial list of the most frequently used reflexive verbs. Please memorize them.

s'appeler	to call oneself	*se coucher*	to go to bed
s'arrêter	to stop	*s'ennuyer*	to be bored
se baigner	to bathe, swim	*se lever*	to get up
		se marier	to get married
se brosser	to brush oneself	*se reposer*	to rest
		se réveiller	to wake up

B. Many reflexive verbs are also nonreflexive.

EX.:	*Elle lave ses vêtements.*	She washes her clothes.
	Elle se lave.	She washes herself.
	Il se réveille à six heures.	He wakes up at six.
	La radio le réveille à six heures.	The radio wakes him up at six.

C. Some nonreflexive verbs that we have studied change their meaning when used in reflexive constructions.

EX.:	*demander*	to ask	*se demander*	to wonder
	entendre	to hear	*s'entendre*	to get along
	tromper	to deceive	*se tromper*	to be mistaken
	trouver	to find	*se trouver*	to be located

D. All reflexive verbs are conjugated in the *passé composé* with *être*. With this fact in mind, simply find the past participle of the verb in question and proceed with the conjugation of *être*. The past participle, of course, agrees in gender and number with the reflexive pronoun, which in turn agrees with the subject. Study the chart of *se laver* in the *passé composé*:

SUBJECT	PRONOUN	AUXILIARY	VERB	ENGLISH
je	**me**	**suis**	**lavé** (e)	I washed myself
tu	**t'**	**es**	**lavé** (e)	you washed yourself
il, elle	**s'**	**est**	**lavé** (e)	he, she, washes himself, herself
nous	**nous**	**sommes**	**lavé(e)s**	we wash ourselves
vous	**vous**	**étes**	**lavé(e)s**	you wash yourselves
ils, elles	**se**	**sont**	**lavé(e)s**	they wash themselves

NOTES:

1. Whenever the auxiliary *être* is used to form the *passé composé,* the past participle, reflexive or nonreflexive, always agrees in number and gender with the subject and/or the pronoun. In the case of the reflexive *passé composé,* the past participle agrees with both the subject and the reflexive pronoun.
2. In the imperative form, the reflexive verbs follow the rules we have learned. However, the *te* becomes *toi* in the imperative form.
   EX.: *Tu te laves.—Lave-toi.* Wash yourself.
   Tu t'occupes de ta soeur.—Occupe-toi de ta soeur. Take care of your sister.

EXERCISES

A. Rewrite the following sentences, in the reflexive form, according to the example.

Example: Je me repose, le gérant se repose aussi.

1. Elle se réveille tard, nous ____________________.
2. Je me brosse les dents, ils ____________________.
3. Tu t'amuses, vous ____________________.
4. Ils s'excusent et nous ____________________.
5. Je me couche à minuit, tu ____________________.
6. Vous vous levez avec peine, ils ____________________.
7. Ils s'amusent et tu ____________________.
8. Vous vous reposez et ils ____________________.
9. Ils s'ennuient et je ____________________.

B. Rewrite the reflexive sentences in the imperative form.

1. Tu te reposes. ____________________.
2. Tu te laves. ____________________.
3. Vous vous dépêchez. ____________________.
4. Nous nous habillons. ____________________.
5. Tu te baignes. ____________________.
6. Vous vous couchez tôt. ____________________.
7. Vous ne vous ennuyez pas. ____________________.
8. Nous ne nous arrêtons pas ici. ____________________.
9. Tu ne t'excuses pas. ____________________.
10. Vous vous brossez les dents (teeth). ____________________.

NOTE:

Reflexive constructions in the imperative form require *toi* instead of *te* in the second person singular in the affirmative *only*.

EX.: *tu t'excuses — excuse-toi*

Lesson 10

À LA GARE
(At the Railroad Station)

le coffre	trunk (car trunk)	**le nord**	North
le contrôleur	ticket collector	**la nuit**	night
la couchette	bunk, berth	**l'ouest (masc.)**	West
la destination	destination	**le panneau**	the road sign
l'endroit (masc.)	place	**le quai**	platform
l'est (masc.)	East	**le rail**	rail
l'express (masc.)	express train	**la route nationale**	highway
l'heure d'affluence (fem.)	rush hour	**la sortie**	exit
l'horaire	schedule, timetable	**la station**	stop, station (subway)
le machiniste	engineer	**le sud**	South
la malle	trunk (suitcase)	**le train**	train
la marque	brand	**la vitesse**	speed
le moyen	the way, means	**le wagon aux bagages**	baggage car
		le wagon-lit	sleeping car
		le wagon-restaurant	dining car
conduire	to drive	**raconter**	to tell (story)
courir	to run	**rentrer**	to return (home)
s'endormir	to fall asleep	**repartir**	to leave again
être pressé	to be in a hurry	**retourner**	to return
indiquer	to indicate	**se sentir**	to feel (oneself)
monter	to go up	**tomber**	to fall
oublier	to forget		

ensemble	together	**plusieurs**	several
à l'étranger	abroad	**plutôt**	rather
en forme	in shape	**en retard**	late
à l'heure	on time	**vite**	fast
incroyable	incredible		

NOTES:

1. The prefix *re* in *repartir* (to leave again), designates repetition of the action of the verb *partir* (to leave).
   EX.: *tomber* to fall — *retomber* to fall again
   venir to come — *revenir* to come again, to come back
   faire to do — *refaire* to do again

2. *Heureusement* (happily) is formed with the feminine singular *(heureuse)* of the adjective *heureux* (happy). The *-ment* ending denotes an adverb. All the adverbs ending in *-ment* are usually formed in the above manner. Ex.: *sérieux* (masc.), *sérieuse* (fem.) *sérieusement,* "seriously." We will study more about these adverbs later in Lesson 15.

PRACTICE THE VOCABULARY:

(Answers for Lesson 10, pp. 147–150)

A. Write the indefinite articles *un, une,* or *des* (pl. form) before the following nouns.

1. ______ couchette
2. ______ wagon aux bagages
3. ______ horaire
4. ______ rails
5. ______ malle
6. ______ train
7. ______ nuit
8. ______ marque
9. ______ quais
10. ______ moyen
11. ______ endroit
12. ______ panneau
13. ______ route
14. ______ coffres
15. ______ station

B. Write the opposite of the following words.

1. le départ ____________
2. le nord ____________
3. l'est ____________
4. monter ____________
5. se réveiller ____________
6. la sortie ____________
7. gagner ____________
8. payer à crédit ____________
9. faible ____________
10. baisser ____________

C. Fill in the blanks with the *passé composé* of the given verbs.

1. Les horaires (changer) ______________________ hier.
2. Le taux d'interêt (augmenter) ______________________ de cinq pour cent.
3. Le train de six heures du soir (arriver) ______________________ à l'heure.
4. Juliette et moi (oublier) ______________________ de remercier la concierge.
5. Charles (repartir) ______________________ en France.
6. Heureusement que la semaine (finir) ______________________.
7. La caissière (être) ______________________ gentille avec moi.
8. Nous (avoir) ______________________ de la chance de trouver un taxi.
9. Ils (envoyer) ______________________ un mandat international de cent dollars.
10. Vous (avoir) ______________________ raison d'être heureux.

DIALOGUE *À la gare Saint Lazare*

JULIETTE: Ah! Voilà Charles. Il a l'air un peu perdu! Charles, par ici!

CHARLES: Salut, Juliette! Attends une minute, je voudrais dire au revoir à Monsieur Legrand.

JULIETTE: As-tu fait un bon voyage? Pour quelqu'un qui a passé la nuit dans le train, tu as l'air bien reposé.

CHARLES: Oui, je me sens en forme. J'avais la couchette supérieure dans le wagon-lit, et après le dîner au wagon-restaurant, j'ai pris un verre avec Monsieur Legrand. Ensuite je suis monté à ma couchette et quand je me suis réveillé, nous étions à la gare!

JULIETTE: C'est parfait, parce que j'ai plusieurs projets pour notre premier jour ensemble à Paris.

CHARLES: Très bien, attends ici une minute, je vais aller trouver ma malle, regarde s'il y a un taxi près d'ici.

JULIETTE: D'accord, j'y vais tout de suite. Vous êtes libre, Monsieur?

LE CHAUFFEUR: Oui, Mademoiselle, c'est pour vous?

JULIETTE: Oui, et pour mon ami. Il arrive avec sa malle.

LE CHAUFFEUR: Excusez-moi, je dois ouvrir le coffre.

JULIETTE: Ta malle a l'air vraiment lourde. Heureusement que j'ai trouvé un taxi tout près.

CHARLES: Oui, nous avons de la chance. Les taxis ne sont pas toujours libres pendant les heures d'affluence.

(Juliette et Charles sont à l'intérieur du taxi)

CHARLES:	La première chose que je vais faire demain, c'est acheter une carte orange et faire tout Paris. Monsieur Legrand m'a expliqué tous les avantages de cette carte-là.
JULIETTE:	C'est une idée excellente, merci. J'ai décidé d'accepter.
CHARLES:	D'accepter quoi?
JULIETTE:	L'invitation d'aller avec toi acheter la carte orange, et faire le tour de Paris.
CHARLES:	Ah! Les femmes sont incroyables! Comment as-tu deviné ce que j'avais en tête?
JULIETTE:	Je suis intelligente!
CHARLES:	Non, tu es maligne!
JULIETTE:	Regarde, nous sommes arrivés; le temps passe si vite quand je suis avec toi!

DIALOG *At the Saint-Lazare Train Station*

JULIETTE:	Ah! There's Charles. He seems a little lost. Charles, over here!
CHARLES:	Hi, Juliette! Wait a minute, I would like to say goodbye to Mr. Legrand.
JULIETTE:	Did you have a good trip? For someone who spent the night on a train, you look well rested.
CHARLES:	Yes, I feel in shape. I had the upper bunk (berth) in the sleeping car, and after dinner I had a drink with Mr. Legrand in the dining car. Then I went up to my bunk and when I woke up, we were at the train station!
JULIETTE:	That's perfect, because I have several plans in mind for our first day in Paris together.
CHARLES:	Very well, wait here a minute, I'm going to go find my trunk. See if there is a taxi nearby.
JULIETTE:	Agreed, I'm going there right away. Are you available, sir?
THE CHAUFFEUR:	Yes Miss, is it for you?
JULIETTE:	Yes, and my friend. He's coming (arriving) with his trunk.
THE CHAUFFEUR:	Excuse me, I have to open the car trunk.
JULIETTE:	The trunk seems really heavy. Fortunately I found a taxi very near.
CHARLES:	Yes, we are lucky. Taxis are not always available during rush hours.

(Juliette and Charles are inside the taxi)

CHARLES:	The first thing I'm going to do is buy an orange card and tour all of Paris. Mr. Legrand explained to me all the advantages of that card.
JULIETTE:	It's an excellent idea, thanks. I've decided to accept.
CHARLES:	To accept what?
JULIETTE:	The invitation to go with you to buy the orange card and tour Paris.
CHARLES:	Ah! Women are incredible! How did you guess what I had in mind?
JULIETTE:	I am intelligent!
CHARLES:	No, you are shrewd!
JULIETTE:	Look, we've arrived; time goes so fast when I'm with you!

NOTES:

1. *La Gare Saint-Lazare* is one of the most important train stations in Paris. It is also a subway stop and is connected to the government regulated SNCF, which stands for the Société Nationale des Chemins de Fer. All the railroads in France are controlled by the SNCF which started in 1938. *La Gare Saint-Lazare* is said to serve 1300 travelers a minute during the evening peak hours.

2. *La carte orange* is an orange card that may be bought at any subway window; it allows the holder to use it on buses and subways for an unlimited number of trips throughout Paris within a given month. Besides being practical, it's also economical.

3. *Le coffre* is the trunk, when cars are in question. It is a safety deposit box, when the subject is a bank.

4. *Y* is a pronoun replacing a place, as in *Es-tu allé au cirque? Oui j'y suis allé.* Yes I went there.

5. *L'heure d'affluence* literally means "the hour of the crowd" (otherwise known as the rush hour) and is usually used in the plural.

6. *Libre:* free (taxi), does not mean *gratis,* but available. Free of charge is translated in French by *gratuit* (masc.) or *gratuite* (fem.).

7. Note that *maligne* is the feminine form of *malin* (masc.).

DIALOG EXERCISES

Answer all the questions according to the text.

1. Où est Juliette? ____________________.
2. Que dit Juliette quand elle voit Charles? ____________________.
3. Que répond Charles? ____________________.
4. À qui Charles voudrait dire au revoir? ____________________.
5. Où Charles a-t-il passé la nuit? ____________________.

6. Quel est l'opposé (opposite) de fatigué? ______.
7. Pourquoi Charles est en forme? ______.
8. Qu'est-ce que Charles fait après le dîner? ______.
9. Que fait le chauffeur quand Charles arrive? ______.
10. Qu'est-ce que Charles veut acheter? ______.
11. Quelle est l'invitation que Juliette n'a jamais reçue? ______ ______.
12. Juliette n'est pas intelligente, mais plutôt? ______.
13. Comment Juliette a-t-elle changé la conversation? ______ ______.
14. Juliette est-elle très sarcastique quand elle dit "le temps passe vite avec toi"? ______.

GRAMMAR I The imperfect indicative *(imparfait)*.

A. Study the imperfect endings in the chart below.

SUBJECT	VERB: TROUVER	IMPERFECT ENDING	ENGLISH
je	**trouv**	**ais**	I used to find
tu	**trouv**	**ais**	you used to find
il, elle, on	**trouv**	**ait**	he, she, it used to find
nous	**trouv**	**ions**	we used to find
vous	**trouv**	**iez**	you used to find
ils, elles	**trouv**	**aient**	they used to find

1. The *imparfait* (imperfect) has several English equivalents: *il trouvait* can mean "he found," "he was finding," and "he used to find."
2. The imperfect is used to describe continuous or habitual actions that existed for indefinite durations. This, in fact, is the reason that this tense is called imperfect—we never know when the action at the imperfect began, nor when it ended.

   EX.: *Elle regardait la télévision tous les soirs.* She watched television every night. (habitual, repetitious)
   La maison était grande et belle. The house was large and beautiful. (description)

3. The imperfect is also used to describe emotions and feelings; it is used to state a date, time of day, or someone's age in the past.
4. A verb having *-ier* in the infinitive, such as *associer* (to associate) or *étudier* (to study)—where the first person plural is *nous associons* and *nous étudions*—has *associ* and *étudi* when we drop the *-ons*. The imperfect will then be *nous associions* and *nous étudiions,* with the *i* doubled in the first and second persons of the plural.

   EX.: *nous associions, nous étudiions*
   vous associiez, vous étudiiez

B. Memorize the imperfect of *être,* the only exception to the rule for forming the imperfect of all French verbs.

SUBJECT	IMPERFECT OF ÊTRE	ENGLISH
j'	**étais**	I was, used to be, was being
tu	**étais**	you were, used to be, etc.
il, elle, on	**était**	he, she, it was, used to be, etc.
nous	**étions**	we were, used to be, etc.
vous	**étiez**	you were, etc.
ils, elles	**étaient**	they were, etc.

EXERCISES

A. Rewrite the following sentences in the imperfect indicative.

1. Ils ont réussi à faire des économies (savings). ______________.
2. Mes parents et moi sommes d'accord sur ce sujet (subject). ______________ ______________.
3. Les voisins ont commencé à nous inviter. ______________.
4. La route nationale est pleine (full) de panneaux. ______________ ______________.
5. Nos amis n'ont pas hésité une minute. ______________.
6. Vous m'encouragez tous les jours. ______________.
7. Il est midi pile et il ne déjeûne pas. ______________.

8. À minuit nous entendons des bruits (noises). ____________________.
9. Nous pouvons sortir plus tard. ____________________.
10. Il veut faire la connaissance de Juliette. ____________________.

B. Write complete sentences using the imperfect indicative and adding necessary connecting words, articles, prepositions, adjectives, etc.

1. nous/avoir/plusieurs/heures/route nationale ____________________.
2. mon mari/donner/argent/pendant/semaine ____________________.
3. chaque (every) jour/voisin/inviter/ma sœur ____________________.
4. nous/partir/en vacances/ensemble ____________________.
5. ces garçons/être/Amérique/Canada ____________________.
6. nous/faire/promenade/le soir ____________________.
7. après le travail/je/faire/des courses ____________________.
8. ils/rentrer/souvent/très tard ____________________.
9. nous/être/avec/Jean/jour/fête ____________________.
10. nous/être/heureux/avec/voisins ____________________.

C. Rewrite the following paragraph, replacing all the verbs with the imperfect indicative, then read the new paragraph aloud.

Je fais mes débuts en français, les leçons sont parfois difficiles, mais je fais mon possible pour les comprendre. Je suis occupé l'après-midi, mais j'étudie le matin et quelquefois (sometimes) j'essaie de finir les exercices le soir. La leçon cinq est très longue parce qu'elle a plusieurs pages de révision (review). Je veux bien continuer l'étude du français parce que j'aime beaucoup la langue, et parce que j'ai envie d'aller en France.

GRAMMAR II Contrast of the *imparfait* and *passé composé*.

A. The two main verb tenses in French are the *imparfait* (imperfect) and the *passé composé* (compound past). We have just learned that the *imparfait* is used in descriptive past actions conveying repetition, habit, and continuity. The *passé composé,* which we have also learned, differs from the *imparfait* in that it is used in actions that are neither continuous nor descriptive.

B. The *passé composé* conveys something that began and ended in the past, without any consideration as to how long that action lasted.

EX.: *J'ai fini mon travail.* (I started *mon travail* and completed it.) The main distinction, then, could be summarized this way:

a. *imparfait* past continuous action with no specific beginning nor end.

b. *passé composé* past completed action without continuity or duration.

C. The *passé composé* also can convey a one-time event that happened in the past, as in *J'ai visité Versailles l'année dernière* (last year).

D. Remember that the *imparfait* always relates what was going on and how things were, while the *passé composé* interrupts these continuous, repetitious, habitual situations:

EX.: *Il est venu pendant que je mangeais.* He came while I was eating.

NOTE:

The imperfect reflexive verbs follow the same pattern as the nonreflexive constructions.

EX.: *Nous nous lavons. Nous nous lavions.*
(We were washing ourselves.)

EXERCISES

A. Write complete sentences using the *imparfait* and *passé composé,* as appropriate. Follow the example.

Example: Juliette était gentille, mais hier elle m'a blessé. (she hurt me)

1. Juliette/venir/toujours à midi, mais aujourd'hui elle/venir/en retard ______
______.
2. Elle/croire/à mes promesses, mais soudain (suddenly) elle/changer
______.
3. Elle/penser/toujours à moi mais lundi elle/oublier/mon anniversaire ______
______.
4. Elle/aimer/mes histoires mais hier elle/trouver/ma plaisanterie (joke) ennuyeuse (boring) ______.
5. Le soir elle/étudier/mais hier elle/sortir/avec Pierre ______
______.
6. Elle me/téléphoner/le matin, mais aujourd'hui elle/ne pas me téléphoner
______.

7. Juliette/vouloir/aller camper mais elle/refuser/d'aller avec moi
____.

8. Juliette/pouvoir/me faire rire, mais hier elle me/faire/pleurer (to cry)
____.

9. Elle m'/attendre/toujours, mais aujourd'hui elle/décider/de partir sans moi (without me) ____.

10. Elle/être/souvent polie, mais hier elle/insulter/ma sœur ______________
____.

B. Complete the sentences using the *imparfait* and/or the *passé composé*, as required. Remember to use the *imparfait* in descriptive past actions (habitual, continuous, repetitious) and the *passé composé* in past completed actions (actions begun and ended in the past).

Example: Je ne (aller) __________ au cinéma hier, je (rester) __________ à la maison. Je ne suis pas allé(e) au cinéma hier, je suis resté(e) à la maison.

1. Juliette (vouloir) __________ faire la connaissance d'Antoine, mais il n(e) (venir) __________ avec Charles.
2. Ma sœur et moi (faire) __________ une promenade quand nous (rencontrer) __________ Jacques.
3. J' (avoir) __________ froid quand je (retourner) __________ de l'aéroport.
4. J' (avoir) __________ faim alors j(e) (manger) __________ tout (all) le pain.
5. Hier, j(e) (rester) __________ au lit parce que j(e) (être) __________ malade (ill).
6. Je (s'ennuyer) __________ alors mon ami m(e) (raconter) __________ une histoire.
7. J(e) (monter) __________ dans ma couchette et j(e) (commencer) __________ à lire.
8. L'heure d'affluence (être) __________ toujours entre quatre heures et cinq heures.
9. Le contrôleur (vérifier) __________ nos billets pendant que (while) nous (manger) __________.
10. Nous (aller) __________ à l'étranger l'année dernière (last year).

GRAMMAR III The days of the week, months of the year, dates, and ordinal numbers 1-100.

A. *Les jours de la semaine* (days of the week):
In French, the days of the week start with *Monday,* are *not capitalized,* and are all masculine.

B. *Les mois de l'année* (the months of the year):
The months of the year are *not capitalized* in French, and are also masculine.

C. Memorize the chart below.

LES JOURS (DAYS)	ENGLISH	LES MOIS (MONTHS)	ENGLISH
lundi	Monday	**janvier**	January
mardi	Tuesday	**février**	February
mercredi	Wednesday	**mars**	March
jeudi	Thursday	**avril**	April
vendredi	Friday	**mai**	May
samedi	Saturday	**juin**	June
dimanche	Sunday	**juillet**	July
		août	August
		septembre	September
		octobre	October
		novembre	November
		décembre	December

NOTES:

1. In French, to ask what day it is, we say,
Quel jour sommes-nous? What day is it? (are we?)
Then we answer either by simply stating the day, *lundi, mardi,* etc., or by repeating the verb *être, nous sommes mardi.*

2. Remember that *le,* before any day of the week, means that the action takes place every week on that same day.

   EX.: *Le dimanche ils vont à l'église.*
   On Sunday they go to church (every Sunday).

   Le is also used when a specific date is called for.

   EX.: *Le 20 décembre nous partons en vacances.*

3. The adjective *prochain* (masc.) is used to indicate the next day, week, month, or year.

EX.:	*la semaine prochaine*	next week
	lundi prochain	next Monday
	février prochain	next February
	l'année prochaine	next year

4. French uses the day of the week alone, when English requires "this," "that," "on," etc.

   EX.: *Jeudi, il va faire des courses.*
   (This) Thursday, or (On) Thursday, he's going shopping.

5. In French, the months are expressed either alone, when used with *prochain,* or with *en,* to translate the English "in," as in "in February" *en février.* We also may say *au mois de février*—in the month of February. However, *en* is the more common usage.

   EX.: *En septembre nous allons à Paris.*
   En juillet nous allons à Nice.

   It's not incorrect to say *au mois de septembre* and *au mois de juillet.*

D. Ordinal numbers 1–100.

1. Ordinal numbers are formed on the cardinal numbers by adding *-ième* to the cardinal number, except for one *(un)* and first (*premier,* or *première,* fem.).

EX.:	*un, premier*	first
	deux, deuxième	second (the *x* of *deuxième* is pronounced *z*)
	trois, troisième	third

2. When a cardinal number ends with *e* as in *quatre,* the *e* is dropped and we have

   quatrième fourth

NOTES:

1. The *x's* in *sixième* and *dixième* are pronounced *z.*
2. The *f* in *neuf* becomes *v* in *neuvième.*
3. The *x* in *soixante* becomes *ss*—soissantième for pronunciation.
4. After *soixante,* the ordinal number is indicated by *dix,* as in *soixante-dix, soixante-dixième.* The same applies to *quatre-vingt-dix* (90), quatre-vingt-dixième.
5. Ordinal numbers can also be written by adding *è* or *ème* to Arabic numbers: 1*er,* 2*è,* 3*ème,* 5*è,* 6*ème,* etc.

CULTURAL NOTE:

The French enjoy more holidays than Americans, because most French holidays are religious in nature. Thus, besides *la Fête Nationale,* which is the 14th of July, *la Fête de la Victoire* (Armistice Day) which is November 11th, and *la fête du Premier Mai* which is their Labor Day, the French have the following holidays:

Le jour de l'An (New Year's Day)—1*er* janvier.
Le lundi de Pâques (Easter Monday)—mars ou avril.
L'Ascension (Ascension Day)—mai, jeudi
L'Assomption (Assumption Day)—15 août.
La Toussaint (All Saints Day)—1*er* novembre.
Noël (Christmas)—25 décembre.

Note also that when French people take a long holiday weekend (4 days), they say *"Faire le pont."* Literally, it means, "to make the bridge."

EXERCISES

A. Practice the days of the week and the months of the year.

1. What is the difference between the days of the week in French and in English? ______________.
2. With what day does the French week start? ______________.
3. What is the gender of days and months in French? ______________ ______________.
4. What does the definite article *le,* before a weekday, mean? ______________ ______________.
5. How do we translate "this Saturday," "on Thursday," "that Friday" into French? ______________.
6. Write in French, "next Sunday" ______________, "next July" ______________, "next year" ______________.
7. How is the French ordinal number formed? ______________.
8. With which ordinal numbers does *x* become *z*? ______________.
9. With which ordinal number does *x* become *ss*? ______________.
10. Say, and then write, in French: "The first day of the week is Monday." ______________.

B. Translate into French.

1. Next week we are going to buy some furniture. ______________________.
2. The second week in July, my friend went to Nice. ______________________.
3. In March we drove to the airport together. ______________________.
4. The ninth month of the year is September. ______________________.
5. Every Tuesday I take piano lessons. ______________________.
6. Next October my husband is leaving for Paris. ______________________.
7. The hundredth passenger won the jackpot! ______________________.

ANSWERS FOR LESSONS 6-10

Lesson 6

Vocabulary

Practice A.
1. beau
2. compose
3. montagnes
4. disponible
5. aimable
6. la commode
7. clef
8. tapageurs

B.
1. I
2. H
3. G
4. B
5. A
6. J
7. C
8. D
9. E
10. F

Dialog Exercises

A.
1. Ils sont à l'Hôtel Rivoli.
2. Il parle à la concierge.
3. Il est à Nice.
4. Ils veulent une chambre à deux places.
5. Odette est l'amie de Jacques.
6. La chambre est parfaite.
7. Elle est au sixième étage.
8. Elle donne sur la plage.

B.
1. grande et belle
2. bijoux
3. sarcastiques
4. est grand et beau
5. bijoux

Grammar I and II

Practice A.
1. to be
2. pouvoir, vouloir
3. verb and noun
4. check a dictionary
5. verb + direct inf.
   verb + prep. de
   verb + prep. à
6. conseiller, défendre, demander, ordonner, suggérer
7. no

B.
1. Nous avons faim aujourd'hui.
2. Odette a peur de Jacques.
3. J'ai envie de danser.
4. La concierge a l'air gentille.
5. J'ai soif quand je suis ici.
6. J'ai besoin de faire des courses.
7. J'ai l'intention de réussir.
8. Nous avons de la chance d'être ici.

Grammar III

Practice A.
1. Cet avion est immense.
2. Ces repas sont délicieux.
3. J'aime cette maison.
4. J'achète ces escargots.

5. Cette armoire n'est pas grande.
6. Cette fille à la robe verte est ma voisine.
7. Ces croissants sont bien chauds.
8. Ce lit et ce matelas sont neufs.

B.
1. cette salade-ci ou cette salade-là
2. cet arbre-ci ou cet arbre-là
3. cette taie-ci ou cette taie-là
4. ce lavabo-ci ou ce lavabo-là
5. ces escargots-ci ou ces escargots-là
6. ce gâteau-ci ou ce gâteau-là
7. ce fauteuil-ci ou ce fauteuil-là
8. cette commode-ci ou cette commode-là
9. cette pizza-ci ou cette pizza-là
10. ces bijoux-ci ou ces bijoux-là

C.
1. E
2. F
3. G
4. I
5. H
6. J
7. B
8. C
9. A
10. D

Lesson 7

Vocabulary

Practice
1. organise
2. voiture
3. décore
4. passe-temps
5. occupée
6. prochain
7. font la grève
8. sauvages
9. amuse-gueules
10. triste
11. Vive la musique!
12. le futur
13. Zut!
14. renseignements

Dialog Exercises

A.
1. Allo? Pierre est là s'il vous plaît?
2. Bonjour Robert, quoi de neuf?
3. Robert téléphone à Pierre pour l'inviter à l'anniversaire de Juliette.
4. Non, il n'accepte pas tout de suite.
5. Pierre accepte l'invitation parce qu'il ne travaille pas le samedi.
6. Pierre doit apporter des ballons et des glaçons.
7. Jacqueline va jouer de la guitare.
8. La voyante Madame Soleil va lire le futur.
9. La date de la fête est le samedi, 12 mars.
10. L'âge officiel de la majorité est vingt-et-un ans.

11. Non, la question d'âge n'est pas importante.
12. Pierre pense que cette question d'âge est plutôt psychologique.
13. Pierre veut danser avec Madame Soleil.
14. Cette fête d'anniversaire est spéciale parce que c'est l'âge officiel de la majorité.

B.
1. décorer
2. fêter
3. occuper
4. bavarder
5. progresser
6. unir
7. vouloir
8. rêver
9. inviter
10. organiser

Grammar I

Practice
1. votre (ta)
2. nos
3. son
4. ton
5. Ma
6. Mes
7. Leur
8. vos
9. leur
10. nos

Exercises A.
1. Elle décore sa maison.
2. Il téléphone à son ami.
3. Ils, elles attendent leur mère.
4. Il cherche sa voiture.
5. Elle veut son argent.
6. Elle adore ses enfants.
7. Elle change ses armoires de place.
8. Il mange ses biscuits.
9. Elle vend ses bijoux.
10. Il apporte ses ballons.

B.
1. Oui, c'est son chien.
2. Oui, ce sont ses amis.
3. Oui, ce sont ses fauteuils.
4. Oui, c'est son amie.
5. Oui, c'est son cousin.
6. Oui, ce sont ses sœurs.
7. Oui, c'est son mari.
8. Oui ce sont leurs employés.
9. Oui c'est leur chat.
10. Oui, c'est leur armoire.

Grammar II

Practice A.
1. Ce sont les tiens.
2. . . . la tienne.
3. . . . les miens.
4. . . . les leurs.
5. . . . les vôtres.
6. . . . les nôtres.
7. . . . les leurs.
8. . . . les siens.
9. . . . le sien.
10. . . . les tiennes.
11. . . . la sienne.
12. . . . le tien?
13. . . . les leurs.
14. . . . la tienne.
15. . . . la nôtre.
16. . . . la vôtre?
17. . . . des leurs.
18. . . . les siennes.
19. . . . du mien.
20. . . . des vôtres.

B.
1. les vôtres.
2. la vôtre.
3. le mien.
4. la sienne.
5. la leur.
6. le nôtre.
7. les miennes.
8. le nôtre.
9. les nôtres.
10. les vôtres.

Grammar III

Practice
1. Jacques l'adore.
2. Le propriétaire l'appelle.
3. Je le regarde.
4. Il les achète.
5. Il ne l'a pas.
6. Vous les refusez.
7. Nous les organisons.
8. Tu veux la manger?
9. Tu le fêtes demain.
10. Ils l'aiment bien.
11. Elle les achète.
12. Je la décore.
13. Je le loue.
14. Je les invite.

Grammar IV

Practice A.
1. Cherchons Jeanette.
2. Ne fumez jamais.
3. Sois gentille avec moi.
4. Ayons beaucoup d'argent.
5. N'aie pas peur.
6. Ne soyez pas triste.
7. Faîtes vos courses le matin.
8. Ne va pas au cinéma aujourd'hui.
9. Racontez-moi une histoire.
10. Attendez votre père.
11. Choisissons le fauteuil rouge.
12. Fais le ménage le lundi.

B.
1. Sois patient.
2. Attendons l'avion.
3. Achetez les meubles.
4. Va à la plage.
5. Ne regardez pas la television.
6. Ne faîtes pas la sieste.
7. Ayons de la chance maintenant.
8. Ne jouez pas au football.
9. Finis la conversation.
10. Fais attention.

Lesson 8

Vocabulary

Practice A.
1. le
2. le
3. l'
4. la
5. le
6. le
7. les
8. le
9. la
10. la
11. le
12. la
13. le
14. la
15. les

B. 1. Les enfants s'amusent à l'épicerie.
2. L'épicier et le vendeur (la vendeuse) travaillent pour le gérant.
3. Quand je vais au supermarché, j'aime prendre mon temps.
4. Pour faire un gâteau, j'ai besoin d'huile, d'oeufs, de farine, et de sucre.
5. Le vendeur (la vendeuse) me rend la monnaie.
6. Je fréquente souvent l'épicerie du coin.
7. Ma sœur ne sait pas (ne peut pas) faire bouillir l'eau.
8. Quand j'ai soif, j'aime prendre un verre avec des amis (des amies).

Dialog Exercises

A. 1. Parce qu'elle a des invités.
2. Elle veut acheter un peu de tout.
3. Elle dit un joli rôti d'agneau, quelque chose d'extra.
4. Elle ne trouve pas la crème fraîche.
5. Elle va à la laiterie pour acheter la crème fraîche.
6. Elles sentent encore l'odeur des champs.
7. Parce que l'arôme des fraises a parfumé l'épicerie.
8. Qu'il a aiguisé son sens olfactif.
9. Oui, il plaisante avec elle.
10. Oui, parce qu'elle plaisante avec l'épicier.

B. 1. C
2. D
3. A
4. E
5. B

Grammar I and II

Practice A. 1. J'ai acheté mes meubles au grand magasin.
2. L'arôme des fraises a parfumé la cuisine.
3. Charles a voyagé avec sa fiancée.
4. Le douanier a pu nous aider.
5. Nous avons choisi la lampe rouge.
6. La vendeuse nous a rendu la monnaie.
7. Juliette a voulu organiser un pique-nique.
8. Vous avez eu soif quand il a fait chaud.
9. Qu'est-ce que Jacques a-t-il fait quand il a bu? (a fait)?
10. Pourquoi Juliette a été (a-t-elle été) triste?

B.
1. Mes parents sont revenus du restaurant.
2. Il est allé à New York et elle est arrivée à Boston.
3. Nous sommes montés (montées) au cinquième étage.
4. Vous êtes devenue ma belle-sœur.
5. Elle est sortie avec son mari.
6. Juliette est arrivée pour l'anniversaire de son frère.
7. Elles sont restées avec leur tante.
8. Les feuilles sont tombées de l'arbre.

C.
1. Je suis venu(e) vous voir avant de partir.
2. J'ai eu de l'argent, mais je l'ai dépensé.
3. J'ai été invité(e) au dîner *(or)* à dîner.
4. Vous êtes descendu(e) prendre un verre.
5. J'ai voulu un pot de crème fraîche.
6. Ils sont partis sans dire "merci."
7. Nous n'avons pas perdu nos clefs.
8. Ils n'ont pas bu de vin.
9. Il est revenu avec des fleurs.
10. Elle a aimé la musique.

Grammar III

Practice
1. Il y a beaucoup de vin dans le réfrigérateur.
2. Il y a une table, mais il n'y a pas de chaises.
3. Il y a un gérant mais il n'y a pas de vendeuses.
4. Il n'y a pas de viande avec ce repas.
5. Il y a une clef pour la chambre, mais il n'y a pas de clef pour la commode.
6. Il y a des fruits et des légumes à l'épicerie.
7. Il y a eu une fête d'anniversaire ici.

Exercise
1. Il ne faut pas regarder la télé.
2. Il faut trouver les clefs pour l'armoire.
3. Pourquoi a-t-il fallu changer d'avion?
4. Il faut organiser le voyage.
5. Il faut atterrir à "Bagdad by the Bay."
6. Il ne faut pas perdre son temps à fumer.
7. Il faut manger quand on a faim.

Lesson 9

Vocabulary

Practice A.

1. forte
2. satisfaite
3. reconnaissante
4. sérieuse
5. mensuelle
6. annuelle
7. luxueuse
8. gagnante
9. gentille
10. patiente
11. prudente
12. courageuse
13. vieille
14. sportive
15. naïve

B.

1. emprunter
2. valeur
3. actionnaire
4. annuelle
5. bavard
6. satisfait
7. place
8. plaisanter
9. vraiment
10. finir

C.

1. ferme
2. caissière me donne . . . à remplir
3. taux . . . bas.
4. impôts
5. guichet des investissements
6. je suis à sec
7. je paie à crédit
8. il faut payer comptant
9. à la caisse d'Epargne
10. des devises . . . augmente

Dialog Exercises

A.

1. Il veut ouvrir un compte.
2. Jacques apporte deux chèques.
3. Il le touche.
4. Il le dépose dans les nouveaux comptes.
5. Il doit l'endosser.
6. Parce que le chèque est déjà endossé.
7. Elle lui donne des chèques provisoires.
8. Pour les chèques imprimés à son nom.
9. Il dépose soixante-quinze dollars.
10. Il dépose vingt-cinq dollars.

B.

1. F
2. G
3. H
4. A
5. B
6. I
7. E
8. J
9. D
10. C

Grammar I

Exercises A.

1. indirect object nouns
2. direct object answers: what, whom
   indirect object answers: to what, to whom, of what, etc.
3. *lui* and *leur*
4. the preposition *à*
5. They immediately precede the verb.

B.

1. leur demande
2. m'a téléphoné
3. lui avons parlé
4. nous rend
5. me demande
6. vous ai téléphoné
7. nous a montré
8. lui ressemble
9. veut leur parler
10. lui écrire

Grammar II

Practice A.

1. When the action of a verb reflects on the subject.
2. The verb always has a reflexive pronoun.
3. They both precede the verb.
4. *Nous ne nous amusons pas.*
5. indirect pronoun
6. *il se lave, ils se lavent, se laver* (infinitive)
7. Je m'amuse.
8. Nous nous arrêtons.
9. Ils s'amusent.
10. Tu te parles.

B.

1. Ma petite sœur se lève tôt le matin.
2. Pendant que je me lave, elle mange.
3. Quand j'ai besoin de me regarder dans le miroir, elle m'appelle.
4. Je me brosse les dents après le petit déjeûner.
5. Ma petite sœur et moi nous nous habillons en même temps.
6. Dès que je finis, je me prépare pour sortir.
7. Ma sœur et ma voisine se promènent après mon départ.
8. J'ai besoin de me coucher de bonne heure ce soir.
9. Mes parents se réveillent souvent plus tôt que moi.
10. Mon ami Mark se marie la semaine prochaine.

Grammar III

Exercises

A.
1. Nous nous réveillons tard aussi.
2. Ils se brossent aussi.
3. Vous vous amusez aussi.
4. Nous nous excusons aussi.
5. Tu te couches aussi.
6. Ils se lèvent aussi.
7. Tu t'amuses aussi.
8. Ils se reposent aussi.
9. Je m'ennuie aussi.

B.
1. Repose-toi.
2. Lave-toi.
3. Dépêchez-vous.
4. Habillons-nous.
5. Baigne-toi.
6. Couchez-vous tôt.
7. Ne vous ennuyez pas.
8. Ne nous arrêtons pas ici.
9. Ne t'excuse pas.
10. Brossez-vous les dents.

Lesson 10

Vocabulary

Practice

A.
1. une
2. un
3. un
4. des
5. une
6. un
7. une
8. une
9. des
10. un
11. un
12. un
13. une
14. des
15. une

B.
1. l'arrivée
2. le sud
3. l'ouest
4. descendre
5. se coucher
6. l'entrée
7. perdre
8. payer comptant
9. fort
10. augmenter

C.
1. ont changé
2. a augmenté
3. est arrivé
4. avons oublié
5. est reparti
6. est finie
7. a été
8. avons eu
9. ont envoyé
10. avez eu

Dialog Exercises

1. Juliette est à la gare.
2. Juliette dit, "Ah! voilà Charles."
3. Charles répond, "Salut, Juliette!"

4. Charles voudrait dire “Au revoir” à Monsieur Legrand.
5. Charles a passé la nuit dans le train.
6. L’opposé de “fatigué” est “reposé.”
7. Charles est en forme parce qu’il a bien dormi.
8. Aprés le diner, Charles prend un verre avec Monsieur Legrand.
9. Quand Charles arrive, le chauffeur ouvre le coffre.
10. Charles veut acheter une carte orange.
11. Juliette n’a jamais reçu l’invitation d’aller avec Charles.
12. Juliette n’est pas intelligente, mais plutôt maligne.
13. Juliette a changé la conversation avec: “Regarde nous sommes arrivés.”
14. Oui, Juliette est très sarcastique quand elle dit, “Le temps passe vite quand je suis avec toi!”

Grammar I

Exercises

A.

1. Ils réussissaient à faire des économies.
2. Mes parents et moi étions d’accord sur ce sujet.
3. Les voisins commençaient à nous inviter.
4. La route nationale était pleine de panneaux.
5. Nos amis n’avaient pas hésité une minute.
6. Vous m’encouragiez tous les jours.
7. Il était midi pile et il ne déjeûnait pas.
8. À minuit nous entendions des bruits.
9. Nous pouvions sortir plus tard.
10. Il voulait faire la connaissance de Juliette.

B.

1. Nous avions plusieurs heures de route nationale.
2. Mon mari me donnait de l’argent pendant la semaine.
3. Chaque jour le voisin invitait ma sœur.
4. Nous partions en vacances ensemble.
5. Ces garçons étaient de l’Amérique et du Canada.
6. Nous faisions une promenade le soir.
7. Après le travail je faisais des courses.
8. Ils rentraient souvent très tard.
9. Nous étions avec Jean le jour de la fête.
10. Nous étions heureux avec nos voisins *(or)* avec les voisins.

C. Je faisais mes débuts en français, les leçons étaient parfois difficiles, mais je faisais mon possible pour les comprendre. J’étais occupé (e) l’après-midi, mais j’étudiais le matin et quelquefois j’essayais de finir les exercices le soir. La leçon cinq était très longue parce qu’elle avait plusieurs pages de révision. Je voulais continuer l’étude du français parce que j’aimais beaucoup la langue, et parce que j’avais envie d’aller en France.

Grammar II

Exercises A.

1. Juliette venait toujours à midi, mais aujourd'hui, elle est venue en retard.
2. Elle croyait à mes promesses, mais soudainement, elle a changé.
3. Elle pensait toujours à moi, mais lundi elle a oublié mon anniversaire.
4. Elle aimait mes histoires, mais hier elle a trouvé ma plaisanterie ennuyeuse.
5. Le soir elle étudiait, mais hier elle est sortie avec Pierre.
6. Elle me téléphonait le matin, mais aujourd'hui elle ne m'a pas téléphoné.
7. Juliette voulait aller camper, mais elle a refusé d'aller avec moi.
8. Juliette pouvait me faire rire, mais hier elle m'a fait pleurer.
9. Elle m'attendait toujours, mais aujourd'hui elle a décidé de partir sans moi.
10. Elle était souvent polie, mais hier elle a insulté ma sœur.

B.

1. Juliette voulait faire la connaissance d'Antoine, mais il n'est pas venu avec Charles.
2. Ma sœur et moi faisions une promenade quand nous avons rencontré Jacques.
3. J'avais froid quand je suis retourné(e) de l'aéroport.
4. J'avais faim alors j'ai mangé tout le pain.
5. Hier, je suis resté(e) au lit parce que j'étais malade.
6. Je me suis ennuyé(e) alors mon ami(e) m'a raconté une histoire.
7. Je suis monté(e) dans ma couchette et j'ai commencé à lire.
8. L'heure d'affluence était toujours entre quatre heures et cinq heures.
9. Le contrôleur vérifiait nos billets pendant que nous mangions.
10. Nous sommes allé(e)s à l'étranger l'année dernière.

Grammar III

Exercises A.

1. Days are not capitalized in French.
2. Monday
3. masculine
4. every (repetition)
5. samedi, jeudi, vendredi

6. dimanche prochain, juillet prochain, l'année prochaine
7. cardinal number + -ième
8. deux, six, dix
9. soixante
10. Le premier jour de la semaine est lundi.

B.
1. La semaine prochaine nous allons acheter des meubles.
2. Mon ami est allé(e) à Nice la deuxième semaine de juillet.
3. Nous avons conduit ensemble à l'aéroport en mars.
4. Le neuvième mois de l'année est septembre.
5. Je prends des leçons de piano le mardi.
6. Mon mari part à Paris le mois d'octobre prochain *(or)* en octobre prochain.
7. Le centième passager a gagné le gros lot!

Note: In answers 2, 3, and 5, the months and days could also start the sentence, as in *Le mardi je prends. . . .*

REVIEW EXAM FOR LESSONS 6–10

(Answers, pp. 154–155)

PART I: VOCABULARY

A. Match the two columns.

1. ______ l'eau
2. ______ le matelas
3. ______ le loyer
4. ______ la grève
5. ______ les glaçons
6. ______ les renseignements
7. ______ l'épicier
8. ______ le gérant
9. ______ les œufs
10. ______ le guichet
11. ______ le coffre
12. ______ le comptant
13. ______ le montant
14. ______ le panneau
15. ______ le quai
16. ______ le nord
17. ______ l'heure d'affluence
18. ______ le mécanicien

A. C'est ce qu'on paie au propriétaire
B. Dans les boissons
C. À demander pour savoir quelque chose
D. Propriétaire d'une épicerie
E. Directeur
F. Pour faire une omelette
G. Est sur le lit
H. La caissière
I. Nécessaire quand on a soif
J. Le droit des travailleurs
K. Le total de l'addition
L. Indique la route
M. Les passagers attendent là
N. Il contrôle le train
O. C'est le contraire de "crédit"
P. Dans une banque pour garder les bijoux
Q. Le contraire de sud
R. Il y a beaucoup de voitures

B. Write the opposite of the following words.

1. froid ______
2. heureux ______
3. comptant ______
4. ouvrir ______
5. vendre ______
6. gagner ______
7. faible ______
8. dépenser ______
9. se coucher ______
10. monter ______

C. Complete the following sentences with the correct word.

1. La caissière m'a donné des __________ à remplir pour ouvrir un compte de chèques.
2. Le train de Paris-Marseille n'a pas de __________ alors je n'ai pas dormi.
3. J'étais invité à dîner chez Marie et __________ bien amusé.
4. Quand j'ai de l'argent __________ à la caisse d'épargne.
5. La banque de notre ville avait un taux d'interêt très __________.
6. Quand je vais à l'étranger je dois acheter des __________.
7. Les enfants de ma tante sont mes __________ et mes __________.
8. Le mari de ma sœur est mon __________ et la femme de mon frère est ma __________.
9. Il faut toujours __________ un chèque avant de le toucher.
10. L'agneau, le bœuf ne sont pas des poissons, ce sont des __________.

D. Circle the best answers to complete the statements below.

1. L'hôtel où nous sommes restés est très beau;
   a. il a des fenêtres.
   b. il donne sur la plage.
   c. les meubles sont vieux.
   d. il n'y a pas un lit.

2. Quand la famille est ensemble
   a. nous allons à la banque.
   b. nous cherchons un hôtel.
   c. nous nous amusons bien.
   d. nous sommes fatigués.

3. Il vaut mieux voyager par avion
   a. quand il fait beau.
   b. à la fin de l'année.
   c. quand on est pressé.
   d. quand on n'a pas de voiture.

4. Quand les travailleurs veulent une augmentation de salaire et ne la reçoivent pas,
   a. ils font la grève.
   b. ils ne sont pas à sec.
   c. ils dépensent beaucoup d'argent.
   d. ils ouvrent des comptes ordinaires.

5. Il vaut mieux voyager par train
   a. quand on veut apprécier le paysage.
   b. quand on n'a pas d'avion.
   c. quand on est en retard.
   d. quand on a beaucoup de bagages.

PART II: GRAMMAR

A. Write the correct form of the *imparfait* (imperfect) in the following sentences.

1. Les enfants __________ (jouer) dans le jardin.
2. Les frères __________ (être) très aimables, et les sœurs __________ (vouloir) nous aider aussi.
3. À la banque, ils __________ (pouvoir) nous vendre des actions.
4. Le gérant du supermarché __________ (chercher) la caissière.
5. L'hôtel __________ (être) grand et il y __________ (avoir) un jardin où __________ (pousser) (to grow) de belles fleurs exotiques.
6. Nous __________ (pouvoir) aller à pied à la plage.
7. Nous __________ (étudier) le français tous les soirs.
8. Mon frère __________ (manger) le petit déjeûner quand je __________ (faire) mes devoirs (homework).
9. Nous __________ (danser) et nous __________ (être) heureux avec nos amis.
10. Il y __________ (avoir) beaucoup de travail à faire.

B. Rewrite the verbs, in the following text, in the past tense, using the *imparfait* or the *passé composé* as verb actions dictate.

Nous arrivons à Nice à quatre heures de l'après-midi. Nous sommes fatigués, mais il fait beau et nous marchons vers la plage. Les baigneuses (swimmers, fem.) ressemblent à des vedettes de cinéma (movie stars). Nous avons soif et nous voulons nous asseoir; nous cherchons un restaurant, alors nous trouvons un petit "snack bar." Nous commandons deux bières et deux sandwiches. Nous finissons, nous nous levons et nous continuons notre promenade.

C. Select and write the proper word in French to complete the following sentences.

Example: (Her) vêtements sont neufs.
Ses vêtements sont neufs.

1. Le 20 juin __________ (I went) au théâtre.
2. (These) __________ exercices sont faciles.

3. J'aime mon repas et toi, aimes-tu __________ (yours)?
4. Les enfants amusent souvent __________ (their) parents.
5. Il a choisi cette couchette-ci, et j'ai choisi __________ (that one).
6. Nous avons ouvert (opened) un compte de chèques et ils ont fermé __________ (theirs).
7. Il vaut mieux prendre l'avion de huit heures que __________ (the one) de dix heures.
8. Nous avons habité __________ (this) ville pendant cinq ans.
9. (It is not allowed) __________ de fumer dans le wagon-lit.
10. (My) __________ parents et __________ (those) de mon mari sont partis en vacances ensemble.
11. Les légumes que __________ (I bought) au supermarché sont dans le frigo.
12. Quand tu es pressé __________ (don't walk) __________ (you must, one must) courir.
13. La couchette supérieure est __________ (for him) et la couchette inférieure est __________ (for her).

REVIEW EXAM: ANSWERS

Lessons 6–10

Vocabulary

A.

1. I	7. D	13. K
2. G	8. E	14. L
3. A	9. F	15. M
4. J	10. H	16. Q
5. B	11. P	17. R
6. C	12. O	18. N

B.

1. chaud	6. perdre
2. triste	7. fort
3. crédit	8. économiser
4. fermer	9. se réveiller
5. acheter	10. descendre

C. 1. cartes
2. couchettes *(or)* wagon-lits
3. je me suis
4. je le dépose
5. bas *(or)* haut
6. devises
7. cousins et mes cousines
8. mon beau-frère . . . , ma belle sœur
9. endosser
10. viandes

D. 1. b
2. c
3. c
4. a
5. d *(or)* a

Grammar

A. 1. jouaient
2. étaient . . . voulaient
3. pouvaient
4. cherchait
5. était . . . il y avait . . . poussaient
6. pouvions
7. étudiions
8. mangeait . . . faisais
9. dansions . . . étions
10. avait

B. Nous sommes arrivés à Nice à quatre heures de l'après-midi. Nous étions fatigués, mais il faisait beau et nous marchions vers la plage. Les baigneuses ressemblaient à des vedettes de cinéma. Nous avions soif et nous voulions nous asseoir; nous cherchions un restaurant, alors nous avons trouvé un petit "snack bar." Nous avons commandé deux bières et deux sandwiches. Nous avons fini, nous nous sommes levés et nous avons continué notre promenade.

C. 1. Le 20 juin, je suis allé au théâtre (je suis allée).
2. Ces exercices sont faciles.
3. J'aime mon repas et toi, aimes-tu le tien?
4. Les enfants amusent souvent leurs parents.
5. Il a choisi cette couchette-ci, et j'ai choisi cette couchette-là.
6. Nous avons ouvert un compte de chèques et ils ont fermé le leur.
7. Il vaut mieux prendre l'avion de huit heures que celui de dix heures.
8. Nous avons habité cette ville pendant cinq ans.
9. Il est défendu de fumer dans le wagon-lit.
10. Mes parents et ceux de mon mari sont partis en vacances ensemble.
11. Les légumes que j'ai achetés au supermarché sont dans le frigo.
12. Quand tu es pressé tu ne marches pas, tu cours. *(or)* Il ne faut pas marcher, il faut courir.
13. La couchette supérieure est pour lui, et la couchette inférieure est pour elle.

Lesson 11

LES PARTIES DU CORPS (Parts of the Body)

la barbe	beard	**le genou**	knee
la bouche	mouth	**la gorge**	throat
le bras	arm	**la jambe**	leg
le casse-pieds	pest	**la langue**	tongue
les cheveux (masc)	hair	**la main**	hand
		le menton	chin
la cheville	ankle	**le nez**	nose
le cil	eyelash	**l'œil (masc.)**	eye
le conseil	advice	**l'oreille (fem.)**	ear
le corps	body	**le pied**	foot
le cou	neck	**la poitrine**	chest
la dent	tooth	**le poumon**	lung
le doigt	finger	**la santé**	health
le dos	back	**le sourcil**	eyebrow
l'épaule (fem.)	shoulder	**le sourire**	smile
l'estomac (masc.)	stomach	**le ventre**	belly, abdomen
		le visage	face
le foie	liver	**les yeux (masc.)**	eyes
le front	forehead		
casser	to break	**se réveiller**	to wake up
examiner	to examine	**se sentir**	to feel
guérir	to heal	**soigner**	to take care
poser	to put	**tomber malade**	to get sick
se reposer	to rest	**tousser**	to cough
reposer	to put back	**trébucher**	to trip over
respirer	to breath	**se trouver**	to find oneself

blond	blonde	**lourd**	heavy
brun	brown	**mal**	evil, badly
donc	therefore	**malade**	sick
droit	right	**mieux**	better
gauche	left	**souple**	supple
imprévu	unexpected	**tout**	all, everything
léger	light	**trop**	too much
lentement	slowly		

NOTES:

1. All the verbs in the above vocabulary except *tomber malade* and *trébucher* can be either reflexive or nonreflexive. When some of them change into reflexive, they also change their meaning. One such verb is *sentir*–"to smell" (nonreflexive) and *se sentir*–"to feel" (reflexive); others simply mean what reflexive constructions imply: that the action reflects back to the subject.
   EX.: *guérir quelqu'un* = to heal someone
   se guérir = to heal oneself
   trouver = to find (something, someone)
   se trouver = to find oneself, as in *Je me trouve à Paris.* (I find myself in Paris).

2. *Le mal* literally means "evil," as in *Le bien et le mal,* "good and evil." It is also used as an adverb, as in *C'est très mal fait.* (It is very badly (poorly) done.) *Malade* means "sick" (adjective), and with the article it becomes a noun.
   EX.: *le malade, la malade* the sick one

3. When the adverb *mal* is preceded by *avoir,* it means "to hurt," as in *J'ai mal aux pieds.* My feet hurt.
   Thus, by using *avoir mal* and adding the hurting part of the body, we can make as many sentences as we wish.
   EX.: *Il a mal à la gorge.* He has a sore throat.
   (He hurts at the throat.)

   Note that the expression *avoir mal à, au, aux,* is followed by *à la* for feminine nouns, *au* for masculine singular, and *aux* for both feminine and masculine plurals, as in:
   Elles ont mal aux jambes (fem. pl.). Their legs hurt.
   Il a mal aux bras. (masc. pl.). His arms hurt.

PRACTICE THE VOCABULARY

(Answers for Lesson 11, pp. 220–222)

A. Name all the pairs of the parts of the body, following the example.

Example: J'ai deux mains (hands).

1. J'ai ____________ (eyes).
2. J'ai ____________ (ears).
3. J'ai ____________ (feet).
4. J'ai ____________ (legs).
5. J'ai ____________ (ankles).
6. J'ai ____________ (knees).

7. J'ai __________ (shoulders).
8. J'ai __________ (lungs).
9. J'ai __________ (eyebrows).
10. J'ai __________ (arms).

B. Translate the following sentences into French.

1. They got sick yesterday. __________.
2. Where do you hurt? __________.
3. Was the suitcase heavy? __________.
4. He feels weak. __________.
5. We are able to heal ourselves. __________.
6. Take good care of yourself. __________.
7. How are you? Are you better today? __________.
8. I feel much better when I rest. __________.
9. Give me your hand, I want to see it. __________.
10. I have been sick for a week. __________.

DIALOGUE: *Un portrait*

Le téléphone sonne. Je prends le récepteur. C'est mon frère.

CHARLES: Allo? C'est Charles. Je voulais te dire que ma nouvelle voisine est d'une beauté rare.

MOI: C'est formidable. Est-elle blonde, brune, grande, petite? Dis-moi tout.

CHARLES: D'abord, elle a les cheveux longs et frisés qui lui touchent les épaules. Elle est blonde bien sûr!

MOI: Pourquoi, bien sûr? Qu'est-ce que tu veux dire par là?

CHARLES: Je veux te rappeler, que je ne regarde presque jamais une brune. Bien sûr, je ne parle pas des membres de la famille!

MOI: Heureusement que tu as ajouté ces mots-là. J'allais t'arrêter tout de suite!

CHARLES: Bon, laisse-moi continuer. Elle a une petite bouche, des dents légèrement imparfaites, et un corps de sportive.

MOI: Elle t'a parlé? Comment as-tu découvert que ses dents étaient imparfaites?

CHARLES: Elle ne m'a pas parlé, mais elle m'a fait un grand sourire.

MOI: Tu as l'intention de faire sa connaissance bientôt, n'est-ce pas? Dans ce cas, je te conseille de surveiller ta langue. Surtout ne parle pas de ses cheveux blonds!

CHARLES: Pourquoi pas? Quel mal y-a-t-il à cela?

MOI:	Peut-être qu'elle était brune dans l'autre monde.
CHARLES:	Quel autre monde?
MOI:	Le monde où les hommes ont du tact!
CHARLES:	Tu es vraiment aimable, chère sœur!
MOI:	Je suis en colère parce que tu m'as réveillée.
CHARLES:	Mais il est midi et demi. Tu n'es pas malade j'espère!
MOI:	Je ne suis pas malade, mais je ne me sens pas très bien. Aussi j'ai le droit de dormir tard, le dimanche.
CHARLES:	Excuse-moi et merci pour ton conseil!
MOI:	Au revoir, Charles, bonne chance avec ta blonde!

DIALOG: *A Portrait*

(The telephone rings. I pick up the receiver. It's my brother.)

CHARLES:	Hello! It's Charles. I wanted to tell you that my new neighbor is a rare beauty.
ME:	That's great! Is she blond, brunette, tall, petite? Tell me everything.
CHARLES:	First, she has long curly hair, which touches her shoulders. She is blond, of course!
ME:	Why, of course? What do you mean by that?
CHARLES:	I want to remind you that I almost never look at a brunette. Of course, I'm not speaking about members of the family!
ME:	It's fortunate that you added those words. I was going to cut you off right away!
CHARLES:	Well, let me continue. She has a small mouth, teeth slightly imperfect, and the body of a sports enthusiast.
ME:	Did she talk to you? How did you discover her teeth were imperfect?
CHARLES:	She didn't speak to me, but she gave (made) me a big smile.
ME:	You intend to make her acquaintance soon, don't you? In that case, I advise you to watch your tongue. Most of all, do not speak about her blond hair!
CHARLES:	Why not? What bad is there in that?
ME:	Perhaps she was a brunette in the other world!
CHARLES:	What other world?
ME:	The world where men have some tact!
CHARLES:	You are truly kind, dear sister!
ME:	I am angry because you woke me.
CHARLES:	But it's half past noon. You're not sick, I hope!
ME:	No, I'm not sick, but I don't feel very well. Also I have the right to sleep late on Sunday!
CHARLES:	Excuse me, and thanks for your advice!
ME:	Goodbye, Charles, and good luck with your blonde!

DIALOG EXERCISES

A. According to the dialog, answer the following questions with complete sentences.

1. Qui est Charles? ____________________
2. Que voulait-il dire? ____________________
3. Les cheveux de la voisine sont ________________________________, ____________________ et ____________________.
4. Pourquoi la sœur de Charles est-elle en colère? ____________________
5. Est-ce que les cheveux de "Moi" sont blonds? ____________________
6. Pourquoi "Moi" a-t-elle dormi tard? ____________________
7. À quelle heure le téléphone a-t-il sonné? ____________________
8. Est-ce que "Moi" est polie, aimable, sarcastique? ____________________
____
9. De quel monde est Charles? ____________________
10. Comment sont les dents de la voisine? ____________________
11. Est-ce que la voisine a parlé à Charles? ____________________
12. Comment la voisine a-t-elle montré ses dents? ____________________
13. Est-ce que "Moi" est malade? ____________________
14. Est-ce que Charles a fait la connaissance de la voisine? ____________________

B. Complete the following sentences, following the example.

Example: Nous sautons (jump) avec les jambes.

1. Nous marchons avec ____________________.
2. Nous regardons avec ____________________.
3. Nous sentons avec ____________________.
4. Nous entendons avec ____________________.
5. Nous écrivons avec ____________________.
6. Nous mangeons avec ____________________.
7. Nous mâchons (chew) avec ____________________.
8. Nous touchons avec ____________________.

GRAMMAR I Comparisons of inequality.

A. Study the following table.

FRENCH	ENGLISH
plus + adjective	more + adjective
moins + adverb + **que**	less + adverb + than
plus de + noun	more + noun
moins de + noun	less + noun

B. Where the English adjective takes the comparative ending *-er,* or *more* + the adjective, French always uses the expression *plus . . . que* and *plus de . . . que*. French uses *plus . . . que* with adverbs or adjectives.

EX.: *Elle est plus riche que lui.* She is richer than he (is).
Il sort plus souvent qu'elle. He goes out more often than she (does).

C. With nouns expressing numbers or amounts, French uses *plus de . . . que.*

EX.: *J'ai plus d'argent que lui.* I have more money than he (does).
J'ai plus d'amis que lui. I have more friends than he.

D. The expressions *moins . . . que* and *moins de . . . que* follow the same rules as *plus . . . que* and *plus de . . . que*. With adjectives and adverbs of inequality, the English equivalent of *moins de . . . que* is "fewer than."

E. The expression *moins de . . . que* is used with nouns expressing numbers and amounts, like *plus de . . . que* above.

EX.: *Il a moins de problèmes que moi.* He has fewer problems than I.
Nous avons moins de patience que vous. We have less patience than you.

F. *Plus . . . que* and *moins . . . que* are always placed *after* the verb.

EX.: *Elle gagne plus que lui.* She earns more than he.
Ils mangent moins que nous. They eat less than we.

PRACTICE THE COMPARATIVES

A. Complete the following exercise.

1. The expressions *plus . . . que* and *moins . . . que* are used with verbs, adverbs, and ____________________.
2. The expressions *plus de . . . que* and *moins de . . . que* are only used with ____________________.
3. What expression is used with numbers and amounts? ____________________ ____________________.
4. The English comparatives *-er* and *more* are translated into French by ____________________ and ____________________.
5. The English equivalent of "less than" in French is ____________________.
6. How do you say in French: "He is more serious than she"? ____________________ ____________________.
7. Say and then write in French: "She has less than twenty dollars." ____________________.
8. Say and then write in French: "We talk more seriously than you." ____________________.
9. Where are the comparatives *plus . . . que* and *moins . . . que* placed in relation to the verb? ____________________.
10. When does French use *moins de . . . que?* ____________________.

B. Complete the sentences with the appropriate comparative.

1. Elle s'est reveillée (later than) ____________________ lui.
2. En magique, la main est (quicker than) ____________________ l'œil.
3. Payer comptant est (easier than) ____________________ payer à crédit.
4. En general les malles sont (heavier than) ____________________ les valises.
5. Ils voyagent à l'étranger (more often than) ____________________ nous.
6. Les femmes sont (more sociable than) ____________________ nous.
7. Les petites filles sont (less talkative than) ____________________ les petits garçons.
8. Le nez de Pinocchio est (longer than) ____________________le mien.
9. Elle dépense (more money than) ____________________ lui.
10. Elle est (less intelligent than) ____________________ vous.

GRAMMAR II Comparisons of equality. Superlatives.

A. Study comparisons of equality with adjectives and adverbs.

FRENCH	ENGLISH
aussi + adjective + **que**	as + adjective + as
aussi + adverb + **que**	as + adverb + as

NOTE:

Following are examples.

EX.: *Elle est aussi intelligente que moi* (adj). She is as intelligent as I.
Elle parle aussi bien que moi (adv.) She speaks as well as I.

B. Study comparisons of equality with verbs and nouns.
French uses *autant . . . que* and *autant de . . . que* with verbs and nouns to translate the English "as much . . . as" or "as many . . . as."

EX.: *Il parle autant que moi* (verb). He speaks as much as I do.
Il a autant d'amis que moi (noun). He has as many friends as I do.

Notice that *autant de . . . que* is used in French only with nouns expressing amounts and numbers (just like *plus de . . . que* and *moins de . . . que*), while in English "as much" and "as many" are used with verbs as well as with nouns.

C. French superlatives are formed by adding *le, la,* or *les* to the comparative of the adjective, thus agreeing in number and gender with the nouns they modify.

EX.: *Il est intelligent.* He is intelligent.
Il est plus intelligent. He is more intelligent.
Il est le plus intelligent. He is the most intelligent.

D. There are some French adjectives and adverbs that have irregular comparatives and superlatives. Study the following chart.

ADJECTIVE/ ADVERB	COMPARATIVE	SUPERLATIVE	ENGLISH
bon	**meilleur**	**le meilleur**	good, better, the best
bien	**mieux**	**le mieux**	well, better, the best
mal	**pire**	**le pire**	bad, worse, the worst

NOTE:

1. The feminine of the adjective *bon* is *bonne,* the masculine plural is *bons,* and the feminine plural is *bonnes.*
   EX.: *La salade est bonne.*
   Le vin est bon.
   La salade et le vin sont bons.
   Les salades sont bonnes.
   Les vins sont bons.

2. The superlatives *le (la, les) meilleur (e, s, es)* also agree in number and gender with the nouns they modify.
   EX.: *J'ai mangé la meilleure salade.*
   J'ai bu le meilleur vin.
   J'ai bu les meilleurs vins.
   J'ai mangé les meilleures salades.

PRACTICE THE GRAMMAR

Practice the comparative of equality and the superlative in the following exercise.

1. What are the French equivalents of "as . . . as" and "as much as" and "as many as"? ______________________.
2. When does French use *autant de . . . que?* ______________________.
3. How is *autant de . . . que* translated in English? ______________________.
4. What does French use to form the superlative of an adjective? ______________________
   ______________________.
5. What is important about the formation of French superlatives? ______________________
   ______________________.
6. Give the French equivalent of "the best books." ______________________.
7. Say and then write in French, "Their books are better." ______________________
   ______________________.
8. Say and then write in French, "They speak better." ______________________
   ______________________.
9. Say and then write in French, "He feels worse." ______________________.
10. Say and then write in French, "He feels as bad as you do." ______________________
    ______________________.

EXERCISE

Change the expressions *plus . . . que, plus de . . . que* into *moins . . . que* and *moins de . . . que*. Follow the example.

Example: Il y a plus de garcons que de filles.
Il y a moins de filles que de garçons.

1. Nous avons plus de courage que vous. ______________________.
2. Jean et Juliette attendent plus longtemps (longer) que vous. ______________________.
3. Les voisins sont plus charmants que vous. ______________________.
4. La concierge est plus sérieuse que la téléphoniste. ______________________.
5. La banque est plus près que la caisse d'épargne. ______________________.
6. Les enfants sont plus bavards que les parents. ______________________.

GRAMMAR III Future indicative of regular and irregular verbs.

A. Study the forms of the future indicative of regular verbs shown on the chart below.

SUBJECT	PARLER	CHOISIR	ATTENDRE
je	**parler ai**	**choisir ai**	**attendr ai**
tu	**parler as**	**choisir as**	**attendr as**
il, elle, on	**parler a**	**choisir a**	**attendr a**
nous	**parler ons**	**choisir ons**	**attendr ons**
vous	**parler ez**	**choisir ez**	**attendr ez**
ils, elles	**parler ont**	**choisir ont**	**attendr ont**

1. The future tense in French is very simply formed by adding the future tense endings to the infinitive of the verbs. These endings are: *-ai, -as, -a, -ons, -ez,* and *-ont.*
2. The final *e* of the verbs ending in *-re* is dropped, as with *attendré-ai.* The endings for the future tense of regular verbs are always regular.

   EX.: *manger* *je manger-ai*
   finir *je finir-ai*
   prendre *je prendr-ai*

B. Some verbs have stem changes or irregular stems. These irregularities are also found in the future tense. For example, we have already studied spelling changes in the verbs *acheter* and *payer.* The future tense of these verbs is:

acheter: *j'achèterai*
tu achèteras, etc.
payer: *je paierai*
tu paieras, etc.

C. Study the verbs with irregular stems.

aller	**j'irai**	**tu iras**	**il, elle ira**	**etc.**
avoir	**j'aurai**	**tu auras**	**il, elle aura**	**etc.**
devoir	**je devrai**	**tu devras**	**il, elle devra**	**etc.**
être	**je serai**	**tu seras**	**il, elle sera**	**etc.**
faire	**je ferai**	**tu feras**	**il, elle fera**	**etc.**
pouvoir	**je pourrai**	**tu pourras**	**il, elle pourra**	**etc.**
savoir	**je saurai**	**tu sauras**	**il, elle saura**	**etc.**
venir	**je viendrai**	**tu viendras**	**il, elle viendra**	**etc.**
voir	**je verrai**	**tu verras**	**il, elle verra**	**etc.**
vouloir	**je voudrai**	**tu voudras**	**il, elle voudra**	**etc.**

1. The verbs listed in the chart all have very irregular stems. Once you've memorized the stems, however, you'll find the future endings follow the regular pattern.
2. The future tense, in French, is used in the same way as in English. However, French uses the future tense with dependent

clauses, starting with *quand* (when), *lorsque* (when), and *dès que* (as soon as), whereas English uses the present tense.

EX.: *Je te raconterai une histoire quand je reviendrai.*
I'll tell you a story when I come back. (present)
Je pourrai te parler lorsque je finirai mon travail.
I'll be able to talk to you when I finish my work. (present)
Je téléphonerai dès que je rentrerai.
I will telephone (you) as soon as I return. (present)

PRACTICE THE FUTURE TENSE

1. Write the endings of the future tense:
   ________, ________, ________, ________, ________, ________.
2. To what verb form does French add these endings in order to form the future tense? ____________.
3. Do the future tense endings ever change? ____________.
4. Do the future tense stems change with irregular verbs?
   ____________.
5. Where does French use the future tense where English does not?
   ____________.
6. Say and then write in French, "They will be able to."
   ____________.
7. Say and then write in French, "They will know more than we."
   ____________.
8. What is the future tense of *il faut?* ____________.
9. What is the future tense of *il vaut mieux?* ____________.
10. Say and then write in French, "He will eat as soon as he comes back."
    ____________.

EXERCISE

Rewrite the sentences below in the future tense.

1. Ma sœur est invitée chez la voisine. ____________
2. Nous trouvons un petit hôtel charmant. ____________
3. Vous pouvez m'aider à préparer le dîner. ____________

4. Juliette travaille à la banque. ____________________
5. Nous allons à Paris après la Noël. ____________________
6. Elle apprend à jouer de la harpe. ____________________
7. Nous savons écrire le chinois (Chinese). ____________________

Lesson 12

À LA PHARMACIE (At the Drugstore)

l'alimentation (fem.)	food	**la goutte**	drop
la balance	scale	**la lame (de rasoir)**	blade
le barbier	barber	**le narcotique**	narcotic
la boucherie	butcher's	**le peigne**	comb
la boulangerie	bakery	**la pipe**	pipe
la brosse (à dents, à cheveux)	brush (tooth, hair)	**le plâtre**	plaster
le calmant	sedative	**le plombage**	filling (tooth)
le compte-goutte	eye dropper	**la poissonnerie**	fish market
la crise	attack, crisis	**la poudre**	powder
la diète	diet	**le rasoir**	razor
la drogue	drug	**le régime**	diet
l'espoir (masc.)	hope	**le soulagement**	relief
		le syrop	syrup
		le talc	talcum
		le tube	tube
abuser	to abuse	**grossir**	to gain weight
alimenter	to feed	**s'habituer**	to get used to
avaler	to swallow	**passer (se)**	to pass
devoir . . . à	to owe to	**plomber**	to fill (tooth)
durer	to last	**se raser**	to shave
écouter	to listen	**répondre**	to answer
équilibrer	to balance	**soulager (se)**	to relieve
compliqué(e)	complicated	**gros, grosse**	fat
grâce à	thanks to	**inoxidable**	rust proof
gras, grasse	fat	**longtemps**	long time

maigre	thin, skinny	**sain(e)**	healthy
mince	slender	**sévère**	strict
pendant	during, for	**simple**	uncomplicated
récent(e)	recent		

NOTES:

1. *Devoir* means "to have to," as in *Je dois manger.* (I must eat.) *Devoir . . . à* means "to owe (something) to someone."
   EX.: *Je te dois dix francs.* I owe you ten francs.
   Combien je vous dois? How much do I owe you?

   Notice that the indirect pronoun is required (*me, te, lui, elle,* etc.)

2. *La diète* means a low-calorie diet, *se mettre à la diète* means to put oneself on a low-calorie diet, *diète absolue* is a starvation diet. *Régime* also means "diet," but could imply other restrictions (salt, sugar, butter, etc.)

3. *Gros, grosse* means fat (adj.) as in *Cet homme est gros.* (This man is fat.) *Gras, grasse* also means "fat" (adj.), but when applied to people, it carries a pejorative meaning. When we speak of foods or things, *gras(se)* means greasy, as in *Cette soupe est grasse.* (This soup is greasy.)

CULTURAL NOTE:

The local *pharmacie* and the *pharmacien* (pharmacist) are where the French search for advice and remedies for minor ailments. The doctor is called upon only in serious cases. The local *pharmacien* becomes a trusted friend whose advice and treatment are taken very seriously. These people know their over-the-counter drugs very well and are able to help their clients make the best decisions for whatever ails them. What ails most French people is their liver—*le foie.* The French *ont mal au foie,* as often as Americans get a headache. The only difference is that the French blame all their discomforts on their liver.

PRACTICE THE VOCABULARY

(Answers for Lesson 12, pp. 222–224)

A. Write *un* or *une* before the following nouns.

1. _____ talc
2. _____ brosse
3. _____ pipe
4. _____ drogue
5. _____ peigne
6. _____ diète
7. _____ rasoir
8. _____ lame
9. _____ boulangerie
10. _____ plâtre
11. _____ compte-goutte
12. _____ régime
13. _____ calmant
14. _____ balance
15. _____ narcotique

B. Which words from the vocabulary relate to the following?

1. grossir ______________________
2. calmer ______________________
3. le dentifrice ______________________
4. la barbe ______________________
5. le poisson ______________________
6. plomber ______________________
7. balancer ______________________
8. alimenter ______________________
9. rasoir ______________________
10. maigrir ______________________

C. Review the future tense by completing the sentences with the appropriate future forms.

1. Mon mari __________ avant de sortir (se raser).
2. Si elle ne mange pas aujourd'hui elle __________ (maigrir).
3. Le calmant que le docteur m'a prescrit ne __________ pas prêt demain (être).
4. Il __________ acheter un compte-goutte (faut).
5. Elle __________ toute la pâte dentifrice en une semaine (user).
6. Juliette n'aime pas les médicaments, elle __________ le syrop malgré elle (avaler).
7. Ils __________ (perdre) leurs privilèges dès qu'ils les __________ (abuser).

DIALOGUE *La pharmacie du coin*

LE PHARMACIEN:	Bonjour Madame Bellan. Comment allez-vous aujourd'hui?
MME BELLAN:	Pas très bien. J'ai eu une crise de foie ce matin et je n'avais plus de pilules pour me soulager. Vous savez de quoi je parle, n'est-ce pas?
LE PHARMACIEN:	C'était par ordonnance, Madame Bellan?
MME BELLAN:	Oui, c'était l'ordonnance du docteur Blanchard.

LE PHARMACIEN:	Ah! La voilà. C'était un calmant, c'est ce que je pensais.
MME BELLAN:	Vous croyez que c'est sain de prendre ces pilules trois fois par jour?
LE PHARMACIEN:	Cela ne vous fera pas de mal si vous vous arrêtez dès que votre crise de foie sera passée. Vous savez que le meilleur conseil en médecine est: "user sans abuser."
MME BELLAN:	Vous donnez toujours de bons conseils. C'est grâce à vous que ma grippe est passée en deux jours, alors que ma fille a gardé le lit pendant une semaine.
LE PHARMACIEN:	Voilà votre médicament, Madame Bellan.
MME BELLAN:	Je voudrais aussi un tube de pâte dentifrice, des losanges pour la gorge et un paquet de lames de rasoir.
LE PHARMACIEN:	Voici le tout. Passez à la caisse s'il vous plaît.
MME BELLAN:	Combien je vous dois pour le tout?
LE PHARMACIEN:	Ça vous fait un total de quarante-deux francs. Merci Madame Bellan, j'espère que votre crise de foie passera bientôt.

DIALOG *The Corner Pharmacy (drugstore)*

THE PHARMACIST:	Good morning Mrs. Bellan. How are you today?
MRS. BELLAN:	Not very well. I had a liver attack this morning and I had no more pills to relieve me. You know what I'm talking about, don't you?
THE PHARMACIST:	Was it by prescription, Mrs. Bellan?
MRS. BELLAN:	Yes, it was Dr. Blanchard's prescription.
THE PHARMACIST:	Ah! There it is. It was a sedative, just what I thought.
MRS. BELLAN:	Do you believe it's safe to take these pills three times a day?
THE PHARMACIST:	That will not do you any harm (hurt), if you stop as soon as your liver attack is gone. You know that the best advice in medicine is "use without abuse" (to use without abusing).
MRS. BELLAN:	You always give good advice. It's thanks to you that my flu is gone in two days, while my daughter stayed in bed for a week.
THE PHARMACIST:	There's your medicine, Mrs. Bellan.
MRS. BELLAN:	I would also like a tube of toothpaste, throat losenges, and a pack of razor blades.
THE PHARMACIST:	Here's everything. Go to the cash register, please.
MRS. BELLAN:	How much do I owe you for everything?
THE PHARMACIST:	It comes to a total of forty-two francs. Thank you, Mrs. Bellan. I hope your liver attack will soon go away.

NOTES:

The verb *passer* means "to pass," but depending on the context it may mean "to walk over to" as in *passez à la caisee,* or "to go away" as in *la crise passera. Se passer* means "to be happening" as in *qu'est ce qui ce passe?* (What's happening?)

DIALOG EXERCISES

A. Answer in short complete sentences the following questions.

1. Pourquoi Mme Bellan est-elle allée à la pharmacie?
   ____________________.
2. Qu'est-ce qui soulage Mme Bellan? ____________________.
3. Qui est-ce qui a prescrit les pilules? ____________________.
4. Quel genre de médicament est-ce? ____________________.
5. Pourquoi Mme Bellan est-elle inquiète? ____________________.
6. Quel est le meilleur conseil du pharmacien? ____________________.
7. How do you say in French "That won't hurt you"? ____________________.
8. Mme Bellan voudrait aussi un ____________________ des ____________________ et des ____________________.
9. Quel est le prix de tout ce que Mme Bellan a acheté? ____________________
   ____________________.
10. Quelle autre (what other) maladie Mme Bellan et sa fille avaient-elles avant la crise de foie? ____________________.

B. Review the rules of the *passé composé* and the *imparfait* for this summary of the dialog.

Madame Bellan ne se ____________ (sentir) pas bien, alors elle ____________ (aller) voir son pharmacien. Le pharmacien lui ____________ (conseiller) de prendre le calmant que le docteur a prescrit. Elle ____________ (acheter) le médicament et elle ____________ (payer) quarante-deux francs. Mme Bellan ____________ (faire) d'autres (other) achats. Avant la crise de foie Mme Bellan ____________ (avoir) la grippe pendant deux jours, mais sa fille ____________ (garder) le lit pendant une semaine. Mme Bellan ____________ (soulager) de savoir que le médicament ne lui fera pas mal.

C. Match the two columns.

1. Le pharmacien donne de bons conseils.
2. Elle est un peu bavarde.
3. Les médicaments ne sont pas chers.
4. La crise du malade passera.
5. Le secret est de ne rien abuser.
6. La grippe peut durer très longtemps.
7. Parfois les parents sont trop sévères.
8. Le calmant soulagera la malade.

A. The secret is to abuse nothing.
B. The sedative will relieve the sick lady.
C. The flu can last a long time.
D. Sometimes parents are too strict.
E. Medicines are not expensive.
F. The pharmacist gives good advice.
G. She is a bit talkative.
H. The sick man's attack will go away.

GRAMMAR I Present subjunctive of regular verbs.

So far, most of the verb tenses you've learned were in the indicative which, as its name implies, is used to indicate facts, ask questions, or make statements. We need the subjunctive to express moods, feelings, attitudes, or opinions about people, things, and actions.

A. French uses the subjunctive more frequently than English. Note that the subjunctive requires a dependent clause starting with *que* (that). Study the present subjunctive of the regular verbs below:

SUBJECT	PARLER	CHOISIR	ATTENDRE
que je	**parle**	**choisisse**	**attende**
que tu	**parles**	**choisisses**	**attendes**
qu' il, elle, on	**parle**	**choisisse**	**attende**
que nous	**parlions**	**choisissions**	**attendions**
que vous	**parliez**	**choisissiez**	**attendiez**
qu' ils, elles	**parlent**	**choisissent**	**attendent**

NOTES:

The subjunctive endings are the same for all French verbs except *avoir* and *être.* These endings are: *-e, -es, -ions, -iez, -ent.*

With the regular verbs ending in: *-er, -ir,* and *-re,* the subjunctive stem is the same as the *imparfait* stem, which is formed by dropping the *-ons* from the *nous* form of the present indicative and adding *-ions,* as in *nous parlions.*

EX.: nous choisiss/ons choisissions
nous attend/ons attendions

The subjunctive *-er, -ir,* and *-re* stems are:

parl **e, es, e, ions, iez, ent**
choisiss **e, es, e, ions, iez, ent**
attend **e, es, e, ions, iez, ent**

B. Uses of the subjunctive.

1. The subjunctive is used to express the speaker's opinions, or attitudes, about an action.
2. The French subjunctive has several English equivalents.

   EX.: *que tu parles* may be translated: "that you speak," "that you may speak," "that you are speaking," "that you do speak," "that you will speak," or "you to speak," as in *je veux que tu parles.* (I want you to speak.)

3. The subjunctive is used to express personal feelings such as emotions, doubts, uncertainty, possibility, and volition.
4. The subjunctive is used in expressing subjective views about the actions, as well as the concept of necessity:

   EX.: *Je veux que tu partes.* I want you to leave. (volition, command)
   Il faut que tu partes. You must leave. (necessity)
   Il doute que tu sortes. He doubts that you will leave. (doubt)
   C'est possible que nous partions. It is possible that we will leave. (possibility)

PRACTICE THE SUBJUNCTIVE PRESENT

A. Answer the following questions.

1. Where do you find the subjunctive stem in a French verb? ________________
____.
2. Give the subjunctive form of *nous formons* ____________________.
3. Name two French verbs that do not follow the rule of the subjunctive endings: ____________________ and ____________________.

4. What is the French equivalent of, "that he will finish"? ____.
5. If the subjunctive is used to express subjective actions to be formed, how do you say in French, "I want you to wait here"? ____________________.
6. What kind of clauses does the subjunctive require? ____.
7. In a subjunctive sentence, the independent clause is in what form? ____.
8. How do you say in French, "It's possible that she may leave"? ____.
9. The subjunctive is used to express personal feelings. Name two: __________ and ____________________.
10. How do you say in French, "We want you to listen"? ____.

B. Express orders in the following sentences, according to the example.

Example: Le docteur veut que tu gardes (garder) le lit.

1. Il veut que nous ____________ (acheter) les médicaments.
2. Il est content que je ____________ (finir) de parler.
3. Nous désirons que tu ____________ (attendre) ton ami.
4. Il faut que vous ____________ (demander) une augmentation.
5. Elle insiste que nous ____________ (refuser) de sortir.

GRAMMAR II Present subjunctive of stem-changing verbs: *essayer, appeler, commencer,* and *manger.*

Study the stem-changing verbs in the following chart.

SUBJECT	ESSAYER	APPELER	COMMENCER	MANGER
j' (e)	**essai e**	**appelle**	**commence**	**mange**
tu	**essai es**	**appelles**	**commences**	**manges**
il, elle, on	**essai e**	**appelle**	**commence**	**mange**
nous	**essay ions**	**appelions**	**commencions**	**mangions**
vous	**essay iez**	**appeliez**	**commenciez**	**mangiez**
ils, elles	**essai ent**	**appellent**	**commencent**	**mangent**

NOTES:

1. The changes that occur in stem-changing verbs are usually in the spelling, which in turn brings changes in the pronunciation.
2. In Lesson 5, we listed the categories of stem-changing verbs which indicated that *g* and *c* sounds in *manger* and *commencer* needed an *e* and a cedilla in the present indicative of the *nous* forms to keep the softer sounds of those consonants. In the subjunctive of such verbs, neither *e* nor a cedilla is needed because we already have the vowels *e* and *i* throughout the conjugated forms. Indicative: *nous mangeons, nous commençons;* subjunctive: *nous mangions, nous commencions.*
3. In the verb category of *appeler,* as in *j'appelle,* the *e* of the stem is pronounced as if it had a grave (`) accent every time it is followed by a double *l.*
4. The verb category of *essayer* reflects the same changes occurring in the indicative. Notice, however, that the *nous* and *vous* forms in the subjunctive are the same as the *imparfait.* Only the meaning of the sentence can alert you to the form of the verb. Study this example:

   Quand nous étions (imparfait) *jeunes, nos parents voulaient*
   que nous essayions (subjunctive) *beaucoup de choses.*

PRACTICE

A. Practice the present subjunctive of the stem-changing verbs.

1. Where do changes occur in stem-changing verbs? ____________________
____.
2. Name two verbs of the *appeler* category: ____________________ and ____________________.
3. Name two verbs of the *manger* category: ____________________ and ____________________.
4. Name two verbs in the *essayer* category: ____________________ and ____________________.
5. Why are the *cedilla* in *nous commençons,* and the *e* in *nous mangeons,* necessary? ____________________.
6. Which two verb forms are similar in the *imparfait* indicative and present subjunctive of the *essayer* verb category? ____________________.
7. How do you say in French, "I want you to pay your bills"? ____________________
____.
8. How do you say in French, "They may want you to call a doctor"? __________
____.
9. How do you say in French, "She may insist I stay in bed"? ____________________
____.
10. How do you say in French, "I want you to start studying French"? __________
____.

B. Write the subjunctive forms of the following:

1. nous ____________ (voyager)
2. tu ____________ (partager)
3. nous ____________ (épeler - to spell)
4. vous ____________ (employer)
5. nous ____________ (acheter)
6. nous ____________ (balancer)
7. ils ____________ (acheter)
8. vous ____________ (changer)
9. tu ____________ (rappeler)
10. je ____________ (payer)

GRAMMAR III Present subjunctive with impersonal expressions: *il faut, il vaut mieux,* etc.

A. The subjunctive occurs after impersonal expressions that designate the same instances in which the subjunctive is used: doubt, uncertainty, possibility, necessity, volition, etc. The subjunctive occurs after an impersonal expression followed by *que*. Study the following examples.

EX.: Il faut *que tu partes.* (necessity)
Il est douteux *que tu paies* ta facture. (bill) (doubt)
Il vaut mieux *que vous partiez.* (subjective opinion)
Il est possible *que vous appeliez* la police. (possibility)

B. The subjunctive does not occur in impersonal expressions that convey certainty or probability.

EX.: *Il est certain qu'elle va partir. Il est vrai qu'elle partira bientôt.*

C. The subjunctive does not have a future tense, so the present tense refers to both present and future. This was mentioned earlier in the possible English translations of the present subjunctive.

EX.: *Il est bon qu'elle parte.* It's good for her to leave (now or later).

D. Memorize the following impersonal expressions requiring the subjunctive.

1. Expressions of doubt:
   il est douteux que . . .

2. Expressions of necessity:
   il faut que . . .
   il est nécessaire que . . .
   il est exigé (required) que . . .

3. Expressions with subjective view of action:
   il est temps que . . .
   il est important que . . .
   il est juste que . . .
   il vaut mieux que . . .
   il est bon que . . .
   il est naturel que . . .

PRACTICE

A. Rewrite the following sentences in the present subjunctive, introducing your sentences with the impersonal expression between parentheses.

Example: Nous ne fumons pas. (il est necessaire)
Il est necessaire que nous ne fumions pas.

1. Elle parle souvent. (il faut) ____________.
2. Vous vous reposez. (il est bon) ____________.
3. Nous essayons tout. (il est important) ____________.
4. Vous commencez votre travail à l'heure. (il est naturel) ____________ ____________.
5. Elle ne jugera personne. (il est certain) ____________.
6. Vous voyagerez en France bientôt. (il est juste) ____________.
7. Nous ne répondons pas souvent. (il est nécessaire) ____________ ____________.
8. Notre réputation grandit à travers la ville. (il est temps) ____________ ____________.
9. Nous finirons cet exercise aujourd'hui. (il vaut mieux) ____________ ____________.
10. Nous payerons notre facture demain. (il est douteux) ____________ ____________.

B. Write the given verbs in the required mood and form according to the meaning of the context.

Example: Il est vrai qu'elle (partir) ____________ demain.
Il est vrai qu'elle partira demain. (no subjunctive is required in certainty clauses)

1. Nous doutons beaucoup que vous (finir) ____________ cette bouteille de vin.
2. Vos parents sont heureux que vous ____________ (réussir) à vos examens.
3. Nous pensons que c'est juste que vous ____________ (payer) vos impôts (taxes).
4. Nous sommes sûrs que vous ____________ (aller) demain à la plage.

5. Il est vrai que nous __________ (être) toujours avec vous.
6. Il est important que vous __________ (partager) votre argent avec moi.
7. Mes parents sont contents que je __________ (partir) en France.
8. Nous doutons que les voisins __________ (acheter) notre voiture.
9. Il vaut mieux que nous __________ (commencer) à économiser de l'argent.
10. Il est certain que tu __________ (payer) ta facture bientôt.

Lesson 13

LA VOITURE (The Automobile)

l'accélérateur (masc.)	accelerator	**le feu**	stop light
l'agent (masc.)	policeman	**le frein**	brake
l'aile (fem.)	fender	**l'indicateur (masc.)**	signal
l'arrière (masc.)	back	**la jauge**	gauge
l'avant (masc.)	front	**le klaxon**	horn
la batterie	battery	**lampe de poche**	flashlight
le bouton	button	**le moteur**	motor
le capot	hood	**la panne**	car breakdown
la carte grise	title	**le pare-brise**	windshield
la carte routière	road map	**le phare**	headlight
la ceinture	belt	**la plaque**	license plate
le chauffage	heating	**la plaque d'immatriculation**	license plate
la contravention	traffic ticket	**le pneu**	tire
la crevaison	flat tire	**la roue**	wheel
le démarreur	starter	**la station service**	gas station
l'embrayage (masc.)	clutch	**le trottoir**	pavement
l'essuie-glace (masc.)	windshield wiper	**la vitesse**	speed
		le volant	steering wheel

allumer	to turn on a light	**guider**	to guide
capoter	to turn over	**heurter**	to hit, run into
défendu	forbidden	**marcher**	to work (machine)
dégonfler	to deflate	**nettoyer**	to clean
démarrer	to start	**ralentir**	to slow down
dépanner	to repair (car)	**reculer**	to back up
éteindre	to turn off	**remorquer**	to tow
faire le plein	to fill the tank	**stationner**	to park
freiner	to brake	**tomber**	to fall
gonfler	to inflate		
assuré(e)	insured	**sans cesse**	constantly
automatique	automatic	**sec, sèche**	dry
comfortable	comfortable	**selon**	according
luxueux(euse)	luxurious	**usé(e)**	used, worn out
manuel(elle)	manual	**volontiers**	gladly, willingly
d'occasion	second hand		

NOTES:

1. *L'arrière* (the back of the car) and *l'avant* (the front) are both masculine, because the word *le côté* is understood: *le côté avant* and *le côté arrière*. *Arrière* is also used with *pneu* and *aile*. *L'aile* literally means "the wing of a bird," but in cars it means "the fender," as in *l'aile arrière* (rear fender).

2. *Marcher* means "to walk." However, when speaking of machines, motors, or anything that works with motors, *marcher* means "to work."
   EX.: *Ma montre marche bien.* My watch works well.

   Familiar expressions heard frequently are:
   Comment ça marche? How are things?
   Tout marche très bien. All is very well.

3. *Être en panne* and *tomber en panne* are two expressions which mean "to have car trouble" (breakdown). *Avoir une panne sèche* means to be out of gas.

4. *Allumer* means "to light." When we say *allumer les phares,* it means "to turn on the headlights." *Les allumettes* (matches) is the noun derived from *allumer*. *Volontiers* (willingly, gladly) derives from *la volonté* (will), *vouloir* (to want).

CULTURAL NOTE:
In the past ten years, owning a car has become such a top priority for the typical French family that today, France ranks third in Europe—after Germany and Sweden—in private car ownership. France also boasts some 54,000 miles of well-kept national highways and allows its citizens to drive at a speed limit of 80 miles per hour on superhighways (55 miles per hour everywhere else). This gives license to the French to develop a driving style which earns them a reputation of high-speed drivers among their European neighbors.

PRACTICE THE VOCABULARY

(Answers for Lesson 13, pp. 224–226)

A. Write *un* or *une* before the following words.

1. _____ agent	5. _____ essuie-glace	9. _____ pneu
2. _____ klaxon	6. _____ crevaison	10. _____ aile
3. _____ phare	7. _____ roue	11. _____ceinture
4. _____ panne	8. _____ pare-brise	12. _____ lampe de poche

B. Write the vocabulary words that relate to each of the following. Review the vocabulary carefully for this exercise.

1. accéléré __________	6. capoter __________
2. avancer __________	7. les freins __________
3. le gonflage __________	8. les assurances __________
4. chauffer __________	9. le stationnement __________
5. dépanner __________	10. la lumière __________

DIALOGUE *Jacques est en panne*

JACQUES: Marc, tu voudrais attendre à côté de la voiture? Je vais essayer de téléphoner à mon mécanicien; je reviens tout de suite.

MARC: D'accord, mais ne tarde pas, et si tu peux, apporte-moi quelque chose à boire. J'ai vraiment soif.

(quelques minutes plus tard)

JACQUES: Je n'ai pas trouvé mon mécanicien alors un employé de garage a offert de nous aider.

MARC: C'est parfait. Où est ma boisson?

JACQUES: Ah! Excuse-moi, j'ai complètement oublié.

L'EMPLOYÉ: (LE GARAGISTE) Voyons, d'abord il faut lever le capot, ensuite, dîtes-moi exactement ce qui s'est passé pendant que je vérifie les choses.

JACQUES: Je conduisais comme d'habitude, et tout d'un coup le moteur a commencé à ralentir. Je pousse sur l'accélérateur et rien n'arrive. Alors j'ai tourné le volant à droite et je me suis stationné ici à côté du trottoir.

LE GARAGISTE: Allumez les phares, s'il vous plaît; tout marche bien de ce côté-là. Eteignez-les maintenant. Voyons, les freins sont bons, les indicateurs marchent bien. Avez-vous fait un réglage récemment?

JACQUES: Oui, le mois dernier exactement.

LE GARAGISTE: La seule chose qui reste à vérifier c'est l'essence et l'huile.

JACQUES: Vous savez, depuis que mon jauge d'essence ne marche plus, j'ai été en panne à trois reprises.

LE GARAGISTE: C'est ça alors, c'est une panne sèche; c'est facile à vérifier. Je vais retourner au garage et apporter un bidon d'essence.

MARC: Tu devrais faire réparer ta jauge? Ce n'est pas amusant pour deux docteurs de gaspiller une heure si stupidement.

JACQUES: Tu as raison, mais j'ai si peu de temps pour m'occuper de ma voiture. Tu sais comment c'est, on travaille comme des esclaves dans cette profession.

MARC: Eh bien, alors tu pourrais dire que tu n'as pas gaspillé une heure; tu t'es reposé une heure.

JACQUES: Avoir une panne sèche n'est pas le genre de repos que j'ai l'intention de recommencer, crois-moi.

DIALOG *Jacques' Car Breaks Down*

JACQUES: Marc, would you wait next to the car? I'm going to try to call my mechanic; I'll be right back.

MARC: O.K., but don't be long, and if you can, bring me something to drink. I'm really thirsty.

(a few minutes later)

JACQUES: I did not find my mechanic, so the garage attendant offered to help us.

MARC: That's perfect. Where is my drink?

JACQUES: Ah! I'm sorry, I completely forgot.

GARAGE ATTENDANT: Let's see, first we have to raise the hood, then, tell me exactly what happened while I check things.

JACQUES: I was driving as usual, and all of a sudden the motor started to slow down. I pushed on the gas pedal, and nothing happened. So I turned the steering wheel to the right and parked next to the pavement.

GARAGE ATTENDANT: Turn the headlights on, please; all is working well from that side. Turn them off now. Let's see,

	the brakes are good, the signals are working well. Did you check your car recently?
JACQUES:	Yes, last month, exactly.
GARAGE ATTENDANT:	The only thing left to check (verify) is the gas and the oil.
JACQUES:	You know, since my gas gauge broke, I've had car trouble on three occasions.
GARAGE ATTENDANT:	That's it, then, you're out of gas; that's easy to check. I'm going to go back to the garage and bring a gas can.
MARC:	You should have your gas gauge repaired. It's not amusing for two doctors to waste one hour so stupidly!
JACQUES:	You are right, but I have so little time to take care of my car. You know how it is, we work like slaves in this profession.
MARC:	Well then, you could say that you did not waste one hour; you rested for one hour!
JACQUES:	Being out of gas is not the kind of rest I intend to repeat, believe me.

NOTES:

1. *La révision* means review (studies, accounts, etc.). *La révision* is a car check, *la révision générale* is a tune-up.

2. *Faire* + infinitive, such as *faire nettover, faire réparer,* means to have someone else do the work and is translated in English by "to have" + past participle. *(Le) faire réparer* (to have (*it*) repaired), *(le) faire nettoyer* (to have (*it*) cleaned).

DIALOG EXERCISES

A. Answer the following questions with short and precise answers.

1. Où Marc doit-il attendre Jacques? ________________.
2. Quelle est la profession de Jacques et de Marc? ________________.
3. Pourquoi Jacques est-il revenu avec un employé de garage, et non avec son mécanicien? ________________.
4. Qu'est ce que Jacques a oublié de faire? ________________.
5. Quelles sont les trois choses que le garagiste a vérifiées? ________________, ________________, et ________________.
6. Pourqoui le moteur a-t-il ralenti? ________________.
7. Où Jacques a-t-il stationné la voiture? ________________.

B. Review the subjunctive.

Suppose that Marc is giving some advice to Jacques on how to take better care of himself and his car. All the given verbs are regular. Write their appropriate subjunctive forms.

All sentences start by: *Jacques, il faut que . . .*

1. tu ______________________ (commencer) à prendre soin de ta santé.
2. tu ______________________ (se reposer) plus souvent.
3. tu ______________________ (partir) en vacances bientôt.
4. tu ______________________ (garder) ta voiture en meilleur état.
5. tu ______________________ (essayer) de quitter ton travail plus tôt.
6. tu ______________________ (s'arrêter) de rester tard dans ton bureau.
7. tu ______________________ (gaspiller) moins de temps.
8. tu ______________________ (surveiller) ta santé plus sérieusement.

GRAMMAR I Present subjunctive of irregular verbs.

A. Study the chart below with the subjunctive of *avoir, être,* and *savoir.*

SUBJECT	AVOIR	ETRE	SAVOIR
que j'(e)	**aie**	**sois**	**sache**
que tu	**aies**	**sois**	**saches**
qu'il, elle, on	**ait**	**soit**	**sache**
que nous	**ayons**	**soyons**	**sachions**
que vous	**ayez**	**soyez**	**sachiez**
qu'ils, elles	**aient**	**soient**	**sachent**

NOTE:

Except for the *nous* and *vous* forms of *avoir* and *être,* the other subjunctive stem endings are all regular.

B. Study the present subjunctive of the irregular verbs *aller, connaître,* and *vouloir.*

SUBJECT	ALLER	CONNAÎTRE	FAIRE
j'(e)	**aille**	**connaisse**	**fasse**
tu	**ailles**	**connaisses**	**fasses**
il, elle, on	**aille**	**connaisse**	**fasse**
nous	**allions**	**connaissions**	**fassions**
vous	**alliez**	**connaissiez**	**fassiez**
ils, elles	**aillent**	**connaissent**	**fassent**

NOTES:

1. Notice that when irregularities occur within subjunctive stems, they usually take place at the *nous* and *vous* forms.
2. The *nous* and *vous* forms *allions, alliez, connaissions,* and *connaissiez* are identical to the *nous* and *vous* forms of the *imparfait* (imperfect indicative) of those verbs.

C. Study the present subjunctive of the irregular verbs *pouvoir* and *vouloir.*

SUBJECT	POUVOIR	VOULOIR
que je	**puisse**	**veuille**
que tu	**puisses**	**veuilles**
qu'il, elle, on	**puisse**	**veuille**
que nous	**puissions**	**voulions**
que vous	**puissiez**	**vouliez**
qu'ils, elles	**puissent**	**veuillent**

NOTES:

1. Notice the *nous et vous* forms of *vouloir* are identical to the *imparfait* (imperfect indicative) forms.

2. The most commonly used form of the imperative of *vouloir* is *veuillez* which is usually found in endings of business letters. Most French business letters end with *Veuillez agréer nos salutations les plus distinguées.* (Kindly accept our most distinguished greetings.)

EXERCISE

Rewrite the following sentences, using *il faut que, il est important que, il est nécessaire que, il est douteux que* so that each sentence makes sense.

Example: 1. Marc doit attendre. Il faut que Marc attende.

1. La voiture est en panne. Marc doit attendre. ____________________.
2. Marie va au cinéma sans son fiancé. ____________________.
3. Monsieur Bertrand connaît les projets de Jacques. ____________________ ____________________.
4. Vous devez aller chercher un mécanicien. ____________________.
5. Nous avons besoin d'avoir du courage. ____________________.

GRAMMAR II Contrast of the indicative and subjunctive.

A. The uses of the indicative and subjunctive:
   1. Most of the verbs you have learned in previous lessons have been in the indicative. We use the indicative to make statements and to ask questions, while we need the subjunctive to express opinions, attitudes, and feelings, rather than facts.
   2. A sentence requiring the subjunctive has two clauses: an independent one requiring the indicative, and a dependent one with *que* (that) requiring the subjunctive.

      EX.: *Je veux qu'elle fasse le ménage.* I want *(indicative)* her to do (that she does) *(subjunctive)* the housework.

   3. However, if the main clause contains a verb of information or knowledge of fact, the verb in the dependent (subordinate) clause will require the indicative.

      EX.: *Je sais qu'il partira demain.* I know he will leave tomorrow.

   You have studied many verbs and expressions of information in the previous lessons and dialogs. Now, review the following table which lists more of the verbs and expressions of information that use the indicative.

communiquer	(to communicate)	**il est certain**	(it's certain)
déclarer	(to declare)	**il est clair**	(it's clear)
écrire	(to write)	**il est sûr**	(it's sure)
informer	(to inform)	**il est vrai**	(it's true)
lire	(to read)	**il est évident**	(it's evident)
reconnaître	(to recognize)		

B. The subjunctive after verbs of command, wishing, etc.

1. The subjunctive is needed if the main clause (independent) contains a verb expressing an opinion, a wish, a feeling, or something that is not a fact. Included in this category are verbs of command, forbidding, wishing, volition, doubt, request, suggestion, possibility, etc.

   EX.: *J'exige qu'il sorte* I require that he leave (I require him to leave.)

   You recall that the subject of the independent clause is frequently different from that of the dependent clause. However, if the subject is the same, the infinitive is used.

   EX.: *Je veux partir* I want to leave.

2. In Lesson 12 you studied several verbs and expressions of command, doubt, volition, possibility, etc. The following table lists other verbs and expressions that use the subjunctive.

conseiller	(to advise)	**il est défendu**	(it's forbidden)
défendre	(to forbid)	**il est impératif**	(it's imperative)
demander	(to ask)	**il est important**	(it's important)
désirer	(to desire)	**il est inutile**	(it's useless)
préférer	(to prefer)	**il est utile**	(it's useful)
regretter	(to regret)		

C. Verbs using both the subjunctive and indicative forms.

1. The verbs *croire* (to believe) and *penser* (to think), when used in an affirmative main clause (independent), are followed by an indicative subordinate clause (dependent).

   EX.: *Je pense qu'elle est gentille* I think she's kind.
   Je crois qu'elle est gentille I believe she's kind.

2. However, when *croire* and *penser* are used in an interrogative or negative independent clause, they are followed by a subjunctive subordinate (dependent) clause.

   EX.: *Penses-tu qu'elle soit gentille?* Do you think she's kind?
   Je ne pense pas qu'elle soit gentille. I don't think she's kind.
   Croyez-vous qu'elle soit gentille? Do you believe she's kind?
   Vous ne croyez pas qu'elle soit gentille. You don't believe she's kind.

3. The verb *dire* (to say, to tell) may use both indicative and subjunctive forms. *Dire* with the indicative relates a fact, while *dire* with the subjunctive may suggest an order or a command. Study the two examples.

   EX.: *Je lui ai dit qu'il est gentil.* I told him that he is kind.
   Je lui ai dit qu'il soit gentil; or . . . *qu'il faut qu'il soit gentil.* I told him to be kind.

PRACTICE

A. Show understanding of the contrast between the indicative and the subjunctive by completing the following exercise.

1. Name one major difference between the indicative and the subjunctive. ____________________.

2. When is the infinitive used instead of the subjunctive in a sentence with two clauses? ____________________.

3. Write a French sentence using the infinitive. ____________________ ____________________.

4. Rewrite this sentence using the subjunctive. *Ils pensent que nous aimons le vin blanc.* ____________________.

5. When do the verbs *croire* and *penser* require the subjunctive? ____________________.

6. What is the French equivalent of "I don't think he can (is able to) change"?
   ______________________.
7. Which verb may be followed by both the indicative and the subjunctive in all forms and tenses? ______________________.
8. Rewrite this sentence using the subjunctive: *Vous dites qu'il a de la chance.*
   ______________________.

B. Use the indicative and the subjunctive according to the ideas conveyed by the verbs between parentheses.

Example: Nous savons que vous <u>êtes</u> (être) français.

1. Ils doutent toujours que nous ____________ (pouvoir) finir notre travail à l'heure.
2. Il est vrai que les parents n(e) ____________ (avoir) pas toujours la meilleure réponse.
3. Pourquoi pense-t-il que les femmes ne ____________ (être) pas sûres de leurs talents?
4. Il est préférable que les politiciens ____________ (faire) moins de publicité.
5. On dit-que la patience ____________ (pouvoir) former le caractère.
6. Nous sommes certains que les médicaments ____________ (aller) guérir le malade.
7. Nous ne doutons pas que les voyageurs ____________ (connaître) bien leur itinéraire.

GRAMMAR III Review of the subjunctive and the impersonal expressions.

A. In reviewing the contrasts between the subjunctive and the indicative forms, the most important point to retain is that information (fact) = indicative *versus* influence (emotion) = subjunctive. In a subjunctive sentence, the speaker voices an opinion, an attitude, a wish, a doubt, a concern, a denial, and other personal feelings of emotion. In a subjunctive sentence, the main clause is in the indicative; the dependent clause is always introduced by *que*.

MAIN CLAUSE	DEPENDENT CLAUSE
subject + verb (indicative) + *que*	*subject + verb (subjunctive)*

B. The subjunctive is used in all the impersonal expressions you have learned except those expressing certainty, fact, or information.

C. Review the following examples of subjunctive usage.

1. Emotion	*Le malade est heureux que le médicament le guérisse.*
2. Doubt, uncertainty	*Nous ne sommes pas sûrs que nous puissions venir demain.*
3. Desire, volition	*Le patron veut que tu fasses bien ton travail.*
4. Necessity	*Il est nécessaire que tu saches ce qu'on dit.*
5. Regret	*Je regrette que vous soyez malade.*
6. Demand, command	*J'exige que vous me rendiez mon argent.*

D. Study the following examples of the use of the indicative and subjunctive with *penser* and *croire.*

1. *Penser* + affirmative + indicative: *Je pense qu'il est gentil.*
2. *Penser* + interrogative, negative + subjunctive:
   a. *Penses-tu qu'il soit gentil?*
   b. *Je ne pense pas qu'il soit gentil.*
3. *Croire* + affirmative + indicative: *Je crois qu'il est gentil.*
4. *Croire* + interrogative, negative + subjunctive:
   a. *Crois-tu qu'il soit gentil?*
   b. *Je ne crois pas qu'il soit gentil.*

E. Review the following table of impersonal expressions requiring the subjunctive.

DESIRE, NECESSITY	EMOTION	DOUBT, POSSIBILITY
il est important que	**il est bon que**	**il est normal que**
il est nécessaire que	**il est dommage que** (it's too bad that)	**il est possible que**
il est essentiel que	**il est juste que**	**il semble que**
il est exigé que (it's required that)	**il est préférable que**	
	il est utile, inutile que **il vaut mieux que**	

F. Review the following impersonal expressions requiring the indicative.

il est certain que	**il est probable que**
il est clair que	**il est sûr que**
il est évident que	**il est vrai que**

NOTE:

Anytime any of the above expressions is in the negative or interrogative form, the subjunctive is required because the certainty becomes doubt and the probability becomes a possibility.

EX.: *Il n'est pas sûr qu'il puisse finir demain.*
Est-il sûr qu'il puisse finir demain?

REVIEW EXERCISE

In the sentence, *Je veux que vous sachiez tout,* replace the *je veux* by the given expressions and complete the sentence.

Example: Je pense Je pense que vous savez tout.

1. Je sais ______________________.
2. Crois-tu ______________________.
3. Il est évident ______________________.
4. Nous savons ______________________.
5. Il est certain ______________________.
6. Il est probable ______________________.
7. Il est impossible ______________________.
8. Je ne crois pas ______________________.
9. Je suis sûr ______________________.
10. Il est défendu ______________________.

Lesson 14

L'ORDINATEUR ET LES PÉRIPHÉRIQUES (The Computer and the Peripherals)

l'alimentation (fem.)	supply	**le disque**	disk
la bande	tape	**l'écran (masc.)**	screen
le bilan	outcome, balance sheet	**l'ensemble (masc.)**	together, whole, entirety
le BUS	BUS	**l'entrée (fem.)**	entrance (input)
le BUS d'entrée	input	**l'imprimante (fem.)**	printer
le BUS de sortie	output	**l'ingénieur (masc.)**	engineer
la carte perforée	punch card	**le listing**	printout
la cassette	cassette tape	**le logiciel**	software
le circuit	circuit	**la machine à écrire**	typewriter
le clavier	keyboard	**le magnétophone**	tape recorder
la colle	glue	**la manette**	hand lever
la configuration	configuration	**le marchand**	shopkeeper
le crayon	pencil	**le marteau**	hammer
le critère	criterion	**le matériel**	hardware
la dactylo	typist	**le mensuel**	monthly
le dessin industriel	industrial design	**le microprocesseur**	microprocessor
disponible	available	**le modem**	modulator

l'ordinateur (masc.)	computer	**le silicium**	silicon
		la sortie	exit (output)
le papier	paper	**le stylo**	pen
la puce	chip	**le stylo lumineux**	light pen
le RAM	RAM		
le registre	register	**la table traçante**	plotter
le ROM	ROM		
le ruban	ribbon	**le tournevis**	screwdriver
le schéma	diagram, sketch	**la vidéo**	video cassette
accéder	to reach	**manier**	to handle
brancher	to connect	**marchander**	to haggle over
coller	to glue, stick	**perforer**	to pierce
enseigner	to teach	**résoudre**	to solve
épargner	to save, spare	**réussir**	to succeed
falloir	to have to	**suivre**	to follow
fumer	to smoke	**taper à la machine**	to type
imprimer	to print		

NOTES:

1. Although the French government recently imposed a law that requires the use of French terms in computer language, there are no words in French for BUS, ROM, RAM, and REM. The matching of computer terms with existing French words is not without humor. Consider the word *la puce* (the flea), that small exasperating insect that bites everywhere with the assurance it will not be caught. *La puce* (the flea) is now "the chip" in computer lingo.

2. *L'imprimante* (the printer) is derived from the word *imprimer* (to print); *imprimant* is the present participle—corresponding to the *-ing* ending in English. This participle is also used as an adjective in French and as such agrees with the noun it precedes.

   EX.: *thé-dansant* (tea party with dancing), *soirée-dansante* (evening party with dancing).

3. *Ensemble* is an adverb as well as a noun. When used with an article, it is a noun, as in *l'ensemble des questions* (all the questions together); when used with verbs it is an adverb, as in *nous sommes tous ensemble* (we are all together). *Ensemble* is also used as a noun when speaking of matching pieces of women's clothing.

   EX.: *L'ensemble bleu est très joli.* (The blue suit is very pretty.)

   A man's suit is called *un costume.*

4. *Coller* "to stick" or "to glue together" relates to the noun *la colle,* which means "glue." This word is found in several expressions.

   EX.: *Ça colle?* Is everything O.K.?
   Ça ne colle pas avec ma sœur, avec lui, avec elle, etc.
   Le collant, as a noun, means "tights" (gym tights or panty hose).
   Collant, used as a present participle, translates "clinging" or "tight," when speaking about clothes.

   EX.: *Une robe collante,* a clinging dress, *or* a tight dress.

PRACTICE THE VOCABULARY

(Answers for Lesson 14, pp. 226–228)

A. Indicate gender of following nouns.

Example: le clavier masc.

1. clavier ______
2. listing ______
3. vidéo ______
4. tournevis ______
5. marteau ______
6. silicium ______
7. cassette ______
8. ruban ______
9. stylo ______
10. sortie ______
11. entrée ______
12. puce ______
13. ordinateur ______
14. bande ______
15. papier ______
16. logiciel ______
17. crayon ______
18. bilan ______

B. Write verbs related to the following nouns.

Example: le comptable compter

1. la solution ______
2. l'imprimante ______
3. la colle ______
4. l'écriture ______
5. le dessin ______
6. la branche ______
7. la sortie ______
8. l'entrée ______
9. la vente ______
10. l'amour ______
11. l'allumette ______
12. la comptabilité ______
13. la conduite ______
14. la décision ______
15. la transformation ______

C. Write nouns related to the following verbs.

Example: décider la décision

1. acheter ______
2. commencer ______
3. décider ______
4. suivre ______
5. réussir ______
6. entrer ______

7. préférer ______
8. imprimer ______
9. coller ______
10. conduire ______
11. sortir ______
12. accéder ______

D. Write the adjectives related to the following nouns:

Example: beauté <u>beau, belle</u>

1. joie ______
2. sourire ______
3. beauté ______
4. courtoisie ______
5. gentillesse ______
6. mois
7. politesse ______
8. brouillard ______
9. soleil ______
10. lumière ______
11. jour ______
12. grandeur ______

DIALOGUE *Une idée excellente!*

(Charles décide d'acheter un ordinateur et demande à son ami Roland de lui donner des conseils. Roland vient de terminer des études d'informatique.)

CHARLES: Ça y est! J'ai décidé d'économiser mon argent et d'acheter un ordinateur.

ROLAND: Idée excellente, mon ami! C'est un appareil fascinant! Mais je t'avertis, c'est très cher.

CHARLES: Oui, je sais. C'est pour cela que j'ai fait des économies toute l'année.

ROLAND: Très bien. Je connais quelqu'un qui est dans cette branche, et qui te vendra ce qu'il te faut à crédit. Il faudra signer un contrat qui t'obligera à faire des versements mensuels, pour ton ordinateur tout neuf.

CHARLES: C'est chouette! Alors viens avec moi, présente-moi à ton ami, et sois mon professeur d'informatique pour quelques heures.

ROLAND: Il y a longtemps que je n'ai parlé à cet ami-là, mais allons-y quand même. Je suis sûr qu'il sera content de nous voir.

CHARLES: Regarde cette machine, quelle beauté!

ROLAND: Cet appareil que tu vois n'est qu'un des périphériques. Il y a un tas d'autres pièces nécessaires au fonctionnement complet de ce que tu appelles "la machine."

CHARLES: Explique-moi, s'il te plaît.

ROLAND: Voilà, regarde le schéma sur cette feuille volante: l'ordinateur c'est l'unité centrale qui comprend l'écran-vidéo, le clavier, la cassette, le disque, la table traçante et le listing. Sans tous ces accessoires, ou périphériques, l'unité centrale n'est qu'une machine sourde et muette.

CHARLES: Tu veux dire que ce sont ces périphériques qui permettent à l'ordinateur de communiquer avec l'extérieur?

ROLAND: Oui, mais seulement en partie, car il faudrait quelqu'un pour manier le système. Cet ensemble d'appareils constitue le système informatique appelé configuration.

CHARLES: Cela devient de plus en plus compliqué, mon vieux.

ROLAND: Ce n'est vraiment pas si compliqué que ça. Rappelle-toi que faire de l'informatique nécessite le côté matériel et le côté logiciel. C'est ce que les Américains appellent "hardware" et "software."

CHARLES: Le matériel est donc l'opposé du logiciel?

ROLAND: Oui, en effet. Le matériel ou "hardware" est le côté purement mécanique et électronique de l'informatique, alors que le logiciel ou "software" est réservé à l'art de faire dialoguer les appareils de la configuration. En effet, c'est la composition du programme.

CHARLES: Mais alors il faut être ingénieur et écrivain à la fois pour faire de l'informatique?

ROLAND: Tu as raison. Si tu veux être l'ingénieur-système, tu dois apprendre à manier la plume aussi bien que le tournevis. Mais si tu veux un ordinateur pour ton usage personnel, c'est facile à apprendre.

CHARLES: C'est exactement ce que je veux. Je te laisse le soin de devenir l'ingénieur-système.

DIALOG: *An Excellent Idea!*

(Charles decides to buy a computer and asks his friend Roland to give him advice. Roland has just finished data processing school.)

CHARLES: That's it! I have decided to save my money and buy a computer.

ROLAND: Excellent idea, my friend! It's a fascinating gadget. But I warn you, it's very expensive.

CHARLES: Yes, I know. That is the reason I saved all year.

ROLAND: Very well, I know someone who is in that area (business), and who will sell you on credit what you need. You will have to sign a contract which will commit you (oblige) to make (pay) monthly installments for your brand new (all new) computer.

CHARLES: That's super! Come with me then, introduce me to your friend, and be my data processing teacher for a few hours.

ROLAND: It's been a long time since I have spoken to that friend, but let's go anyway. I am sure he will be happy to see us.

CHARLES: Look at this beauty of a machine!

ROLAND: That apparatus (gadget) you see is nothing but one of the peripherals. There are a whole lot of parts necessary for the complete functioning of what you call "the machine."

CHARLES: Explain to me, please.

ROLAND: Here, look at the sketch on this flier: the computer is the central unit, which includes the screen, the keyboard, the cassette, the disk, the plotter, and the printout. Without all these accessories, or peripherals, the central unit is nothing but a deaf and mute machine.

CHARLES: You mean (you want to say) that it is these peripherals that allow the computer to communicate with people?

ROLAND: Yes, but only in part, for it would need someone to make the system work (to handle). This set of parts constitutes the data processing system called configuration.

CHARLES: This is becoming more and more complicated, my dear friend.

ROLAND: It's not really that complicated. Remember that data processing involves (necessitates) the hardware side and the software side. It is what the Americans call "hardware" and "software."

CHARLES: Hardware is then the opposite of software?

ROLAND: Yes, in fact hardware is the part (side) of data processing which is purely mechanical and electronic, while software is the art of making the system parts talk to one another. In other words, it's the programming.

CHARLES: One must be an engineer and a writer at the same time.

ROLAND: You're right. If you want to be an engineer in electronics, you must learn how to handle the pen as well as the screwdriver. But if you want a computer for your personal use, it is easy to learn.

CHARLES: That's exactly what I want. You can be the electronics engineer (I leave the care to you).

LES PÉRIPHÉRIQUES (PERIPHERALS)
UN SCHÉMA (A SKETCH)

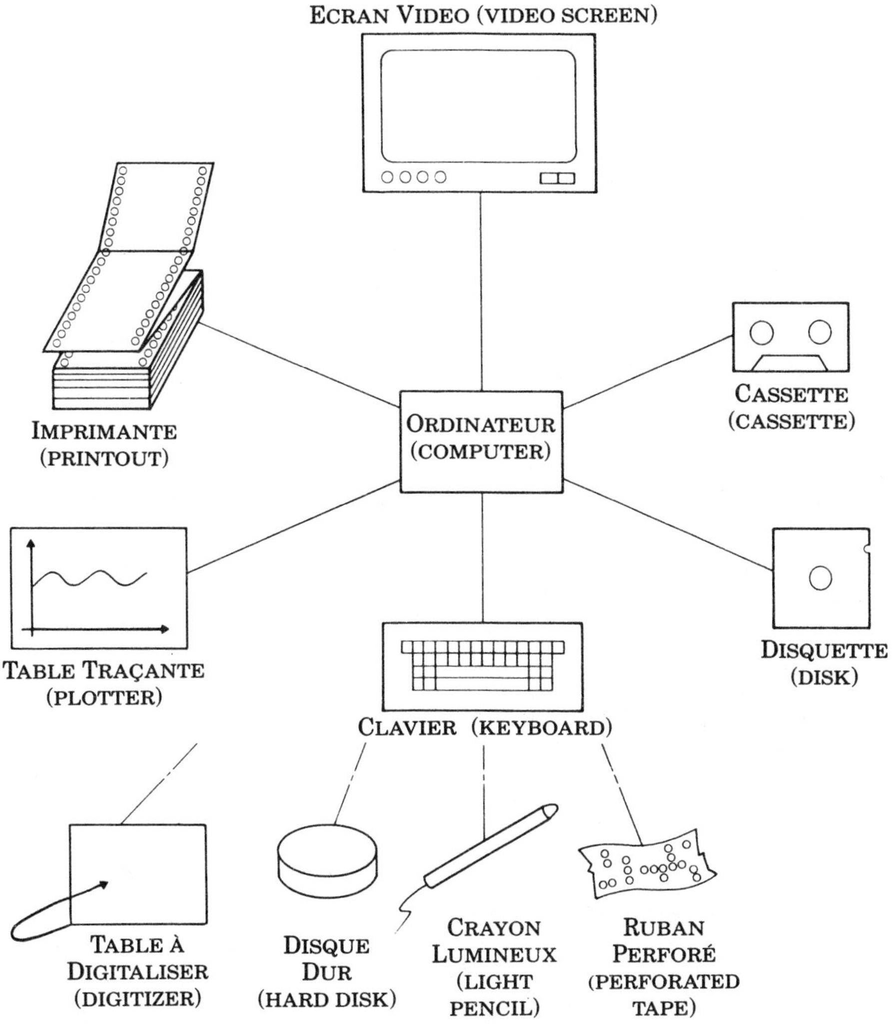

DIALOG EXERCISES

A. Answer True (T) or False (F).

1. Charles veut acheter un ordinateur. ____________
2. Roland ne sait rien au sujet de l'informatique. ____________

3. Roland est un ami de Charles. ___________
4. Charles sait beaucoup de choses au sujet des ordinateurs. ___________
5. Roland et Charles sont allés au cinéma. ___________
6. Roland n'aime pas l'informatique. ___________
7. Charles n'achètera jamais d'ordinateur. ___________
8. Roland vient d'acheter un ordinateur. ___________
9. Charles a acheté beaucoup d'accessoires. ___________
10. Charles demande à Roland de l'aider. ___________
11. Roland et Charles ont passé l'après-midi au parc. ___________
12. Charles est fasciné par les appareils d'informatique. ___________
13. Charles et Roland sont très riches. ___________
14. Charles est un ingénieur-système. ___________
15. Roland a fait des études d'informatique. ___________

B. Write the following sentences in the first person or third person according to given text.

Example: Dites que vous acheterez un ordinateur. J'achèterai un ordinateur.

1. Dites que vous travaillez sans cesse.
2. Dites que vous aimez étudier l'informatique.
3. Dites que vous allez enseigner la biologie.
4. Dites que vous ne savez pas conduire.
5. Dites que votre ordinateur marche très bien.
6. Dites qu'il faut travailler pour vivre.
7. Dites qu'il y aura de la place pour votre ami(e).
8. Dites que les périphériques sont des appareils électroniques.
9. Dites que le travail, c'est la santé; le repos c'est la conserver.
10. Dites que la puce de l'ordinateur est une des parties essentielles de l'informatique.
11. Dites que vous venez de rentrer d'un long voyage.
12. Dites que vous allez faire des versements mensuels.
13. Dites que le matériel est aussi compliqué que le logiciel.

GRAMMAR I Immediate past: **venir de** with the infinitive.

Besides the *imparfait* and the *passé composé,* which convey the past tense, French has an additional past tense called "the immediate past." The English equivalent is a verb used with the adverb "just," as in "I just finished my lunch." To translate the immediacy of a past action as a second is taking place, French uses a present tense form of *venir de* followed by the infinitive of the action verb.

EX.: *Il vient de rentrer.* He just came back.
Nous venons de finir notre leçon. We just finished our lesson.

Venir de is conjugated as the verb *venir* would be. *Venir de* in the imperfect becomes the English pluperfect.

EX.: *Elle vient de partir.* She just left.
Elle venait de partir. She had just left.

PRACTICE THE IMMEDIATE PAST

Write in French the complete sentences required.

1. (He just telephoned you.) ____________________.
2. (We just sent) votre lettre. ____________________.
3. (They just bought) une voiture. ____________________.
4. (I just connected) la table traçante. ____________________.
5. (She just went out.) ____________________.
6. (You just solved) notre problème. ____________________.

GRAMMAR II Immediate future. *Aller* with the infinitive.

A. In French, there is an additional future tense that is formed with *aller* (to go), followed by the infinitive of the action verb.

EX.: *Je vais faire le marché.* I'm going grocery shopping.

This is the French equivalent of the English "to be going to" with the infinitive.

Note that the French does not use the same verbal form *-ant,* which would be the literal English translation of "-ing."

EX.: *Je vais acheter un stylo.* I'm going to buy a pen.
Ils vont apprendre l'informatique. They're going to learn data processing.

B. An important rule to remember here is that when two verbs follow each other, the second verb is always an infinitive.
EX.: *Il veut chanter à l'opéra.* He wants to sing at the opera.
Elle aime faire du ski. She likes to ski.

PRACTICE THE IMMEDIATE FUTURE

Write in French the complete sentences required.

1. (I'm going to sell my car.) ____________________.
2. (He was going to have lunch) avec nous. ____________________.
3. (Are you going to drive) jusqu' à New York? ____________________.
4. (Are you going to teach) à Los Angeles? ____________________.
5. (Are they going) rester avec nous? ____________________.
6. (You are going to use) votre ordinateur. ____________________.

GRAMMAR III Impersonal expressions.

A. Remember how we stressed the absence of the English *it* as a neuter gender of nouns? Well, in French we do have this neuter gender, but only in connection with the verbs that are called impersonal *(expressions impersonnelles)*. These impersonal expressions are always used in the third person singular. They are *il faut* (one must, one has to), *c'est* (it's), and *il y a* (there is, there are).
EX.: *Il faut travailler.* One has to work.
C'est gentil à vous. It's nice of you.
Il y a des gens chez vous. There are people at your home.

B. These expressions follow the rules of the regularities or irregularities of their verbs. For example, *il faut* is the third person singular of the verb *falloir*. It is important to note that this verb is used *only* in the third person. As a result, it is doubly impersonal since it can't be used with any other pronoun besides *il*.
EX.: *il faut* one must, has to
il fallait one had to
il faudra one will have to
il faudrait one would have to

C. Unlike *falloir,* which can be used only with the third person singular *il,* the verbs *être* (to be) and *avoir* (to have) are conjugated in all persons, singular and plural. However, in the two impersonal ways they are used here, *c'est* (it's) and *il y a* (there is, there are), they always remain in the third person singular.

EX.: *C'est dommage.* It's a pity.
C'était dommage. It was a pity.
Il y a du bruit. There is noise.
Il y avait du bruit. There was noise.

D. Since *il y a* and *c'est* are formed with the verbs *avoir* and *être,* they follow the rules of their respective conjugations in all forms and tenses.

EX.: *Il y aura de la place.* There will be room.
Ce sera dommage. It will be a pity.

NOTE:

The *c'* in *c'est* is *ce* + *est.* The first vowel is always dropped when the following word starts with a vowel or a mute *h.* Thus, *ce est* becomes *c'est, le homme* becomes *l'homme.* In other constructions, the *c'* regains its vowel, as in *ce sera* (it will be), *ce serait* (it would be).

EXERCISES

A. Practice the impersonal expressions with *falloir* and *devoir* by translating the expression in parentheses, using the tense indicated.

Example: Il fallait (had to) acheter du pain.
Note: The negative form takes on a slightly different meaning. *Il ne faut pas* is equivalent to *défense de* + infinitive, as in *défense de fumer* (no smoking, no smoking allowed).

1. ____________ (did not have to) acheter du pain.
2. ____________ (will have to) être gentil.
3. ____________ (would have to) suivre les règles.
4. ____________ (has to) se reposer.
5. ____________ (had to drive) doucement.
6. ____________ (has had to) finir le travail.
7. ____________ (does not have to) être méchant.
8. ____________ (would not have to) rester debout.

9. ___________ (will not have to) s'asseoir par terre.
10. ___________ (has to learn) ses leçons.

B. Practice the impersonal expressions with *être* by translating the expressions in parentheses, using the tense indicated.

Example: (It's difficult.) C'est difficile.

1. (It's a pity.) ____________________.
2. (It would be nice.) ____________________.
3. (It will be correct.) ____________________.
4. (It is not) ____________________ votre faute.
5. (It was a pity.) ____________________.
6. (It would have been nice.) ____________________.
7. (It was not necessary.) ____________________.
8. (It will not be) ____________________ compliqué.
9. (It has been a pleasure.) ____________________.
10. (It has not been) ____________________ comme d'habitude.

C. Practice the impersonal expressions with *avoir* by translating the expressions in parentheses, using the tense indicated.

Example: (There will be room.) Il y aura de la place.

1. (There are a lot of people.) ____________________.
2. (There is enough sun.) ____________________.
3. (There will be a rainbow.) ____________________.
4. (There is some kindness.) ____________________.
5. (There are not enough computers.) ____________________.
6. (There would be a contract.) ____________________.
7. (There has been noise.) ____________________.
8. (There will be a new screen.) ____________________.
9. (There were enough accessories.) ____________________.
10. (There are many French people in San Francisco.) ____________________.

Lesson 15

MOTS APPARENTÉS ET FAUX AMIS (Cognates and False Friends)

This chapter is the culmination of your newly acquired French Vocabulary and syntax. It's intended to remind you that you have a chance to enrich your French vocabulary, on your own, by some 2,000 cognates.

Cognates are words that may have the same sounds, spellings, and meanings as known English words. Some have all of the preceding. Many will resemble so closely the English words that by applying the rules set forth in this chapter, you will be able to form your own French equivalents. This chapter will not overlook *les faux amis* (false friends)—these are French words that have exactly the same spelling as English words, but convey a completely different meaning. The French word *sensible,* for example, means "sensitive," "touchy," while in English it conveys common sense. This chapter will list the most frequently used *faux amis.*

Cognates such as "garage," "automobile," "vague," "vain," and "primordial" belong to the category of hundreds of cognates that have the same meaning, spelling, and sound as in English. There are, however, hundreds of other cognates that have the same meaning conveyed by the English words but are not spelled exactly like them. These cognates are found in nouns, adjectives, verbs, and adverbs. While it will be impossible to list all English cognates, the following pages will provide the necessary guidelines to assist you in converting your own English words into new French ones.

FRENCH NOUNS WITH ENGLISH ENDINGS

Please study the charts and word ending conversion below.

FRENCH NOUNS	FRENCH ENDINGS	ENGLISH ENDINGS	
l'anatomie (fem.)	**-ie**	(anatomy)	**-y**
la chambre	**-re**	(chamber)	**-er**
le dictionnaire	**-aire**	(dictionary)	**-ary**
la liberté	**-té**	(liberty)	**-y**
le moteur	**-eur**	(motor)	**-or**
la république	**-que**	(republic)	**-ic**
le snobisme	**-isme**	(snobism)	**-ism**
l'urgence (fem.)	**-ence**	(urgency)	**-ency**

NOTE:

Notice that all word transformations take place in the word endings.

FRENCH ADJECTIVES WITH ENGLISH ENDINGS

FRENCH ADJECTIVES	FRENCH ENDINGS	ENGLISH ENDINGS	
américain	**-ain**	(American)	**-an**
canadien	**-ien**	(Canadian)	**-ian**
comique	**-ique**	(comical)	**-ical**
contraire	**-aire**	(contrary)	**-ary**
délicieux	**-eux**	(delicious)	**-ous**
pessimiste	**-iste**	(pessimistic)	**-istic**
populaire	**-aire**	(popular)	**-ar**
progréssif	**-if**	(progressive)	**-ive**

NOTE:

Notice that both French adjectives and nouns ending in *-aire* correspond to the English ending "-ary," and that both French adjectives and nouns ending in *-iste* have the English ending "ist" for nouns and "istic" for adjectives.

FRENCH VERBS WITH ENGLISH ENDINGS

FRENCH VERBS	FRENCH ENDINGS	ENGLISH ENDINGS	
admirer	**-er**	(to admire)	**-e**
analyser	**-yser**	(to analyze)	**-yze**
célébrer	**-er**	(celebrate)	**-ate**
finir	**-ir**	(to finish)	**-ish**
organiser	**-iser**	(to organize)	**-ize**

FRENCH ADVERBS WITH ENGLISH ENDINGS

French adverbs ending in *-ment,* as in *directement, sérieusement,* etc., correspond to the English ending "-ly," as in "directly," "seriously." All the French adjectives ending in *-eux (euse)* which have the English ending "-ous," follow the *-ment,* "-ly" equivalent in the respective adverbs.

EX.: *délicieux, délicieusement,* delicious, deliciously

NOTES:

1. Both French and English have identical scientific and technical terms. The spelling may vary slightly from French into English, but all words are easily recognized.
   EX.: *analyse, artère, ordre, alcali, acide, angle, triangle, vitamine, protéine, oxygène,* etc.

2. French nouns ending in *-ance, -ence, -able, -ible, -sion, -tion, -ude, -ure, -ment* are similar in both languages.
   EX.: *élégance, différence, agréable, précision, éducation, certitude, culture, département.*

   Certain months of the year are also easily recognizable.
   EX.: *septembre, octobre, novembre, décembre, mars, avril, mai.*

FRENCH FAUX AMIS (false friends)

As stated earlier, there are many French words that can be misleading, thus their nickname of "false friends." Below is a short list of such *faux amis*.

FRENCH FAUX AMIS	TRANSLATION	ENGLISH FALSE FRIENDS
anniversaire	birthday	not: anniversary
assister (à)	to attend	not: to help or assist
la cave	cellar	not: a cave
commander	to order (meal, etc.)	not: to command
demander	to ask for	not: to demand
la lecture	reading	not: a lecture, lesson
la location	rent, renting	not: a location, place
rester	to stay, to remain	not: to rest
sensible	sensitive	not: sensible

There are no set rules for *faux amis*. You should, however, be aware of their existence. When a phrase does not make sense with a cognate, you know it's a false friend.

Following is a summary of cognate endings in nouns, adjectives, adverbs, and verbs.

FRENCH ENDINGS	EQUIVALENT ENGLISH ENDINGS
-ie, geographie	-y, geography
-té, possibilité	-y, possibility
-eur, labeur (noun)	-or, labor
-ique, logique	-ic, logic
-isme, optimisme	-ism, optimism
-iste, chimiste	-ist, chemist
-ien, musicien	-ian, musician
-ain, africain	-an, African
-eux, furieux	-ous, furious
-if, décisif	-ive, decisive
-iste, optimiste (adj.)	-istic, optimistic
-er, arriver	-e, to arrive
-er, célébrer	-ate, to celebrate
-ier, simplifier	-y, to simplify
-ir, nourrir	-ish, to nourish
-iser, organiser	-ize, to organize
-yser, analyser	-yze, to analyze
-ment, arrangement (n.)	-ment, arrangement
-ment, immédiatement (adj.)	-ly, immediately

UNDERSTANDING COGNATES

(Answers for Lesson 15, pp. 228–230)

A. What are the English cognates for the following words?

1. capacité ___________
2. géométrie ___________
3. analogie ___________
4. monstre ___________
5. ordinaire ___________
6. ferveur ___________
7. musique ___________
8. estuaire ___________
9. sérieux ___________
10. logique ___________
11. australien ___________
12. abusif ___________
13. actif ___________
14. modérer ___________
15. temporaire ___________
16. affirmer ___________
17. bannir ___________
18. chimiste ___________
19. offrir ___________
20. absolument ___________
21. dangereux ___________
22. cultiver ___________
23. irriter ___________
24. multiplier ___________

GRAMMAR I Conditional form of regular verbs.

A. To form the conditional of a regular verb in French, we add the endings of the *imparfait* to the infinitive. Study the chart below.

SUBJECT	PARLER	CHOISIR	ATTENDRE
je	**parler ais**	**choisir ais**	**attendr ais**
tu	**parler ais**	**choisir ais**	**attendr ais**
il, elle, on	**parler ait**	**choisir ait**	**attendr ait**
nous	**parler ions**	**choisir ions**	**attendr ions**
vous	**parler iez**	**choisir iez**	**attendr iez**
ils, elles	**parler aient**	**choisir aient**	**attendr aient**

1. The verb stem of the conditional is the infinitive, just as we have seen in the future tense.
2. To this stem are added the conditional endings, which are the same as those of the *imparfait: -ais, -ais, -ait, -ions, -iez,* and *-aient*. These endings are added to the infinitives of regular verbs. If a verb has an *e* in the infinitive, this vowel is dropped, as in *apprendre*.

   EX.: *j' apprendre-ais* I would learn.
   tu apprendre-ais You would learn.

B. Uses of the *conditionnel* (conditional).

1. The conditional is used with wishes and requests. Using the conditional makes a request softer and more polite. Compare these two examples:

   Je voudrais un livre. I would like a book.
   Je veux un livre. I want a book.

   The request in example *a* is more polite than *b*.
2. The conditional is also used to indicate a projected action that is to occur sometime in the future.

   EX.: *Elle savait qu'il téléphonerait après de dîner.* She knew he would call after dinner.
3. English uses the conditional to express habits that occurred in the past. This form is rendered in French by *l'imparfait.*

   EX.: *À Paris, je me promenais toujours le matin.* In Paris, I would always take a walk in the morning.

PRACTICE THE CONDITIONAL

A. Complete the following exercise by writing in French the required response.

1. What is the verb stem of the conditional in French? ____________________

   ____
2. In English, the conditional is formed by *would* + infinitive. How is it formed in French? ____________________
3. When is the conditional used to convey politeness? ____________________

   ____
4. What tense does French use to convey the English conditional expressing habits occurring in the past? ____________________
5. Give the conditional form of *ils* ____________________ *(finir)* and of *elle* ____________________ *(rendre)*.

____

B. Change the verb forms from the *passé composé* to the conditional.

1. j'ai acheté ____________
2. nous avons examiné ____________
3. nous sommes partis ____________
4. ils sont sortis ____________
5. elle a mangé ____________
6. nous avons admiré ____________
7. elle a appris ____________
8. il a fini ____________
9. tu as préparé ____________
10. tu t'es ennuyé(e) ____________

C. Change the verb forms from the present to the conditional.

1. nous partons ____________
2. elle joue ____________
3. vous sortez ____________
4. il s'amuse ____________
5. tu attends ____________
6. ils achètent ____________
7. tu manges ____________
8. nous finissons ____________
9. elle admire ____________
10. ils aiment ____________

GRAMMAR II Contrast of the future and conditional of irregular verbs.

A. Memorize the following chart with *être* and *avoir*.

SUBJECT	FUTURE (ÊTRE)	CONDITIONAL (ÊTRE)	FUTURE (AVOIR)	CONDITIONAL (AVOIR)
je	**serai**	**serais**	**aurai**	**aurais**
tu	**seras**	**serais**	**auras**	**aurais**
il, elle, on	**sera**	**serait**	**aura**	**aurait**
nous	**serons**	**serions**	**aurons**	**aurions**
vous	**serez**	**seriez**	**aurez**	**auriez**
ils, elles	**seront**	**seraient**	**auront**	**auraient**

NOTES:

1. All irregular verbs in the future tense are irregular in the conditional. This means that the list of irregular verbs given in Lesson 11 will have the same irregular changes, to which are added the regular conditional endings.
2. The same rules apply in changes of spelling or accentuation in stem-changing verbs such as *acheter* (to buy) or *appeler* (to call).
   EX.: *acheter, j'achèterai, j'achèterais,* etc.
   appeler, j'appellerai, j'appellerais, etc.

B. Memorize the irregular verbs in the future and conditional forms below.

INFINITIVE	FUTURE	CONDITIONAL
aller	**j'irai**	**j'irais**
devoir	**je devrai**	**je devrais**
faire	**je ferai**	**je ferais**
pouvoir	**je pourrai**	**je pourrais**
savoir	**je saurai**	**je saurais**
venir	**je viendrai**	**je viendrais**
voir	**je verrai**	**je verrais**
vouloir	**je voudrai**	**je voudrais**

C. Study the irregular impersonal expressions in the future and conditional forms.

IMPERSONAL	FUTURE	CONDITIONAL
il faut	**il faudra**	**il faudrait**
il vaut	**il vaudra**	**il vaudrait**

PRACTICE

A. Practice the irregular future and conditional forms.

1. All the verbs that are irregular in the future are also irregular in ________ ________________.
2. The conditional of *savoir* is *je* ________________.
3. If the future of *il peut* is *il pourra,* what is the conditional? ________ ________________.
4. If the future of *nous apprenons* is *nous apprendrons,* what is the conditional? ________________.
5. If the future of *tu sais* is *tu sauras,* what is the conditional? ________ ________________.
6. If the future of *il doit* is *elle devra,* what is the conditional? ________ ________________.
7. If the future of *tu fais* is *tu feras,* what is the conditional? ________ ________________.
8. If the future of *vous voyez* is *vous verrez,* what is the conditional? ________ ________________.
9. If the future of *il veut* is *il voudra,* what is the conditional? ________ ________________.
10. If the future of *nous allons* is *nous irons,* what is the conditional? ________ ________________.

B. Complete the sentences with the correct future form of the given verbs.

Example: Jacques et Mac (aller) ironts voir Juliette.

1. Jeudi prochain, je (faire) ________ des courses.
2. Si tu viens nous (pouvoir) ________ faire du ski.
3. Juliette et Charles se (fiancer) ________ le mois prochain.
4. Il y (avoir) ________ beaucoup de loisirs.
5. Vous (savoir) ________ la réponse demain.
6. Tu (aller) ________ avec nous à l'aéroport.
7. Il (faut) ________ travailler lundi prochain.
8. Nous (faire) ________ toute la vaisselle.

9. Il (garder) ___________ le lit jusqu'à demain.
10. Vous (voir) ___________ dès que vous (venir) ___________.

C. Complete the table according to the examples below.

PRESENT	IMPERFECT	FUTURE	CONDITIONAL
1. vous avez	vous aviez	vous aurez	vous auriez
2. tu achètes	___________	___________	___________
3. vous venez	___________	___________	___________
4. elle apprend	___________	___________	___________
5. tu finis	___________	___________	___________
6. elle va	___________	___________	___________
7. tu vois (voir)	___________	___________	___________
8. nous savons	___________	___________	___________
9. elle attend	___________	___________	___________
10. nous avons	___________	___________	___________

GRAMMAR III Formation and usage of adverbs.

A. Usage and placement of adverbs.

1. Adverbs are used to modify adjectives, verbs, and other adverbs. We have learned several adverbs, such as *beaucoup, bien, mal, trop, très, vite, peu, souvent, ici, bientôt, là-bas,* etc.
2. Adverbs usually are placed before adjectives and after verbs.

   EX.: *Il va bien.* He is well.
   Il est très gentil. He is very kind.

3. Adverbs of time and place are usually at the end or the beginning of a sentence.
4. The adverbs of time are: *bientôt, demain,* and *hier.*
   The adverbs of place are: *ici* and *là-bas.*

   EX.: *Nous partons à Nice bientôt.* We are leaving for Nice soon.
   Ils sont heureux ici. They are happy here.

5. Adverbs are placed after *pas* in a negative sentence.
   EX.: *Il ne chante pas souvent.* He does not sing often.
   Il ne mange pas bien. He does not eat well.

6. Adverbs are placed after the auxiliary in the *passé composé* sentences.
   EX.: *Il a beaucoup parlé.* He talked a lot.

B. Formation of adverbs.

1. Most French adverbs are formed by adding *-ment* to the adjective.
   EX.: *vrai, vraiment*
   aimable, aimablement

   The *-ment* is often the equivalent of the English "-ly," as in "quickly."

2. The *-ment* ending is *always* added to the masculine form of the adjective, only. However, if the masculine form ends with a consonant, then *-ment* is added to the feminine form of the adjective. Study the following examples.

EX.:	*poli* (masc.)	*poliment*	
	joli (masc.)	*joliment*	
	heureux (masc.)	*heureuse* (fem.)	*heureusement*
	lent (masc.)	*lente* (fem.)	*lentement*

3. When the masculine form of an adjective ends in *-ent* or *-ant,* the adverb is formed by adding *-emment* to the *-ent* adjective and *-amment* to the *-ant* adjective. Study the following examples.

EX.:	*différent*	*différemment* (differently)
	constant	*constamment* (constantly)

4. Two adverbs do not follow any of the above rules and are the only irregular adverbs in French. They are: *brièvement* (briefly), *gentiment* (kindly). Their adjectives are *bref, brève,* (brief); *gentil, gentille* (kind).

PRACTICE YOUR ADVERBS

A. Answer the following questions.

1. How are adverbs generally formed in French? ____________________.
2. What adjective form is necessary to make an adverb? ________________.
3. When does French require the feminine form of an adjective to make an adverb? ____________________.

4. Where are adverbs of time and place put in a sentence? ________________.
5. Name two adverbs of place: ________________ and ________________.
6. Name two adverbs of time: ________________ and ________________.
7. Where are French adverbs placed in negative sentences? ________________.

B. Give the adverbial equivalent of the following adjectives.

1. gentil ____________
2. heureux ____________
3. actif ____________
4. bref ____________
5. intelligent ____________
6. absolu ____________
7. courant ____________
8. évident ____________
9. triste ____________
10. certain ____________
11. rapide ____________
12. apparent ____________
13. seul ____________
14. élégant ____________

ANSWERS FOR LESSONS 11–15

Lesson 11

Vocabulary

Practice A.

1. J'ai deux yeux.
2. J'ai deux oreilles.
3. J'ai deux pieds.
4. J'ai deux jambes.
5. J'ai deux chevilles.
6. J'ai deux genoux.
7. J'ai deux épaules.
8. J'ai deux poumons.
9. J'ai deux sourcils.
10. J'ai deux bras.

B.

1. Ils sont tombés malades hier.
2. Où avez-vous mal?
3. Est-ce que la malle était lourde?
4. Il se sent faible.
5. Nous pouvons nous guérir.
6. Prends (prenez) soin de toi (de vous).
7. Comment allez-vous? Allez-vous mieux aujourd'hui?
8. Je me sens beaucoup mieux quand je me repose.
9. Donne-moi ta main, je veux la voir (*or*) Donnez-moi votre main . . .
10. J'ai été malade pendant une semaine.

Dialog Exercises

A.

1. Charles est le frère de "Moi."
2. Il voulait dire qu'il avait une nouvelle voisine.
3. Les cheveux de la voisine sont blonds, frisés et longs.
4. La sœur de Charles est en colère parce qu'elle dormait (or) parce que Charles l'a réveillée.
5. Non, les cheveux de "Moi" ne sont pas blonds.
6. "Moi" a dormi tard parce que c'était le dimanche.
7. Le téléphone a sonné à midi et demi.
8. "Moi" est sarcastique.
9. Charles est du monde où les hommes n'ont pas de tact.
10. Les dents de la voisine sont légèrement imparfaites.
11. Non, la voisine n'a pas parlé à Charles.
12. La voisine a montré ses dents quand elle lui a fait un grand sourire.
13. Non, "Moi" n'est pas malade.
14. Non, Charles n'a pas fait la connaissance de la voisine.

B.

1. Nous marchons avec les pieds.
2. Nous regardons avec les yeux.
3. Nous sentons avec le nez.
4. Nous entendons avec les oreilles.
5. Nous écrivons avec la main.

6. Nous mangeons avec la bouche.
7. Nous mâchons avec les dents.
8. Nous touchons avec les doigts (or) avec les mains.

Grammar I

Practice A.
1. adjectives
2. nouns expressing numbers and amounts
3. plus de . . . que
4. plus que . . . and plus de . . . que
5. moins que
6. Il est plus sérieux qu'elle.
7. Elle a moins de vingt dollars.
8. Nous parlons plus sérieusement que vous.
9. after the verb
10. with nouns expressing numbers and amounts

B.
1. plus tard que
2. plus vite que
3. plus facile que
4. plus lourdes que
5. plus souvent que
6. plus sociables que
7. moins bavardes que
8. plus long que
9. plus d'argent que
10. moins intelligente que

Grammar II

Practice
1. aussi . . . que, autant . . . que, and autant de . . . que.
2. with numbers and amounts
3. as many as, as much as
4. uses *le, la, les* + comparatives
5. They agree in number and gender with modifiers.
6. les meilleurs livres
7. Leurs livres sont meilleurs.
8. Ils parlent mieux.
9. Il se sent pire.
10. Il se sent aussi mal que vous.

Exercise
1. Vous avez moins de courage que nous.
2. Vous attendez moins longtemps que . . .
3. Vous êtes moins charmants que les voisins.
4. La téléphononiste est moins sérieuse que la concierge.
5. La caisse d'épargne est moins près que la banque.
6. Les parents sont moins bavards que les enfants.

Grammar III

Practice

1. ai, as, a, ons, ez, ont
2. to the infinitive
3. no
4. yes
5. dependent clause + *when*
6. ils pourront
7. ils sauront plus que nous.
8. il faudra
9. il vaudra mieux
10. il mangera aussitôt qu'il reviendra.

Exercise

1. Ma soeur sera invitée chez la voisine.
2. Nous trouverons un petit hôtel charmant.
3. Vous pourrez m'aider à préparer, le dîner.
4. Juliette travaillera à la banque.
5. Nous irons à Paris après la Noël.
6. Elle apprendra à jouer de la harpe.
7. Nous saurons écrire le chinois.

Lesson 12

Vocabulary

Practice

A.
1. un
2. une
3. une
4. une
5. un
6. une
7. un
8. une
9. une
10. un
11. un
12. un
13. un
14. une
15. un

B.
1. gros
2. calmant
3. dent
4. barbier
5. poissonnerie
6. plombage
7. balance
8. alimentation
9. (se) raser
10. maigre

C.
1. se rasera
2. maigrira
3. ne sera pas
4. faudra
5. usera
6. avalera
7. perdront . . . abuseront

Dialog Exercises

A.
1. Parce qu'elle a une crise de foie.
2. Les pilules la soulagent.
3. Le docteur Blanchard a prescrit les pilules.

4. C'est un calmant.
5. Parce qu'il faut prendre les pilules trois fois par jour.
6. "User mais pas abuser." (*or*) "User sans abuser."
7. Cela ne vous fera pas mal.
8. Un tube de pâte dentifrice, des losanges pour la gorge, et des lames de rasoir.
9. Le prix est de quarante-deux francs.
10. Mme Bellan et sa fille avaient la grippe.

B. sentait, est allée . . . a conseillé . . . a acheté . . . a payé . . . a fait . . . avait . . . a gardé . . . est soulagée

C. 1. F
2. G
3. E
4. H
5. A
6. C
7. D
8. B

Grammar I

Practice A.
1. in the *nous* form of the present indicative
2. que nous formions
3. être et avoir
4. qu'il finisse
5. Je veux que tu attendes ici.
6. a dependent clause with *que* and an independent clause
7. in the indicative
8. Il est possible qu'elle parte.
9. emotion, doubt
10. Nous voulons que vous écoutiez.

B.
1. achetions
2. finisse
3. attendes
4. demandiez
5. refusions

Grammar II

Practice A.
1. in the spelling
2. rappeler, se rappeler, épeler (to spell)
3. changer, ranger (to put away or to put in order)
4. payer, employer
5. to make *c* and *g* into softer sounds
6. nous essayions (and) vous essayiez
7. Je veux que vous payiez votre facture (*or*) que tu paies ta facture.
8. Ils veulent que vous appeliez un docteur.
9. Elle insiste que je reste au lit (*or*) que je garde le lit.
10. Je veux que vous commenciez à étudier le français.

B. 1. que nous voyagions
2. que tu partages
3. que nous épelions
4. que vous employiez
5. que nous achetions
6. que nous balancions
7. qu'ils achètent
8. que vous changiez
9. que tu rappelles
10. que je paie

Grammar III

Practice A. 1. Il faut qu'elle parle souvent.
2. Il est bon que vous vous reposiez.
3. Il est important que nous essayions tout.
4. Il est naturel que vous commenciez . . .
5. Il est certain qu'elle ne jugera personne.
6. Il est juste que vous voyagiez . . .
7. Il est nécessaire que nous ne répondions pas . . .
8. Il est temps que notre réputation grandisse . . .
9. Il vaut mieux que nous finissions . . .
10. Il est douteux que nous payions . . .

B. 1. que vous finissiez
2. que vous réussissiez
3. que vous payiez
4. que vous irez
5. que nous sommes . . .
6. que vous partagiez
7. que je parte
8. que les voisins achètent
9. que nous commencions
10. que tu payeras

Lesson 13

Vocabulary

Practice A. 1. un
2. un
3. un
4. une
5. un
6. une
7. une
8. un
9. un
10. une
11. une
12. une

B. 1. accélérateur
2. avant
3. gonfler
4. chauffage
5. panne
6. capot
7. freiner
8. assuré
9. stationner
10. allumer

Dialog Exercises

A. 1. à côté de la voiture
2. ils sont medecins, docteurs
3. parce qu'il n'a pas trouvé son mécanicien
4. d'apporter une boisson
5. les phares, les freins, les indicateurs
6. parce qu'il n'y a pas d'essence
7. à côté du trottoir

B. 1. que tu commences
2. que tu te reposes
3. que tu partes
4. que tu gardes
5. que tu essaies
6. que tu t'arrêtes
7. que tu gaspilles
8. que tu surveilles

Grammar I

Exercise 1. Il faut que Marc attende.
2. Il est douteux que Marie aille au cinéma sans son fiancé.
3. Il est douteux que Monsieur Bertrand connaisse les projets de Jacques.
4. Il faut que vous alliez chercher le mécanicien.
5. Il est nécessaire que nous ayons du courage.

Grammar II

Practice A. 1. Indicative = fact, subjunctive = opinion
2. When the subject is the same in the two clauses.
3. Je veux chanter (or any verb).
4. Pensent-ils que nous aimions le vin blanc? (*or*) Ils ne pensent pas que nous aimions le vin blanc.
5. in the negative and interrogative forms
6. Je ne crois pas qu'il puisse changer.
7. dire
8. Vous dîtes qu'il ait de la chance.

B. 1. puissions
2. ont
3. soient
4. fassent
5. peut
6. vont
7. connaissent

Grammar III

Review Exercise

1. Je sais que vous savez tout.
2. Crois-tu tout savoir? (*or*) Crois-tu que tu sais tout?
3. Il est évident que vous savez tout.
4. Nous savons que vous savez tout.
5. Il est certain que vous savez tout.
6. Il est probable que vous sachiez tout.
7. Il est impossible que vous sachiez tout.
8. Je ne crois pas que vous sachiez tout.
9. Je suis sûr que vous savez tout.
10. Il est défendu que vous sachiez tout.

Lesson 14

Vocabulary

Practice

A.

1. le (masc.)	7. la (fem.)	13. l' (masc.)
2. le (masc.)	8. le (masc.)	14. la (fem.)
3. la (fem.)	9. le (masc.)	15. le (masc.)
4. le (masc.)	10. la (fem.)	16. le (masc.)
5. le (masc.)	11. l' (fem.)	17. le (masc.)
6. le (masc.)	12. la (fem.)	18. le (masc.)

B.

1. résoudre	9. vendre
2. imprimer	10. aimer
3. coller	11. allumer
4. écrire	12. compter
5. dessiner	13. conduire
6. brancher	14. décider
7. sortir	15. transformer
8. entrer	

C.

1. l'achat	7. la préférence
2. le commencement	8. l'imprimante
3. la décision	9. la colle
4. la suite	10. la conduite
5. la réussite	11. la sortie
6. l'entrée	12. l'accession

D.

1. joyeux, euse	7. poli, polie
2. souriant(e)	8. brumeux (euse)
3. beau, belle	9. ensoleillé (e)
4. courtois, courtoise	10. lumineux (euse)
5. gentil, gentille	11. journalier (ière)
6. mensuel, mensuelle	12. grand (e)

Dialog Exercises

A.

1. T	6. F	11. F
2. F	7. F	12. T
3. T	8. F	13. F
4. F	9. F	14. F
5. F	10. T	15. T

B.
1. Je travaille sans cesse.
2. J'aime étudier l'informatique.
3. Je vais enseigner la biologie.
4. Je ne sais pas conduire.
5. Mon ordinateur marche très bien.
6. Il faut travailler pour vivre.
7. Il y aura de la place pour mon ami(e).
8. Les périphériques sont des appareils électroniques.
9. Le travail c'est la santé; le repos c'est la conserver.
10. La puce de l'ordinateur est une partie essentielle de l'informatique.
11. Je viens de rentrer d'un long voyage.
12. Je vais faire des versements mensuels.
13. Le matériel est aussi compliqué que le logiciel.

Grammar I

Practice
1. Il vient de vous téléphoner.
2. Nous venons d'envoyer votre lettre.
3. Ils viennent d'acheter une voiture.
4. Je viens de brancher la table traçante.
5. Elle vient de sortir.
6. Vous venez de résoudre notre problème.

Grammar II

Practice
1. Je vais vendre ma voiture.
2. Il allait déjeuner avec nous.
3. Allez-vous conduire jusqu'à New York?
4. Allez-vous enseigner à Los Angeles?
5. Vont-ils rester avec nous?
6. Vous allez utiliser votre ordinateur.

Grammar III

Exercises A.
1. Il ne fallait pas acheter du pain.
2. Il faudra être gentil.
3. Il faudrait suivre les règles.
4. Il faut se reposer. (or) On doit se reposer.

5. Il fallait conduire doucement.
6. Il a fallu finir le travail.
7. Il ne faut pas être méchant. (or) On ne doit pas être méchant.
8. On ne devrait pas rester debout. (or) Il ne faudrait pas rester debout.
9. Il ne faudra pas s'asseoir par terre.
10. On doit apprendre ses leçons. (or) Il faut apprendre ses leçons.

B.
1. C'est dommage.
2. Ce serait gentil.
3. Ce sera correct.
4. Ce n'est pas votre faute.
5. C'était dommage.
6. Cela (ça) aurait été gentil.
7. Ce n'était pas nécessaire.
8. Ce ne sera pas compliqué.
9. Cela (ça) a été un plaisir.
10. Cela n'a pas été comme d'habitude.

C.
1. Il y a beaucoup de monde (*or*) de personnes, de gens.
2. Il y a assez de soleil.
3. Il y aura un arc-en-ciel.
4. Il y a de la gentillesse.
5. Il n'y a pas assez d'ordinateurs.
6. Il y aurait un contrat.
7. Il y a eu du bruit.
8. Il y aura un nouvel écran.
9. Il y avait assez d'accessoires.
10. Il y a beaucoup de Français à San Francisco.

Lesson 15

Understanding Cognates

A.
1. capacity
2. geometry
3. analogy
4. monster
5. ordinary
6. fervor
7. music
8. estuary
9. serious
10. logic
11. Australian
12. abusive
13. active
14. moderate
15. temporary
16. affirm
17. banish
18. chemist
19. offer
20. absolutely
21. dangerous
22. cultivate
23. irritate
24. multiply

Grammar I

Practice A.
1. the infinitive
2. by adding to the infinitive the *imparfait* endings
3. with wishes and requests
4. the imperfect
5. ils finiraient, elle rendrait

B.
1. j'achèterais
2. nous examinerions
3. nous partirions
4. ils sortiraient
5. elle mangerait
6. nous admirerions
7. elle apprendrait
8. il finirait
9. tu preparerais
10. tu t'ennuyerais

C.
1. nous partirions
2. elle jouerait
3. vous sortiriez
4. il s'amuserait
5. tu attendrais
6. ils achèteraient
7. tu mangerais
8. nous finirions
9. elle admirerait
10. ils aimeraient

Grammar II

Practice A.
1. the conditional
2. saurais
3. il pourrait
4. nous apprendrions
5. tu saurais
6. elle devrait
7. tu ferais
8. vous verriez
9. il voudrait
10. nous irions

B.
1. ferai
2. pourrons
3. fianceront
4. aura
5. saurez
6. iras
7. faudra
8. ferons
9. gardera
10. verrez, viendrez

C.
1. vous aviez, vous aurez, vous auriez
2. tu achetais, tu achèteras, tu achèterais
3. vous veniez, vous viendrez, vous viendriez
4. elle apprenait, elle apprendra, elle apprendrait
5. tu finissais, tu finiras, tu finirais
6. elle allait, elle ira, elle irait
7. tu voyais, tu verras, tu verrais
8. nous savions, nous saurons, nous saurions
9. elle attendait, elle attendra, elle attendrait
10. nous avions, nous aurons, nous aurions

Grammar III

Practice

A.
1. by adding *-ment* to the adjective
2. the masculine form
3. when the masculine form ends with a consonant
4. the beginning or end of sentences
5. ici (and) là-bas
6. demain (and) bientôt
7. after *pas*

B.
1. gentiment
2. heureusement
3. activement
4. brièvement
5. intelligemment
6. absolument
7. couramment
8. évidemment
9. tristement
10. certainement
11. rapidement
12. apparemment
13. seulement
14. élégamment

REVIEW EXAM FOR LESSONS 11–15

(Answers, pp. 236–237)

Part I: VOCABULARY

A. Match the two columns (some of the articles may not be needed).

1. ______ les poumons
2. ______ le nez
3. ______ les doigts
4. ______ les oreilles
5. ______ la langue
6. ______ la fièvre
7. ______ la grippe
8. ______ le rhume
9. ______ la toux
10. ______ l'ordonnance
11. ______ le remède
12. ______ le calmant
13. ______ la crise
14. ______ le médicament
15. ______ le soulagement
16. ______ la ceinture
17. ______ la matricule
18. ______ l'indicateur
19. ______ la bouche
20. ______ la gorge

A. On sent les fleurs avec . . .
B. On mange et on parle avec
C. On l'utilise pour tourner à droite.
D. On en a besoin, quand on a une voiture
E. C'est prudent de l'attacher quand on conduit
F. Il vient quand on est guéri
G. Nous aide à guérir
H. Quand elle arrive, on a très mal
I. C'est un soulagement
J. C'est souvent un médicament
K. Le docteur écrit le nom des médicaments
L. On l'a quand on a mal à la gorge
M. Commence par un mal de tête
N. C'est un rhume compliqué
O. Elle accompagne la grippe
P. Nous parlons avec la
Q. Nous entendons avec les
R. On touche avec
S. On respire avec
T. Il est difficile d'avaler avec un mal de . . .

B. Complete the sentences with the most appropriate word, using the proper article, and adding *de* or *d'* to verbs when needed.

1. Je ne peux pas m'arrêter si __________ (compte-goutte, espoir, freins) ne marchent pas.
2. J'ai besoin d'acheter deux __________ (voiture, balance, brosses) avant de sortir de la pharmacie.
3. J'ai beaucoup grossi, alors le docteur m'a conseillé de suivre __________ (crise, régime, drogue).
4. Il est impossible de faire marcher le moteur sans __________ (démarreur, essuie-glace, essence).
5. Le garagiste a changé mon pneu parce que j'ai eu une __________ (phare, roue, crevaison).
6. Chaque fois que j'ai __________ (radiologie, maladie, grippe) j'ai très mal à la tête et à la gorge.
7. En France la __________ (matricule, feu rouge, vitesse) limite est de 55 miles.
8. Il est toujours prudent __________ (essayer, attacher, allumer) les ceintures quand on conduit.
9. Quand on doit faire un long voyage il faut faire __________ (nettoyer, ralentir, vérifier) la voiture.
10. J'ai eu une panne sèche parce que j'ai oublié de __________ (dégonfler, faire le plein, faire marche arrière).
11. La voiture a capoté, alors on l'a fait __________ (stationner, remorquer, reculer).
12. On préfère souvent acheter une voiture luxueuse que __________ (occasion, assuré, moteur).

C. Write a related word for each of the following words. (The related word may be a verb, noun, or adjective.)

1. tousser __________
2. soulager __________
3. le repos __________
4. calmer __________
5. grossir __________
6. la balance __________
7. l'allumette __________
8. alimenter __________

9. espérer ____________
10. tard ____________
11. enrhumé ____________
12. ennuyer ____________
13. démarreur ____________
14. dépanner ____________
15. freiner ____________
16. la main ____________
17. la volonté ____________
18. l'habitude ____________
19. maigrir ____________
20. indiquer ____________

D. Select the appropriate answer by circling the letter.

1. L'année prochaine j'achèterai une voiture de luxe.
   a. Ma voiture est toujours en panne.
   b. Il est vrai que ma voiture ne marche pas bien.
   c. Hier j'ai fait nettoyer le pare-brise.
   d. Les freins et l'embrayage sont très importants.

2. Le docteur a prescrit un calmant pour la crise de foie.
   a. Ces crises-là sont souvent désagréables.
   b. Ce genre de crise est fréquent chez les Français.
   c. Le docteur donne de bons conseils.
   d. On trouve des hypochondriaques partout.

3. Les marques de voitures françaises sont populaires ici.
   a. Quand on veut acheter une voiture, on choisit la meilleure marque.
   b. Les Peugeot et les Renault sont partout dans cette ville.
   c. Il aime les voitures françaises.
   d. Les voitures de luxe sont souvent trop chères.

4. Il est toujours prudent de respecter la vitesse limite.
   a. Les Français conduisent aussi vite que les Américains.
   b. Quand on conduit trop vite on peut tamponner une autre voiture.
   c. L'agent a le droit de t'arrêter si tu n'as pas la plaque d'immatriculation

5. Le chauffeur de taxi veut mettre ta malle dans le coffre.
   a. Les chauffeurs de taxi sont souvent pressés.
   b. Les bagages prennent trop de place.
   c. Les bagages et les passagers sont séparés.
   d. Le taxi était libre quand nous sommes arrivés.

6. Crois-tu que maigrir ou grossir est plutôt psychologique?
   a. Cette question ne m'intéresse pas.
   b. La psychologie est une science intéressante.
   c. Le boucher et le boulanger sont des marchands comme l'épicier.

PART II: GRAMMAR

A. Write the appropriate future form of the verbs between parentheses.

1. Les questions ____________ (être) longues.
2. Le médicament la ____________ (soulager) demain.
3. Il ____________ (dire) la vérité à l'agent.
4. Il ____________ (faut) partir bientôt.
5. Nous ____________ (pouvoir) finir ce travail-là.
6. Ils ____________ (aller) avec nous au théâtre.
7. Dimanche prochain tu ____________ (savoir) la vérité.
8. Ils ____________ (avoir) beaucoup de plaisir à vous revoir.
9. Vous ____________ (voir) comme c'est facile de ne pas fumer.
10. Ils ____________ (arriver) à temps pour la Noël.

B. Complete the following sentences with the present indicative or the present subjunctive as required.

1. Il est vrai que nos voisins ____________ (être) toujours absents.
2. Nous voulons que vous ____________ (guérir) très bientôt.
3. Il n'est pas nécessaire que tu ____________ (faire) ce travail-là.
4. Nous sommes certains que vous ____________ (aller) avec nous ce soir.
5. Le sénateur n'est pas sûr qu'il ____________ (pouvoir) gagner l'élection.
6. Ma fiancée veut une chambre qui ____________ (avoir) une grande armoire à clef.
7. Le patron a défendu que nous ____________ (bavarder) entre nous.
8. Il est utile que nous ____________ (savoir) les règles du jeu (rules of the game).
9. Je regrette que la leçon ____________ (être) longue.
10. Il est important qu'ils ____________ (avoir) assez d'argent pour le loyer.

C. Complete the sentences with the most appropriate word or expression.

1. Je ne sais rien qui ____________ l'aider.
   a. soit c. ait
   b. puisse d. fasse

2. Il était ____________ quand il m'a téléphoné.
   a. plus tard c. sans cesse
   b. volontiers d. en panne

3. Elle était très sophistiquée et bien habillée, elle portait ____________ vert.
   a. une robe c. un ensemble
   b. un collant d. un costume

4. Avant de commencer à écrire, je dois ____________ l'imprimante.
   a. imprimer c. résoudre
   b. brancher d. coller

5. Ce n'est pas nécessaire que tu ____________ manier le tournevis pour faire marcher un ordinateur.
   a. ailles c. saches
   b. finisses d. réussisses

6. L'épicier m'a dit qu'il ne vend pas de lait, c'est à la crèmerie que je le ____________.
   a. ferai c. sortirai
   b. irai d. trouverai

7. Quand on conduit, pour changer de la première vitesse à la quatrième, il faut employer ____________.
   a. le signe c. le volant
   b. le phare d. l'embrayage

8. Je lui ai demandé de partir et il a dit "____________."
   a. "Je voudrais bien." c. "Je suis fatigué."
   b. "Je n'ai pas entendu." d. "Je suis pressé."

9. L'épicier, le boucher, et le laitier sont des ____________.
   a. voisins c. amis
   b. marchands commerçants d. hommes

10. Il faut que je ____________ quand j'arrive au feu rouge.
    a. m'arrête c. change de vitesse
    b. freine d. ralentisse

11. Quand j'avais la grippe je ____________ beaucoup.
    a. toussais c. m'amusais
    b. jouais d. dansais

12. Il est illégal que vous ne ___________ pas assuré.
    a. vouliez
    b. soyez
    c. passiez
    d. puissiez

13. Mon professeur parle cinq langues ___________.
    a. terriblement
    b. couramment
    c. sérieusement
    d. complètement

14. Nous voudrions que vous ___________ avec nous.
    a. sortiez
    b. alliez
    c. mangiez
    d. partiez

REVIEW EXAM: ANSWERS

LESSONS 11–16

Vocabulary

A.
1. S
2. A
3. R
4. Q
5. B
6. O
7. N
8. M
9. L
10. K
11. J
12. I
13. H
14. G
15. F
16. E
17. D
18. C
19. P
20. T

B.
1. les freins . . .
2. brosses
3. un régime
4. essence
5. une crevaison
6. la grippe
7. vitesse
8. d'attacher
9. vérifier
10. faire le plein
11. remorquer
12. qu'une d'occasion

C.
1. la toux
2. le soulagement
3. se reposer
4. un calmant
5. gros (grosse)
6. balancer
7. allumer
8. l'alimentation
9. l'espoir
10. tarder (en retard)
11. le rhume (un)
12. l'ennui (un)
13. démarrer
14. une panne (la)
15. les freins
16. manuel, manuelle
17. vouloir
18. s'habituer
19. maigre
20. l'indicateur

D.
1. a
2. b
3. b
4. b
5. c
6. a

Grammar

A.
1. seront
2. soulagera
3. dira
4. faudra
5. nous pourrons
6. iront
7. sauras
8. auront
9. verrez
10. arriveront

B.
1. sont
2. guérissiez
3. fasses
4. irez (or) allez
5. puisse
6. ait
7. bavardions
8. sachions
9. soit
10. aient

C.
1. b
2. d
3. c
4. b
5. c
6. d
7. d
8. a (or) c
9. b
10. a
11. a
12. b
13. b
14. c (or) a

Appendix A

Regular Verbs

This appendix contains examples of the conjugation rules for each of the three regular verb forms; those ending in -ER, -IR, and -RE. All regular verbs follow these rules.

parler to speak

Present Participle
parlant, speaking

Past Participle
parlé, spoken

Imperative
parle
parlons
parlez

Present Indicative
je parle
tu parles
il, elle parle
nous parlons
vous parlez
ils, elles parlent

Imperfect
je parlais
tu parlais
il, elle parlait
nous parlions
vous parliez
ils, elles parlaient

Passé Composé
j'ai parlé
tu as parlé
il, elle a parlé
nous avons parlé
vous avez parlé
ils, elles ont parlé

Future
je parlerai
tu parleras
il, elle parlera
nous parlerons
vous parlerez
ils, elles parleront

Conditional
je parlerais
tu parlerais
il, elle parlerait
nous parlerions
vous parleriez
ils, elles parleraient

Present Subjunctive
que je parle
que tu parles
qu'il, elle parle
que nous parlions
que vous parliez
qu'ils, elles parlent

finir to finish

Present Participle
finissant, finishing

Past Participle
fini, finished

Imperative
finis
finissons
finissez

Present Indicative
je finis
tu finis
il, elle finit
nous finissons
vous finissez
ils, elles finissent

Imperfect
je finissais
tu finissais
il, elle finissait
nous finissions
vous finissiez
ils, elles finissaient

Passé Composé
j'ai fini
tu as fini
il, elle a fini
nous avons fini
vous avez fini
ils, elles ont fini

Future
je finirai
tu finiras
il, elle finira
nous finirons
vous finirez
ils, elles finiront

Conditional
je finirais
tu finirais
il, elle finirait
nous finirions
vous finiriez
ils, elles finiraient

Present Subjunctive
que je finisse
que tu finisses
qu'il, elle finisse
que nous finissions
que vous finissiez
qu'ils, elles finissent

attendre to wait

Present Participle
attendant, waiting

Past Participle
attendu, waited

Imperative
attends
attendons
attendez

Present Indicative
j'attends
tu attends
il, elle attend
nous attendons
vous attendez
ils, elles attendent

Imperfect
j'attendais
tu attendais
il, elle attendait
nous attendions
vous attendiez
ils, elles attendaient

Passé Composé
j'ai attendu
tu as attendu
il, elle a attendu
nous avons attendu
vous avez attendu
ils, elles ont attendu

Future
j'attendrai
tu attendras
il, elle attendra
nous attendrons
vous attendrez
ils, elles attendront

Conditional
j'attendrais
tu attendrais
il, elle attendrait
nous attendrions
vous attendriez
ils, elles attendraient

Present Subjunctive
que j'attende
que tu attendes
qu'il, elle attende
que nous attendions
que vous attendiez
qu'ils, elles attendent

Appendix B

Irregular Verbs

This appendix contains a sampling of the irregular verbs and their conjugations. Most irregular verbs follow the conjugation rules exemplified by the verbs in this section.

aller to go

Present Participle
allant, going

Past Participle
allé(e), gone

Imperative
va (tu)
allons (nous)
allez (vous)

Present Indicative	**Imperfect**	**Passé Composé**
je vais	j'allais	je suis allé(e)
tu vas	tu allais	tu es allé(e)
il, elle va	il, elle allait	il, elle est allé(e)
nous allons	nous allions	nous sommes allé(e)s
vous allez	vous alliez	vous êtes allé(e)s
ils, elles vont	ils, elles allaient	ils, elles sont allé(e)s

Future	**Conditional**	**Present Subjunctive**
j'irai	j'irais	que j'aille
tu iras	tu irais	que tu ailles
il, elle ira	il, elle irait	qu'il, elle aille
nous irons	nous irions	que nous allions
vous irez	vous iriez	que vous alliez
ils, elles iront	ils, elles iraient	qu'ils, elles aillent

avoir to have

Present Participle
ayant, having

Past Participle
eu, had

Imperative
aie
ayons
ayez

Present Indicative	Imperfect	Passé Composé
j'ai	j'avais	j'ai eu
tu as	tu avais	tu as eu
il, elle a	il, elle avait	il, elle a eu
nous avons	nous avions	nous avons eu
vous avez	vous aviez	vous avez eu
ils, elles ont	ils, elles avaient	ils, elles ont eu
Future	**Conditional**	**Present Subjunctive**
j'aurai	j'aurais	que j'aie
tu auras	tu aurais	que tu aies
il, elle aura	il, elle aurait	qu'il, elle ait
nous aurons	nous aurions	que nous ayons
vous aurez	vous auriez	que vous ayez
ils, elles auront	ils, elles auraient	qu'ils, elles aient

boire to drink

Present Participle
buvant, drinking

Past Participle
bu, drunk

Imperative
bois
buvons
buvez

Present Indicative	Imperfect	Passé Composé
je bois	je buvais	j'ai bu
tu bois	tu buvais	tu as bu
il, elle boit	il, elle buvait	il, elle a bu
nous buvons	nous buvions	nous avons bu
vous buvez	vous buviez	vous avez bu
ils, elles boivent	ils, elles buvaient	ils, elles ont bu
Future	**Conditional**	**Present Subjunctive**
je boirai	je boirais	que je boive
tu boiras	tu boirais	que tu boives
il, elle boira	il, elle boirait	qu'il, elle boive
nous boirons	nous boirions	que nous buvions
vous boirez	vous boiriez	que vous buviez
ils, elles boiront	ils, elles boiraient	qu'ils, elles boivent

conduire to drive

Present Participle
conduisant, driving

Past Participle
conduit, driven

Imperative
conduis
conduisons
conduisez

Present Indicative	Imperfect	Passé Composé
je conduis	je conduisais	j'ai conduit
tu conduis	tu conduisais	tu as conduit
il, elle conduit	il, elle conduisait	il, elle a conduit
nous conduisons	nous conduisions	nous avons conduit
vous conduisez	vous conduisiez	vous avez conduit
ils, elles conduisent	ils, elles conduisaient	ils, elles ont conduit

Future
je conduirai
tu conduiras
il, elle conduira
nous conduirons
vous conduirez
ils, elles conduiront

Conditional
je conduirais
tu conduirais
il, elle conduirait
nous conduirions
vous conduiriez
ils, elles conduiraient

Present Subjunctive
que je conduise
que tu conduises
qu'il, elle conduise
que nous conduisions
que vous conduisiez
qu'ils, elles conduisent

connaître to know

Present Participle
connaissant, knowing

Past Participle
connu, known

Imperative
connais
connaissons
connaissez

Present Indicative
je connais
tu connais
il, elle connaît
nous connaissons
vous connaissez
ils, elles connaissent

Imperfect
je connaissais
tu connaissais
il, elle connaissait
nous connaissions
vous connaissiez
ils, elles connaissaient

Passé Composé
j'ai connu
tu as connu
il, elle a connu
nous avons connu
vous avez connu
ils, elles ont connu

Future
je connaîtrai
tu connaîtras
il, elle connaîtra
nous connaîtrons
vous connaîtrez
ils, elles connaîtront

Conditional
je connaîtrais
tu connaîtrais
il, elle connaîtrait
nous connaîtrions
vous connaîtriez
ils, elles connaîtraient

Present Subjunctive
que je connaisse
que tu connaisses
qu'il, elle connaisse
que nous connaissions
que vous connaissiez
qu'ils, elles connaissent

croire to believe

Present Participle
croyant, believing

Past Participle
cru, believed

Imperative
crois
croyons
croyez

Present Indicative
je crois
tu crois
il, elle croit
nous croyons
vous croyez
ils, elles croient

Imperfect
je croyais
tu croyais
il, elle croyait
nous croyions
vous croyiez
ils, elles croyaient

Passé Composé
j'ai cru
tu as cru
il, elle a cru
nous avons cru
vous avez cru
ils, elles ont cru

Future
je croirai
tu croiras
il, elle croira
nous croirons
vous croirez
ils, elles croiront

Conditional
je croirais
tu croirais
il, elle croirait
nouus croirions
vous croiriez
ils, elles croiraient

Present Subjunctive
que je croie
que tu croies
qu'il, elle croie
que nous croyions
que vous croyiez
qu'ils, elles croient

devoir to have to, to owe

Present Participle
devant, having to, owing

Past Participle
dû, had to, owed

Imperative
None

Present Indicative	Imperfect	Passé Composé
je dois	je devais	j'ai dû
tu dois	tu devais	tu as dû
il, elle doit	il, elle devait	il, elle a dû
nous devons	nous devions	nous avons dû
vous devez	vous deviez	vous avez dû
ils, elles doivent	ils, elles devaient	ils, elles ont dû
Future	**Conditional**	**Present Subjunctive**
je devrai	je devrais	que je doive
tu devras	tu devrais	que tu doives
il, elle devra	il, elle devrait	qu'il, elle doive
nous devrons	nous devrions	que nous devions
vous devrez	vous devriez	que vous deviez
ils, elles devront	ils, elles devraient	qu'ils, elles doivent

dire to say

Present Participle
disant, saying

Past Participle
dit, said

Imperative
dis
disons
dîtes

Present Indicative	Imperfect	Passé Composé
je dis	je disais	j'ai dit
tu dis	tu disais	tu as dit
il, elle dit	il, elle disait	il, elle a dit
nous disons	nous disions	nous avons dit
vous dîtes	vous disiez	vous avez dit
ils, elles disent	ils, elles disaient	ils, elles ont dit
Future	**Conditional**	**Present Subjunctive**
je dirai	je dirais	que je dise
tu diras	tu dirais	que tu dises
il, elle dira	il, elle dirait	qu'il, elle dise
nous dirons	nous dirions	que nous disions
vous direz	vous direz	que vous disiez
ils, elles diront	ils, elles diraient	qu'ils, elles disent

dormir to sleep

Present Participle
dormant, sleeping

Past Participle
dormi, slept

Imperative
dors
dormons
dormez

Present Indicative
je dors
tu dors
il, elle dort
nous dormons
vous dormez
ils, elles dorment

Imperfect
je dormais
tu dormais
il, elle dormait
nous dormions
vous dormiez
ils, elles dormaient

Passé Composé
j'ai dormi
tu as dormi
il, elle a dormi
nous avons dormi
vous avez dormi
ils, elles ont dormi

Future
je dormirai
tu dormiras
il, elle dormira
nous dormirons
vous dormirez
ils, elles dormiront

Conditional
je dormirais
tu dormirais
il, elle dormirait
nous dormirions
vous dormiriez
ils, elles dormiraient

Present Subjunctive
que je dorme
que tu dormes
qu'il, elle dorme
que nous dormions
que vous dormiez
qu'ils, elles dorment

écrire to write

Present Participle
écrivant, writing

Past Participle
écrit, written

Imperative
écris
écrivons
écrivez

Present Indicative
j'écris
tu écris
il, elle écrit
nous écrivons
vous écrivez
ils, elles écrivent

Imperfect
j'écrivais
tu écrivais
il, elle écrivait
nous écrivions
vous écriviez
ils, elles écrivaient

Passé Composé
j'ai écrit
tu as écrit
il, elle a écrit
nous avons écrit
vous avez écrit
ils, elles ont écrit

Future
j'écrirai
tu écriras
il, elle écrira
nous écrirons
vous écrirez
ils, elles écriront

Conditional
j'écrirais
tu écrirais
il, elle écrirait
nous écririons
vous écririez
ils, elles écriraient

Present Subjunctive
que j'écrive
que tu écrives
qu'il, elle écrive
que nous écrivions
que vous écriviez
qu'ils, elles écrivent

être to be

Present Participle
étant, being

Past Participle
été, been

Imperative
sois
soyons
soyez

Present Indicative
je suis
tu es
il, elle est
nous sommes
vous êtes
ils, elles sont

Imperfect
j'étais
tu étais
il, elle était
nous étions
vous étiez
ils, elles étaient

Passé Composé
j'ai été
tu as été
il, elle a été
nous avons été
vous avez été
ils, elles ont été

Future	Conditional	Present Subjunctive
je serai	je serais	que je sois
tu seras	tu serais	que tu sois
il, elle sera	il, elle serait	qu'il, elle soit
nous serons	nous serions	que nous soyons
vous serez	vous seriez	que vous soyez
ils, elles seront	ils, elles seraient	qu'ils, elles soient

faire to do, to make

Present Participle
faisant, doing, making

Past Participle
fait, done, made

Imperative
fais
faisons
faites

Present Indicative	Imperfect	Passé Composé
je fais	je faisais	j'ai fait
tu fais	tu faisais	tu as fait
il, elle fait	il, elle faisait	il, elle a fait
nous faisons	nous faisions	nous avons fait
vous faites	vous faisiez	vous avez fait
ils, elles font	ils, elles faisaient	ils, elles ont fait

Future	Conditional	Present Subjunctive
je ferai	je ferais	que je fasse
tu feras	tu ferais	que tu fasses
il, elle fera	il, elle ferait	qu'il, elle fasse
nous ferons	nous ferions	que nous fassions
vous ferez	vous feriez	que vous fassiez
ils, elles feront	ils, elles feraient	qu'ils, elles fassent

falloir to be necessary (impersonal)

Present Participle
None

Past Participle
fallu, was necessary

Imperative
None

Present Indicative	Imperfect	Passé Composé
—	—	—
—	—	—
il faut	il fallait	il a fallu
—	—	—
—	—	—
—	—	—

Future	Conditional	Present Subjunctive
—	—	—
—	—	—
il faudra	il faudrait	qu'il faille
—	—	—
—	—	—
—	—	—

lire to read

Present Participle
lisant, reading

Past Participle
lu, read

Imperative
lis
lisons
lisez

Present Indicative	Imperfect	Passé Composé
je lis	je lisais	j'ai lu
tu lis	tu lisais	tu as lu
il, elle lit	il, elle lisait	il, elle a lu
nous lisons	nous lisions	nous avons lu
vous lisez	vous lisiez	vous avez lu
ils, elles lisent	ils, elles lisaient	ils, elles ont lu

Future	Conditional	Present Subjunctive
je lirai	je lirais	que je lise
tu liras	tu lirais	que tu lises
il, elle lira	il, elle lirait	qu'il, elle lise
nous lirons	nous lirions	que nous lisions
vous lirez	vous liriez	que vous lisiez
ils, elles liront	ils, elles liraient	qu'ils, elles lisent

mettre to put

Present Participle
mettant, putting

Past Participle
mis, put

Imperative
mets
mettons
mettez

Present Indicative	Imperfect	Passé Composé
je mets	je mettais	j'ai mis
tu mets	tu mettais	tu as mis
il, elle met	il, elle mettait	il, elle a mis
nous mettons	nous mettions	nous avons mis
vous mettez	vous mettiez	vous avez mis
ils, elles mettent	ils, elles mettaient	ils, elles ont mis

Future	Conditional	Present Subjunctive
je mettrai	je mettrais	que je mette
tu mettras	tu mettrais	que tu mettes
il, elle mettra	il, elle mettrait	qu'il, elle mette
nous mettrons	nous mettrions	que nous mettions
vous mettrez	vous mettriez	que vous mettiez
ils, elles mettront	ils, elles mettraient	qu'ils, elles mettent

partir to leave

Present Participle
partant, leaving

Past Participle
parti(e), left

Imperative
pars
partons
partez

Present Indicative	**Imperfect**	**Passé Composé**
je pars	je partais	je suis parti(e)
tu pars	tu partais	tu es parti(e)
il, elle part	il, elle partait	il, elle est parti(e)
nous partons	nous partions	nous sommes parti(e)s
vous partez	vous partiez	vous êtes parti(e)s
ils, elles partent	ils, elles partaient	ils, elles sont parti(e)s

Future	**Conditional**	**Present Subjunctive**
je partirai	je partirais	que je parte
tu partiras	tu partirais	que tu partes
il, elle partira	il, elle partirait	qu'il, elle parte
nous partirons	nous partirions	que nous partions
vous partirez	vous partiriez	que vous partiez
ils, elles partiront	ils, elles partiraient	qu'ils, elles partent

pouvoir to be able to

Present Participle
pouvant, being able to

Past Participle
pu, been able to

Imperative
None

Present Indicative	**Imperfect**	**Passé Composé**
je peux	je pouvais	j'ai pu
tu peux	tu pouvais	tu as pu
il, elle peut	il, elle pouvait	il, elle a pu
nous pouvous	nous pouvions	nous avons pu
vous pouvez	vous pouviez	vous avez pu
ils, elles pouvent	ils, elles pouvaient	ils, elles ont pu

Future	**Conditional**	**Present Subjunctive**
je pourrai	je pourrais	que je puisse
tu pourras	tu pourrais	que tu puisses
il, elle pourra	il, elle pourrait	qu'il, elle puisse
nous pourrons	nous pourrions	que nous puissions
vous pourrez	vous pourriez	que vous puissiez
ils, elles pourront	ils, elles pourraient	qu'ils, elles puissent

prendre to take

Present Participle
prenant, taking

Past Participle
pris, taken

Imperative
prends
prenons
prenez

Present Indicative	**Imperfect**	**Passé Composé**
je prends	je prenais	j'ai pris
tu prends	tu prenais	tu as pris
il, elle prend	il, elle prenait	il, elle a pris
nous prenons	nous prenions	nous avons pris
vous prenez	vous preniez	vous avez pris
ils, elles prennent	ils, elles prenaient	ils, elles ont pris

Future	Conditional	Present Subjunctive
je prendrai	je prendrais	que je prenne
tu prendras	tu prendrais	que tu prennes
il, elle prendra	il, elle prendrait	qu'il, elle prenne
nous prendrons	nous prendrions	que nous prenions
vous prendrez	vous prendriez	que vous preniez
ils, elles prendront	ils, elles prendraient	qu'ils, elles prennent

recevoir to receive

Present Participle
recevant, receiving

Past Participle
reçu, received

Imperative
reçois
recevons
recevez

Present Indicative	Imperfect	Passé Composé
je reçois	je recevais	j'ai reçu
tu reçois	tu recevais	tu as reçu
il, elle reçoit	il, elle recevait	il, elle a reçu
nous recevons	nous recevions	nous avons reçu
vous recevez	vous receviez	vous avez reçu
ils, elles reçoivent	ils, elles recevaient	qu'ils, elles ont reçu

Future	Conditional	Present Subjunctive
je recevrai	je recevrais	que je reçoive
tu recevras	tu recevrais	que tu reçoives
il, elle recevra	il, elle recevrait	qu'il, elle reçoive
nous recevrons	nous recevrions	que nous recevions
vous recevrez	vous recevriez	que vous receviez
ils, elles recevront	ils, elles recevraient	qu'ils, elles reçoivent

savoir to know

Present Participle
sachant, knowing

Past Participle
su, known

Imperative
sache
sachons
sachez

Present Indicative	Imperfect	Passé Composé
je sais	je savais	j'ai su
tu sais	tu savais	tu as su
il, elle sait	il, elle savait	il, elle a su
nous savons	nous savions	nous avons su
vous savez	vous saviez	vous avez su
ils, elles savent	ils, elles savaient	ils, elles ont su

Future	Conditional	Present Subjunctive
je saurai	je saurais	que je sache
tu sauras	tu saurais	que tu saches
il, elle saura	il, elle saurait	qu'il, elle sache
nous saurons	nous saurions	que nous sachions
vous saurez	vous sauriez	que vous sachiez
ils, elles sauront	ils, elles sauraient	qu'ils, elles sachent

sentir to smell, to feel

Present Participle
sentant, smelling, feeling

Past Participle
senti, smelled, felt

Imperative
sens
sentons
sentez

Present Indicative	**Imperfect**	**Passé Composé**
je sens	je sentais	j'ai senti
tu sens	tu sentais	tu as senti
il, elle sent	il, elle sentait	il, elle a senti
nous sentons	nous sentions	nous avons senti
vous sentez	vous sentiez	vous avez senti
ils, elles sentent	ils, elles sentaient	ils, elles ont senti
Future	**Conditional**	**Present Subjunctive**
je sentirai	je sentirais	que je sente
tu sentiras	tu sentirais	que tu sentes
il, elle sentira	il, elle sentirait	qu'il, elle sente
nous sentirons	nous sentirions	que nous sentions
vous sentirez	vous sentiriez	que vous sentiez
ils, elles sentiront	ils, elles sentiraient	qu'ils, elles sentent

servir to serve

Present Participle
servant, serving

Past Participle
servi, served

Imperative
sers
servons
servez

Present Indicative	**Imperfect**	**Passé Composé**
je sers	je servais	j'ai servi
tu sers	tu servais	tu as servi
il, elle sert	il, elle servait	il, elle a servi
nous servons	nous servions	nous avons servi
vous servez	vous serviez	vous avez servi
ils, elles servent	ils, elles servaient	ils, elles ont servi
Future	**Conditional**	**Present Subjunctive**
je servirai	je servirais	que je serve
tu serviras	tu servirais	que tu serves
il, elle servira	il, elle servirait	qu'il, elle serve
nous servirons	nous servirions	que nous servions
vous servirez	vous serviriez	que vous serviez
ils, elles serviront	ils, elles serviraient	qu'ils, elles servent

sortir to go out

Present Participle
sortant, going out

Past Participle
sorti(e), gone out

Imperative
sors
sortons
sortez

Present Indicative	**Imperfect**	**Passé Composé**
je sors	je sortais	je suis sorti(e)
tu sors	tu sortais	tu es sorti(e)
il, elle sort	il, elle sortait	il, elle est sorti(e)
nous sortons	nous sortions	nous sommes sorti(e)s
vous sortez	vous sortiez	vous êtes sorti(e)s
ils, elles sortent	ils, elles sortaient	ils, elles sont sorti(e)s
Future	**Conditional**	**Present Subjunctive**
je sortirai	je sortirais	que je sorte
tu sortiras	tu sortirais	que tu sortes
il, elle sortira	il, elle sortirait	qu'il, elle sorte
nous sortirons	nous sortirions	que nous sortions
vous sortirez	vous sortiriez	que vous sortiez
ils, elles sortiront	ils, elles sortiraient	qu'ils, elles sortent

tenir to hold

Present Participle
tenant, holding

Past Participle
tenu, held

Imperative
tiens
tenons
tenez

Present Indicative	**Imperfect**	**Passé Composé**
je tiens	je tenais	j'ai tenu
tu tiens	tu tenais	tu as tenu
il, elle tient	il, elle tenait	il, elle a tenu
nous tenons	nous tenions	nous avons tenu
vous tenez	vous teniez	vous avez tenu
ils, elles tiennent	il, elles tenaient	ils, elles ont tenu
Future	**Conditional**	**Present Subjunctive**
je tiendrai	je tiendrais	que je tienne
tu tiendras	tu tiendrais	que tu tiennes
il, elle tiendra	il, elle tiendrait	qu'il, elle tienne
nous tiendrons	nous tiendrions	que nous tenions
vous tiendrez	vous tiendriez	que vous teniez
ils, elles tiendront	ils, elles tiendraient	qu'ils, elles tiennent

venir to come

Present Participle
venant, coming

Past Participle
venu(e), come

Imperative
viens
venons
venez

Present Indicative	**Imperfect**	**Passé Composé**
je viens	je venais	je suis venu(e)
tu viens	tu venais	tu es venu(e)
il, elle vient	il, elle venait	il, elle est venu(e)
nous venons	nous venions	nous sommes venu(e)s
vous venez	vous veniez	vous êtes venu(e)s
ils, elles viennent	il, elles venaient	ils, elles sont venu(e)s

Future	Conditional	Present Subjunctive
je viendrai	je viendrais	que je vienne
tu viendras	tu viendrais	que tu viennes
il, elle viendra	il, elle viendrait	qu'il, elle vienne
nous viendrons	nous viendrions	que nous venions
vous viendrez	vous viendriez	que vous veniez
ils, elles viendront	ils, elles viendraient	qu'ils, elles viennent

valoir to be worth

Present Participle
valant, being worth

Past Participle
valu, been worth

Imperative
vaux
valons
valez

Present Indicative	Imperfect	Passé Composé
je vaux	je valais	j'ai valu
tu vaux	tu valais	tu as valu
il, elle vaut	il, elle valait	il, elle a valu
nous valons	nous valions	nous avons valu
vous valez	vous valiez	vous avez valu
ils, elles valent	ils, elles valaient	ils, elles ont valu

Future	Conditional	Present Subjunctive
je vaudrai	je vaudrais	que je vaille
tu vaudras	tu vaudrais	que tu vailles
il, elle vaudra	il, elle vaudrait	qu'il, elle vaille
nous vaudrons	nous vaudrions	que nous valions
vous vaudrez	vous vaudriez	que vous valiez
ils, elles vaudront	ils, elles vaudraient	qu'ils, elles vaillent

voir to see

Present Participle
voyant, seeing

Past Participle
vu, seen

Imperative
vois
voyons
voyez

Present Indicative	Imperfect	Passé Composé
je vois	je voyais	j'ai vu
tu vois	tu voyais	tu as vu
il, elle voit	il, elle voyait	il, elle a vu
nous voyons	nous voyions	nous avons vu
vous voyez	vous voyiez	vous avez vu
ils, elles voient	ils, elles voyaient	ils, elles ont vu

Future	Conditional	Present Subjunctive
je verrai	je verrais	que je voie
tu verras	tu verrais	que tu voies
il, elle verra	il, elle verrait	qu'il, elle voie
nous verrons	nous verrions	que nous voyions
vous verrez	vous verriez	que vous voyiez
ils, elles verront	ils, elles verraient	qu'ils, elles voient

vouloir to want

Present Participle
voulant, wanting

Past Participle
voulu, wanted

Imperative
veuille
veuillons
veuillez

Present Indicative	**Imperfect**	**Passé Composé**
je veux	je voulais	j'ai voulu
tu veux	tu voulais	tu as voulu
il, elle veut	il, elle voulait	il, elle a voulu
nous voulons	nous voulions	nous avons voulu
vous voulez	vous vouliez	vous avez voulu
ils, elles veulent	ils, elles voulaient	ils, elles ont voulu
Future	**Conditional**	**Present Subjunctive**
je voudrai	je voudrais	que je veuille
tu voudras	tu voudrais	que tu veuilles
il, elle voudra	il, elle voudrait	qu'il, elle veuille
nous voudrons	nous voudrions	que nous voulions
vous voudrez	vous voudriez	que vous vouliez
ils, elles voudront	ils, elles voudraient	qu'ils, elles veuillent

Appendix C

Verbs with Spelling Changes

This appendix contains a sampling of the verbs that undergo spelling changes when conjugated. These examples should help to define the patterns by which changes occur in verbs with stems that change spelling when conjugated.

acheter to buy

Present Participle
achetant, buying

Past Participle
acheté, bought

Imperative
achète
achetons
achetez

Present Indicative
j'achète
tu achètes
il, elle achète
nous achetons
vous achetez
ils, elles achètent

Imperfect
j'achetais
tu achetais
il, elle achetait
nous achetions
vous achetiez
ils, elles achetaient

Passé Composé
j'ai acheté
tu as acheté
il, elle a acheté
nous avons acheté
vous avez acheté
ils, elles ont acheté

Future
j'achèterai
tu achèteras
il, elle achètera
nous achèterons
vous achèterez
ils, elles achèteront

Conditional
j'achèterais
tu achèterais
il, elle achèterait
nous achèterions
vous achèteriez
ils, elles achèteraient

Present Subjunctive
que j'achète
que tu achètes
qu'il, elle achète
que nous achetions
que vous achetiez
qu'ils, elles achètent

appeler to call

Present Participle
appelant, calling

Past Participle
appelé, called

Imperative
appelle
appelons
appelez

Present Indicative	Imperfect	Passé Composé
j'appelle	j'appelais	j'ai appelé
tu appelles	tu appelais	tu as appelé
il, elle appelle	il, elle appelait	il, elle a appelé
nous appelons	nous appelions	nous avons appelé
vous appelez	vous appeliez	vous avez appelé
ils, elles appellent	ils, elles appelaient	ils, elles ont appelé
Future	**Conditional**	**Present Subjunctive**
j'appellerai	j'appellerais	que j'appelle
tu appelleras	tu appellerais	que tu appelles
il, elle appellera	il, elle appellerait	qu'il, elle appelle
nous appellerons	nous appellerions	que nous appelions
vous appellerez	vous appelleriez	que vous appeliez
ils, elles appelleront	ils, elles appelleraient	qu'ils, elles appellent

s'asseoir to sit down

Present Participle
s'asseyant, sitting down

Past Participle
assis(e), sat down

Imperative
assieds-toi
asseyons-nous
asseyez-vous

Present Indicative	Imperfect	Passé Composé
je m'assieds	je m'asseyais	je me suis assis(e)
tu t'assieds	tu t'asseyais	tu t'es assis(e)
il, elle s'assied	il, elle s'asseyait	il, elle s'est assis(e)
nous nous asseyons	nous nous asseyions	nous nous sommes assis(es)
vous vous asseyez	vous vous asseyiez	vous vous êtes assis(es)
ils, elles s'asseyent	ils, elles s'asseyaient	ils, elles se sont assis(es)
Future	**Conditional**	**Present Subjunctive**
je m'assiérai	je m'assiérais	que je m'asseye
tu t'assiéras	tu t'assiérais	que tu t'asseyes
il, elle s'assiéra	il, elle s'assiérait	qu'il, elle s'asseye
nous nous assiérons	nous nous assiérions	que nous nous asseyions
vous vous assiérez	vous vous assiériez	que vous vous asseyiez
ils, elles s'assiéront	ils, elles s'assiéraient	qu'ils, elles s'asseyent

commencer to start

Present Participle
commençant, starting

Past Participle
commencé, started

Imperative
commence
commençons
commencez

Present Indicative	Imperfect	Passé Composé
je commence	je commençais	j'ai commencé
tu commences	tu commençais	tu as commencé
il, elle commence	il, elle commençait	il, elle a commencé
nous commençons	nous commencions	nous avons commencé
vous commencez	vous commenciez	vous avez commencé
ils, elles commencent	ils, elles commençaient	ils, elles ont commencé

Future	Conditional	Present Subjunctive
je commencerai	je commencerais	que je commence
tu commenceras	tu commencerais	que tu commences
il, elle comencera	il, elle commencerait	qu'il, elle commence
nous commencerons	nous commercerions	que nous commencions
vous commencerez	vous commenceriez	que vous commenciez
ils, elles commenceront	ils, elles commenceraient	qu'ils, elles commencent

envoyer to send

Present Participle
envoyant, sending

Past Participle
envoyé, sent

Imperative
envoie
envoyons
envoyez

Present Indicative	Imperfect	Passé Composé
j'envoie	j'envoyais	j'ai envoyé
tu envoies	tu envoyais	tu as envoyé
il, elle envoie	il, elle envoyait	il, elle a envoyé
nous envoyons	nous envoyions	nous avons envoyé
vous envoyez	vous envoyiez	vous avez envoyé
ils, elles envoient	ils, elles envoyaient	ils, elles ont envoyé

Future	Conditional	Present Subjunctive
j'enverrai	j'enverrais	que j'envoie
tu enverras	tu enverrais	que tu envoies
il, elle enverra	il, elle enverrait	qu'il, elle envoie
nous enverrons	nous enverrions	que nous envoyions
vous enverrez	vous enverriez	que vous envoyiez
ils, elles enverront	ils, elles enverraient	qu'ils, elles envoient

espérer to hope

Present Participle
espérant, hoping

Past Participle
espéré, hoped

Imperative
espère
espérons
espérez

Present Indicative	Imperfect	Passé Composé
j'espère	j'espérais	j'ai espéré
tu espères	tu espérais	tu as espéré
il, elle espère	il, elle espérait	il, elle a espéré
nous espérons	nous espérions	nous avons espéré
vous espérez	vous espériez	vous avez espéré
ils, elles espèrent	ils, elles espéraient	ils, elles ont espéré

Future	Conditional	Present Subjunctive
j'espérerai	j'espérerais	que j'espère
tu espéreras	tu espérerais	que tu espères
il, elle espérera	il, elle espérerait	qu'il, elle espère
nous espérerons	nous espérerions	que nous espérions
vous espérerez	vous espéreriez	que vous espériez
ils, elles espéreront	ils, elles espéreraient	qu'ils, elles espèrent

essayer to try

Present Participle
essayant, trying

Past Participle
essayé, tried

Imperative
essaie
essayons
essayez

Present Indicative
j'essaie
tu essaies
il, elle essaie
nous essayons
vous essayez
ils, elles essaient

Imperfect
j'essayais
tu essayais
il, elle essayait
nous essayions
vous essayiez
ils, elles essayaient

Passé Composé
j'ai essayé
tu as essayé
il, elle a essayé
nous avons essayé
vous avez essayé
ils, elles ont essayé

Future
j'essaierai *or* essayerai
tu essaieras
il, elle essaiera
nous essaierons
vous essairerez
ils, elles essaieront

Conditional
j'essaierais *or* essayerais
tu essaierais
il, elle essaierait
nous essaierions
vous essaieriez
ils, elles essaieraient

Present Subjunctive
que j'essaie
que tu essaies
qu'il, elle essaie
que nous essayions
que vous essayiez
qu'ils, elles essaient

jeter to throw

Present Participle
jetant, throwing

Past Participle
jeté, thrown

Imperative
jette
jetons
jetez

Present Indicative
je jette
tu jettes
il, elle jette
nous jetons
vous jetez
ils, elles jettent

Imperfect
je jetais
tu jetais
il, elle jetait
nous jetions
vous jetiez
ils, elles jetaient

Passé Composé
j'ai jeté
tu as jeté
il, elle a jeté
nous avons jeté
vous avez jeté
ils, elles ont jeté

Future
je jetterai
tu jetteras
il, elle jettera
nous jetterons
vous jetterez
ils, elles jetteront

Conditional
je jetterais
tu jetterais
il, elle jetterait
nous jetterions
vous jetteriez
ils, elles jetteraient

Present Subjunctive
que je jette
que tu jettes
qu'il, elle jette
que nous jetions
que vous jetiez
qu'ils, elles jettent

lever to raise

Present Participle
levant, raising

Past Participle
levé, raised

Imperative
lève
levons
levez

Present Indicative	Imperfect	Passé Composé
je lève	je levais	j'ai levé
tu lèves	tu levais	tu as levé
il, elle lève	il, elle levait	il, elle a levé
nous levons	nous levions	nous avons levé
vous levez	vous leviez	vous avez levé
ils, elles lèvent	ils, elles levaient	ils, elles ont levé
Future	**Conditional**	**Present Subjunctive**
je lèverai	je lèverais	que je lève
tu lèveras	tu lèverais	que tu lèves
il, elle lèvera	il, elle lèverait	qu'il, elle lève
nous lèverons	nous lèverions	que nous levions
vous lèverez	vous lèveriez	que vous leviez
ils, elles lèveront	ils, elles lèveraient	qu'ils, elles lèvent

manger to eat

Present Participle
mangeant, eating

Past Participle
mangé, eaten

Imperative
mange
mangeons
mangez

Present Indicative	Imperfect	Passé Composé
je mange	je mangeais	j'ai mangé
tu manges	tu mangeais	tu as mangé
il, elle mange	il, elle mangeait	il, elle a mangé
nous mangeons	nous mangions	nous avons mangé
vous mangez	vous mangiez	vous avez mangé
ils, elles mangent	ils, elles mangeaient	ils, elles ont mangé
Future	**Conditional**	**Present Subjunctive**
je mangerai	je mangerais	que je mange
tu mangeras	tu mangerais	que tu manges
il, elle mangera	il, elle mangerait	qu'il, elle mange
nous mangerons	nous mangerions	que nous mangions
vous mangerez	vous mangeriez	que vous mangiez
ils, elles mangeront	ils, elles mangeraient	qu'ils, elles mangent

payer to pay

Present Participle
payant, paying

Past Participle
payé, paid

Imperative
paie
payons
payez

Present Indicative	Imperfect	Passé Composé
je paie	je payais	j'ai payé
tu paies	tu payais	tu as payé
il, elle paie	il, elle payait	il, elle a payé
nous payons	nous payions	nous avons payé
vous payez	vous payiez	vous avez payé
ils, elles paient	ils, elles payaient	ils, elles ont payé

Future	**Conditional**	**Present Subjunctive**
je payerai *or* paierai	je payerais	que je paie
tu payeras	tu payerais	que tu paies
il, elle payera	il, elle payerait	qu'il, elle paie
nous payerons	nous payerions	que nous payions
vous payerez	vous payeriez	que vous payiez
ils, elles payeront	ils, elles payeraient	qu'ils, elles paient

préférer to prefer

Present Participle
préférant, preferring

Past Participle
préféré, preferred

Imperative
préfère
préférons
préférez

Present Indicative	**Imperfect**	**Passé Composé**
je préfère	je préférais	j'ai préféré
tu préfères	tu préférais	tu as préféré
il, elle préfère	il, elle préférait	il, elle a préféré
nous préférons	nous préférions	nous avons préféré
vous préférez	vous préfériez	vous avez préféré
ils, elles préfèrent	ils, elles préféraient	ils, elles ont préféré

Future	**Conditional**	**Present Subjunctive**
je préférerai	je préférerais	que je préfère
tu préféreras	tu préférerais	que tu préfères
il, elle préférera	il, elle préférerait	qu'il, elle préfère
nous préférerons	nous préférerions	que nous préférions
vous préférerez	vous préféreriez	que vous préfériez
ils, elles préféreront	ils, elles préféreraient	qu'ils, elles préfèrent

Vocabulary

French–English

This vocabulary contains most of the words used in the first fourteen lessons. Cognates are not all listed, since Lesson 15 provides you with the necessary background to recognize them.

à, at, in, with
abandonner, to leave
abonnement (m.), subscription
abréviation (f.), abbreviation
abriter, to shelter
absence (f.), absence, lack
absent(e), absent
absolu(e), absolute
absolument, absolutely
abstrait(e), abstract
absurde, absurd
abuser, to abuse
à cause de, because of
accéder, to reach
accélérateur (m.), accelerator
accepter, to accept
accès (m.), access
accompagner, to accompany
accorder, to agree
  d'accord, agreed, o.k.
accueil (m.), welcome
accueillir, to welcome, to receive
achat (m.), purchase
acheter, to buy
achever, to achieve, to finish
acide, sour
acier (m.), steel
à côté, near, beside
  à côté de, next to
acquisition (f.), acquisition, purchase
acteur (m.), actor
action (f.), stock
actionnaire (m.), stockholder
actrice (f.), actress
actualités, newsreel
actuellement, now, currently
addition (f.), bill, check, addition
à demain, see you tomorrow
admirer, to admire
adorer, to adore
adresser (se), to contact
aéroport (m.), airport
affaires (f.), belongings, business
affiche (f.), poster
affiché(e), posted
afficher, to post, to display
affirmer, to affirm
âge (m.), age
âgé(e), old
agence (f.), agency
agenda (m.), engagement calendar
agent (m.), agent, policeman
  agent de change (m.), stock broker
  agent de voyage (m.), travel agent
agglomeration (f.), urban area
agir, to take action
agir (se), to be in question
  il s'agit de, it is a question of, it's about

agneau (m.), lamb
agréable, pleasant
agricole, agricultural
agriculteur (m.), farmer
agriculture (f.), agriculture
ah bon!, really?
aide (f.), help
aider, to help
aie!, ouch!
aigu, acute, sharp
ail (m.), garlic
aile (f.), wing, fender
ailleurs, elsewhere
  d'ailleurs, besides
aimable, nice, kind
aimer, to like, to love
ainsi, so, thus
  ainsi de suite, and so forth
air (m.), air, looks
  avoir l'air, to seem, look
  en plein air, in the open
ajouter, to add
à la place de, in place of
à l'heure, on time
aliment (m.), food
alimentaire, related to food
alimentation (f.), food, supply
alimenter, to feed
aller, to go
aller et retour, round trip
allié(e), ally
allo!, hello! (telephone)
allocation (f.), allowance, aid
allumer, to light, to turn on
alors, then, at that time
amant(e), lover
ambiance (f.), mood, atmosphere
amende (f.), fine
amener, to bring
ami(e), friend, boyfriend, girlfriend
amical(e), friendly
amortir, to weaken, to moderate
amour (m.), love
ampoule (f.), medicine capsule, light bulb
amuser, to amuse
amuser (se), to have fun
an (m.), year
ancêtre (m., f.), ancestor
âne (m.), donkey
animer, to bring to life
animer (se), to come to life
année (f.), year
anniversaire (m.), birthday
  anniversaire de mariage (m.), wedding anniversary
annonce (f.), advertisement
  petites annonces, want ads
annuel, yearly
août, August
apercevoir, to notice, to perceive
à peu près, approximately
appareil (m.), device
  appareil photographique (m.), camera
appeler, to call
appeler (se), to be called
apporter, to bring
apprécier, to appreciate
apprendre, to learn
après, after
  d'après, according to
après-demain, the day after tomorrow
après-midi, afternoon
abre (m.), tree
arc (m.), arch
arc-en-ciel (m.), rainbow
argent (m.), money
  argent de poche, spending money
armoire (f.), wardrobe (furniture)
arracher, to pull out
arrêter, to stop
arrêter (se), to stop oneself
arrière (m.), back
arrivée (f.), arrival
arriver, to arrive, to happen
ascenseur (m.), elevator
asseoir (se), to sit down
assez, enough
assiette (f.), plate, dish
assis(e), seated
  être assis(e), to be seated
assister, to attend
assuré, insured
assurer, to insure
assurer (se), to make sure
à temps, on time
  à temps complet, full time
  à mi-temps, part time
à tout à l'heure, see you soon
attacher, to fasten to tie
atteindre, to reach
attendre, to wait for

atterrir, to land
atterrissage (m.), landing
attirer, to attract
attraper, to catch
au contraire, on the contrary
augmentation, increase
augmenter, to increase, to raise
aujourd'hui, today
au lieu de, instead
au revoir, goodbye
aussi, also, too
  aussi tôt que, as soon as
automatique, automatic
auto-stop, hitchhiking
autour, around
autre, other
  l'un l'autre, les uns les autres, each other, one another
avaler, to swallow
avant (m.), front
avant, before
avant-hier, day before yesterday
avec, with
avion (m.), airplane
avoir, to have
  (see Lesson 8 for expressions using *avoir*)
avouer, to admit
avril (m.), April

bagage (m.), luggage
bague (f.), ring
baigner, to bathe
baigner (se), to bathe oneself
baignoire (f.), bathtub
bain (m.), bath
  salle de bains (f.), bathroom
baisser, to lower, to decrease
balance (f.), scale
balcon (m.), balcony
balle (f.), ball
ballon (m.), balloon
banane (f.), banana
bande (f.), tape
banlieue (f.), suburb
banquier (m.), banker
barbe (f.), beard
  quelle barbe!, how terrible!
barbier (m.), barber
bas, low
  à bas, down with
  en bas, downstairs
bateau (m.), boat, ship
batterie (f.), battery
bavard, talkative
bavardage, chit-chat, gossip
bavarder, to chat
beau, handsome
beau-fils (m.), son-in-law
beau-frère (m.), brother-in-law
beau-père (m.), father-in-law
beaux-parents, in-laws
bel(le), beautiful
belle-fille (f.), daughter-in-law
belle-mère (f.), mother-in-law
belle-sœur (f.), sister-in-law
beurre (m.), butter
bibliothèque (f.), library
bien, well, fine
bien sûr, of course
bientôt, soon
biftek (m.), steak
bijou (m.), jewel, jewelry
bijouterie (f.), jewelry store
bilan (m.), outcome, balance sheet
billet (m.), ticket
blanc(he), white
bleu(e), blue
blond(e), blonde
bœuf (m.), beef
boire, to drink
boisson (f.), drink
boîte (f.), box
  boîte de nuit, nightclub
bord (m.), shore, edge
  à bord, on board
  monter à bord, to go on board
bouche (f.), mouth
boucher (m.), butcher
boucher, to cork
boucherie (f.), butcher shop
bougie (f.), candle
bouillir, to boil
boulanger (m.), baker
boulangerie (f.), bakery
bourse (f.), scholarship
  la Bourse, the stock exchange
bouteille (f.), bottle
bouton (m.), button

brancher, to connect
bras (m.), arm
bricoler, to putter around
brosse (f.), brush
brosser, to brush
brosser (se), to brush oneself
bruit (m.), noise
  faire du bruit, to make noise
brûler, to burn
brun(e), brown, dark
bureau (m.), desk, office, den
BUS (m.), BUS
  BUS d'entrée (m.), input
  BUS de sortie (m.), output
but (m.), aim, goal

ça, that
  ça ne fait rien, it doesn't matter
cacher, to hide
cacher (se), to hide oneself
caisse (f.), cashier's office
caissier (m.), cashier
caissière (f.), cashier
calculer, to calculate
calendrier (m.), calendar
calmant (m.), sedative
camion (m.), truck
capitaine (m.), captain
capot (m.), hood
capoter, to turn over
car, for
  le car, the bus (inter-city)
carnet de chèques (m.), checkbook
carte (f.), card
  carte d'embarquement, boarding pass
  carte grise (f.), title
  carte perforée (f.), punch card
  carte postale (f.), postcard
  carte routière (f.), road map
casse-croûte (m.), snack
casse-pieds (m.), pest
casser, to break
cassette (f.), cassette tape
ceci, this
ceinture (f.), belt
  ceinture de sécurité (f.), safety belt
cela, that
célibataire, single
cendrier (m.), ashtray
ces, these
chaise (f.), chair
chambre (f.), room
  chambre à coucher, bedroom
champagne (m.), champagne
chance (f.), luck
chaque, each
  chacun(e), each one
chat (m.), cat
chauffage (m.), heating
cher (m.), dear, expensive
chère (f.), dear, expensive
chercher, to look for
cheval (m.), horse
cheveux (m. plural), hair
cheville (f.), ankle
chien (m.), dog
choix (m.), choice
chose (f.), thing
  quelque chose, something
ci-dessous, below
ci-dessus, above
cigarette (f.), cigarette
cil (m.), eyelash
circuit (m.), circuit
clavier (m.), keyboard
clef (f.), key
client(e), customer
cœur (m.), heart
coffre (m.), safe deposit box, car trunk
colère (f.), anger
  être en colère, to be angry
colle (f.), glue
coller, to glue, to stick
combien, how many, how much
comfortable, comfortable
commander, to order
commandes (f.), controls
comme, as
comme-ci-comme-ça, so-so
commencer, to start
comment, how
commode (f.), dresser
comparer, to compare
composer, to compose, to dial
comptant (m.), cash
compte-goutte (m.), eyedropper
compter, to count
conduire, to drive
configuration (f.), configuration

connaître, to know
conseil (m.), advice
conseiller, to advise
contravention (f.), traffic ticket
contrôleur (m.), ticket collector
corps (m.), body
cou (m.), neck
couchette (f.), bunk, berth
couleur (f.), color
couloir (m.), hallway
cour (f.), yard
courir, to run
cours (m.), course
  cours de change, exchange
course (f.), errand, race
  course de chevaux, horse racing
court(e), short
cousin(e), cousin
couteau (m.), knife
coûter, to cost
  coûter cher, to be expensive
couverture (f.), blanket
crayon (m.), pencil
crédit (m.), bank credit
  à credit (m.), on credit
  carte de crédit, credit card
créer, to create
crème (f.), cream
creux(se), deep
crevaison (f.), flat tire
crevette (f.), shrimp
crise (f.), attack, crisis
critère (m.), criterion
croire, to believe
cuir (m.), leather
cuire, to cook

d'abord, first of all
dactylo (f.), typist
danser, to dance
davantage, more
début (m.), beginning
débuter, to begin
décembre (m.), December
décevoir, to disappoint
décider, to decide
décoller, to take off
décontracté, relaxed
décorer, to decorate
découvrir, to discover
décrire, to describe
décrocher, to unhook
défendu, forbidden
dégonfler, to deflate
dehors, out, outside
déjà, already
déjeuner (m.), lunch
déjeuner, to lunch
délicieux, delicious
demain, tomorrow
demander, to ask
démarrer, to start
démarreur (m.), starter
déménager, to move out
dent (f.), tooth
dépanner, to repair (car)
départ (m.), departure
dépasser, to exceed, to pass someone
dépêcher (se), to hurry
depense (f.), expense
dépenser, to spend
déposer, to deposit
depuis, since
  depuis quand, since when
déranger, to bother, to disturb
de rien, you're welcome
descendre, to go down
déshabiller (se), to undress
desirer, to wish, to desire
dès que, as soon as
dessin (m.), drawing, design
destination (f.), destination
détacher, to unfasten
détruire, to destroy
devant, in front of, before
devenir, to become
deviner, to guess
devise (f.), motto
devises (f.), foreign currency
devoir, to have to, to owe
diète (f.), diet
dimanche, Sunday
dinde (f.), turkey
diner (m.), dinner
diner, to have dinner
dire, to say
discuter, to discuss
disponible, available
disque (m.), disk
doigt (m.), finger
donc, therefore

donner, to give
dormir, to sleep
dos (m.), back
douane (f.), customs
douanier (m.), customs agent
douche (f.), shower
doute (m.), doubt
  sans doute, undoubtedly
  sans aucun doute, without a doubt
douter, to doubt
doux(ce), soft, sweet
drap (m.), sheet
drapeau (m.), flag
drogue (f.), drug
droit(e), straight
  à droite, to the right
  tout droit, straight ahead
drôle, funny
dur(e), hard, harsh
durant, during
durer, to last

eau (f.), water
  eau minérale (f.), mineral water
échange (m.), exchange
échanger, to exchange
école (f.), school
économiser, to save
écouter, to listen
écran (m.), screen
écrire, to write
écrivain (m.), writer
édifice (m.), building
effacer, to erase
égal(e), equal
égarer (se), to get lost, to wander
embarquer, to board
embaucher, to hire
embouteillage (m.), traffic jam
embrasser, to kiss
embrayage (m.), clutch
emmenager, to move in
empêcher, to prevent
employé (m.), employee
emprunt (m.), loan
emprunter, to borrow
enchanté, pleased, enchanted
encore, again
  encore une fois, one more time
encourager, to encourage
endormir (se), to fall asleep
endroit (m.), place
enfant, child
enfin, finally
enlever, to remove
ennuyer, to annoy, to bore
ennuyer (se), to be bored
en retard, late
enseigner, to teach
ensemble, whole, together, entirety
ensemble (m.), lady's suit, garment
ensuite, then, next
entendre, to hear
entendre (se), to get along with
entre, between
entrée (f.), entrance (input)
envoyer, to send
épargne (f.), savings
épargner, to spare, to save
  la Caisse d'Epargne, savings bank
épaule (f.), shoulder
épice (f.), spice
épouser, to marry
époux(se), spouse
équilibrer, to balance
escale (f.), calling place
  faire escale, to stop over
espérer, to hope
espoir (m.), hope
essayer, to try
essuie-glace (m.), windshield wiper
est (m.), east
estomac (m.), stomach
étage (m.), floor, story (in a building)
éteindre, to turn off, to put out
étoile (f.), star
  étoile de cinéma, movie star
étranger, foreigner
être, to be
étroit(e), narrow
étude (f.), study
étudiant(e), student
étudier, to study
évasion (f.), escape
évier (m.), kitchen sink
éviter, to avoid
examiner, to examine
excellent, excellent
express (m.), express train
extraire, to extract
extrait (m.), excerpt, extract

fabriquer, to manufacture
fabuleux, fabulous
facteur (m.), postman
facture (f.), bill
faible, weak
faim (f.), hunger
  avoir faim, to be hungry
faire, to do
  faire le plein, to fill the tank
  (see Lesson 4 for expressions using *faire*)
falloir, to be necessary
  (see Lesson 8 for the impersonal use of *falloir*)
famille (f.), family
farine (f.), flour
faute (f.), mistake
fauteuil (m.), armchair
faux(sse), false, wrong
femme (f.), woman, wife
  femme de chambre (f.), maid
fenêtre (f.), window
fête (f.), party
fêter, to celebrate
feu (m.), fire, stoplight
février (m.), February
fiancé(e), fiancée
fièvre (f.), fever
  avoir de la fièvre, to have a fever
fille (f.), daughter, girl
fils (m.), son
fin (f.), end
finir, to end, to finish
flan (m.), custard
fleur (f.), flower
foie (m.), liver
fonder, to found
fondre, to melt
fonds (m.), capital
forme (f.), shape, form
fort(e), strong
foule (f.), crowd
fouler (se), to sprain
  se fouler la cheville, to sprain one's ankle
fourchette (f.), fork
fournir, to supply
fourrure (f.), fur
fragile, fragile
fraise (f.), strawberry
frapper, to hit, to strike
frein (m.), brake (car)
freiner, to brake
fréquenter, to patronize
frère (m.), brother
frigo (m.), refrigerator
frites (plural), fries
fromage (m.), cheese
front (m.), forehead
fruit (m.), fruit
fruits de mer (m., plural), seafood
fumer, to smoke
  défense de fumer, no smoking (allowed)

gagner, to win, to earn
gant (m.), glove
garçon (m.), boy, waiter
garder, to keep
gaspillage (m.), waste
gaspiller, to waste
gâteau (m.), cake
gauche, left
  à gauche, to the left
genou (m.), knee
gens, people
gentil(le), kind, nice
gérant(e), manager
gérer, to manage
gestion (f.), management
glace (f.), ice cream
glaçon (m.), ice cube
gonfler, to inflate
gorge (f.), throat
gorgée (f.), sip swallow
  à petites gorgées, in small sips
goût (m.), taste
goûter, to taste
goutte (f.), drop
grand(e), big
grand-mère (f.), grandmother
grand-père (m.), grandfather
gratuit(e), free of charge
grève (f.), strike of workmen
gros(se), fat
  le gros lot, the jackpot
grossir, to gain weight
guérir, to heal
guichet (m.), teller window
guider, to guide

habiller, to clothe
habiller (se), to get dressed
habitant (m.), inhabitant
habiter, to live in, to inhabit
haricot vert (m.), green bean
hasard (par), per chance
haut(e), high, elevated
  à haute voix, out loud
hebdomadaire (m.), weekly (journal, magazine)
hésiter, to hesitate
heure (f.), hour
  Quelle heure est-il?, What time is it?
  heure d'affluence (f.), rush hour
heureux(se), happy
heureusement, happily
heurter, to hit, to run into
hier, yesterday
  avant hier, day before yesterday
histoire (f.), story, history
homard (m.), lobster
homme (m.), man
  homme d'affaires (m.), businessman
honneur (m.), honor
horaire (m.), timetable, schedule
hôtesse (f.), hostess
huile (f.), oil
huître (f.), oyster
hypothèque (f.), mortgage

ici, here
  par ici, over here, this way
idolâtrer, to idolize
il y a, there is, there are
impôt (m.), tax
imprévu(e), unexpected
  à limprévu, unexpectedly
imprimante (f.), printer (computer)
imprimer, to print
  imprimerie (f.), printing press
incroyable, incredible
indicateur (m.), signal
indiquer, to indicate
informatique (f.), computer science
ingénieur (m.), engineer
inoxidable, rust proof
inquiet(e), worried
inquiéter(se), to worry, to be anxious
inspecter, to inspect
intérêt (m.), interest
inutile, useless
investir, to invest
investissement (m.), investment
invite(e), guest
inviter, to invite

jamais, never
jambe (f.), leg
jambon (m.), ham
janvier (m.), January
jardin (m.), garden
jauge (f.), gauge
jaune, yellow
jeter, to throw
jeudi (m.), Thursday
jeune, young
  les jeunes gens, young people
jeunesse (f.), youth
joie (f.), joy
joli(e), pretty
jouer, to play
jouet (m.), toy
joueur(se), player
jour (m.), day
journal (journaux) (m.), newspaper(s)
journalier, daily
journée (f.), day
juillet (m.), July
juin (m.), June
jusqu'à, until
  jusque là, up to here
juste, right, just
justement, exactly, as a matter of fact
justice (f.), justice
  palais (m.) de justice, courthouse

kilo (m.), kilo
kilomètre (m.), kilometer
klaxon (m.), horn

là, there
  là-bas, over there
laisser, to leave
laisser tomber, to drop
lait (m.), milk
  lait écrémé, skim milk

laitue (f.), lettuce
lame (f.), blade
  lame de rasoir, razor blade
lampe (f.), lamp
  lampe de poche (f.), flashlight
langouste (f.), crayfish
langue (f.), tongue
large, wide
lavabo (m.), bathroom sink
laver (se), to wash oneself
leçon (f.), lesson
lecture (f.), reading
léger (légère), light
légume (m.), vegetable
lendemain (m.), next day
lent(e), slow
lentement, slowly
lèvre (f.), lip
listing (m.), printout
lit (m.), bed
livre (m.), book
livrer, to deliver
location (f.), rental of anything but a dwelling
logiciel (m.), software
loin de, far from
loisirs (m.), activities
longtemps, a long time
louer, to rent
lourd(e), heavy
loyer (m.), rent (dwelling)
lumière (f.), light
lumineux(se), lighted
  le spot lumineux, spotlight
lundi (m.), Monday
luxueux(se), luxurious
lycée (m.), high school

ma, mon, mes, my
machine (f.), machine
  machine à écrire, typewriter
  machine à laver, washing machine
machiniste (m.), engineer
magasin (m.), store
  Grand Magasin, department store
magnétophone (m.), tape recorder
mai (m.), May
maigre, skinny
main (f.), hand
maintenant, now
mais, but
maison (f.), house
mal, evil, badly
malade, sick
malle (f.), trunk, suitcase
mandat (m.), money order
manette (f.), hand lever
manger, to eat
manier, to handle
manquer, to miss, to lack
manteau (m.), coat, overcoat
manuel, manual
marchand (m.), storekeeper, merchant
marchander, to haggle over
marcher, to walk, to work (machine)
mardi (m.), Tuesday
mari (m.), husband
marier (se), to get married
marque (f.), brand
mars (m.), March
marteau (m.), hammer
matelas (m.), mattress
matériel (m.), hardware
matin (m.), morning
mauvais (e), mean, bad
méchant(e), mean
mélange (m.), mix
melon (m.), melon
mensuel(le), monthly
menton (m.), chin
mer (f.), sea
mercredi (m.), Wednesday
mère (f.), mother
meuble (m.), furniture
meublé, furnished
microprocesseur (m.), microprocessor
mieux, better
  mieux vaut tard que jamais, better late than never
mince, slender
mode (à la), fashionable
modem (m.), modulator
moi, me
moins, less
  à moins que, unless
mois (m.), month
montagne (f.), mountain
montant (m.), amount
monter, to go up
montre (f.), watch
montrer, to show

morceau (m.), piece
mort (f.), death
mot (m.), word
moteur (m.), motor
mourir, to die
moyen (m.), way, means
mûrir, to ripen, to mature
musée (m.), museum
mutuellement, mutually

nager, to swim
nageur(se), swimmer
naissance (f.), birth
naître, to be born
nappe (f.), tablecloth
narcotique (m.), narcotic
neige (f.), snow
neiger, to snow
nettoyage, cleaning
nettoyer, to clean
neuf, nine
neuf(ve), new
neveu (m.), nephew
nez (m.), nose
noir (e), black
nord (m.), north
nourrir, to feed, to nourish
nourrir (se), to eat
nourriture (f.), food
nouveau (elle), new
  de nouveau, again
nouvelle (f.), news, story
nu(e), naked, nude
nuageux(se), cloudy
nuit (f.), night
  il fait nuit, it is dark
nuit blanche, sleepless night

obéir, to obey
obligatoire, mandatory
obtenir, to obtain
occasion, occasion
  d'occasion, secondhand
occupé, busy
occuper, to occupy, to take up space
occuper (se), to take care of
octobre (m.), October
odeur (f.), smell
œil (les yeux) (m.), eye
œuf (m.), egg
oignon (m.), onion
oiseau (m.), bird
oncle (m.), uncle
orange (f.), orange
  jus d'orange (m.), orange juice
  ordinateur (m.), computer
  ordonnace (f.), prescription, order
  ordonner, to prescribe, to order
  oreille (f.), ear
  oreiller (m.), pillow
  organiser, to organise
  orgueil (m.), pride
  oser, to dare
  ou, or
  ou bien, or
où, where
oublier, to forget
ouest (m.), west
ouvrir, to open
ouvrir (se), to open up, to open one's mind

pain (m.), bread
paisible, peaceful
paix (f.), peace
palais (m.), palace
panier (m.), basket
panne (f.), breakdown
panneau (m.), panel, board, road sign
pansement (m.), bandage
papier (m.), paper
  papier de verre, sandpaper
paquet (m.), package
par, by
  par avion, airmail
  par exemple, for example
  par jour, per day
parapluie (m.), umbrella
pare-brise (m.), windshield
parfois, sometimes
parler, to speak
parmi, among
part (f.), share, piece
  à part, separately
partager, to share
partir, to leave
partout, everywhere
passager(ère), passenger
passé(e), past

passe-temps (m.), pastime
passionnant, exciting
pauvre, poor
payer, to pay for
paysage (m.), scenery
peau (f.), skin
peigne (m.), comb
peigner (se), to comb one's hair
peindre, to paint
peine (f.), pain, punishment
  à peine, hardly
peinture (f.), painting
pendant, during, for
penser, to think
penseur(se), thinker
perdre, to lose, to waste
père (m.), father
perforer, to pierce
  carte perforée, punch card
permettre, to allow
permis (m.), license
  permis de conduire, driver's license
personne (f.), person
personne (m.), nobody
petit(e), small
petite-fille (f.), granddaughter
petit-fils (m.), grandson
petits pois (m.), peas
peut-être, maybe
phare (m.), headlight
pied (m.), foot
  marcher à pied, to walk
piéton(ne), pedestrian
pilote (m.), pilot
pipe (f.), pipe
piscine (f.), swimming pool
piste de décollage (f.), runway
placement (m.), investment
placer, to invest
plafond (m.), ceiling
plage (f.), beach
plaindre (se), to complain
plaire, to please
  s'il vous plaît, please
plaisanter, to joke
plaisir (m.), pleasure
plaque (f.), license plate
plat (m.), dish, plate
plâtre (m.), plaster
plein(e), full
plombage (m.), filling (tooth)
plomber, to fill (tooth)
plus, more
plusieurs, several
plutôt que, rather than
pneu (m.), tire
poire (f.), pear
poisson (m.), fish
poissonnerie (f.), fish market
poitrine (f.), chest
poivre (m.), pepper
poli(e), polite
porte (f.), door
porter, to carry
porteur(se), porter
poser, to put
poudre (f.), powder
poulet (m.), chicken
poumon (m.), lung
pourboire (m.), tip
pour-cent (m.), per hundred
pourtant, however
pouvoir, to be able to, can
préférer, to prefer
prendre, to take
préparer, to prepare
près, near, next to
pressé(e), in a hurry
  être pressé(e), to be in a hurry
prêt(e), ready
prêter, to lend
prix (m.), price
prochain(e), next
profiter, to profit, to take advantage of
progrès, progress
promesse (f.), promise
promettre, to promise
propriétaire (m., f.), owner
puce (f.), flea, computer chip
puis, then
puisque, since

quai (m.), platform
quand, when, while
quart (m.), quarter, fourth
que, which, whom, what, that (object)
quel(le), what
quelque, some, any, whatever
  quelque chose, something
quelquefois, sometimes
quelquepart, somewhere
qui, who, that, which (subject)

quitter, to quit, to leave
quoi, what, which

raconter, to tell (a story)
rail (m.), rail
ralentir, to slow down
ramener, to bring back
râpé(e), grated
  fromage râpé, grated cheese
rasoir (m.), razor
rayon (m.), aisle
récent(e), recent
réception (f.), front desk
recevoir, to receive
reconnaissant(e), grateful
reculer, to back up
régime (m.), diet
registre (m.), register
reine (f.), queen
remercier, to thank
remorquer, to tow
remplir, to fill up
rencontre (f.), meeting
rencontrer, to meet
rendre, to give back
renseignement (m.), information
renseigner, to give information
renseigner (se), to get information
rentrer, to come back (home)
renverser, to spill
repartir, to leave again
repas (m.), meal
repos (m.), rest
reposer, to put back
reposer (se), to rest
résoudre, to solve
respirer, to breath
ressembler, to look like
rester, to stay
retard (m.), delay
  être en retard, to be late
retourner, to return
réunion (f.), meeting, reunion
réunir, to reunite, to gather
réussir, to succeed
réussite (f.), success
réveiller, to wake someone
réveiller (se), to wake up
revenir, to come back
rêver, to dream
rez-de-chaussée (m.), ground floor
rhume (m.), cold
  être enrhumé, to have a cold
rien (m.), nothing
rire, to laugh
rire (m.), laughter
riz (m.), rice
robe (f.), dress
roi (m.), king
rôti (m.), roast
roue (f.), wheel
rouge, red
  le feu rouge, the red light
rougir, to blush
route nationale (f.), highway
ruban (m.), ribbon
rythme (m.), rhythm

sa, son, ses, his, hers, its
sable (m.), sand
sac (m.), purse
  sac à dos, backpack
  sac de couchage, sleeping bag
sain(e), healthy
salade (f.), salad
salaire (m.), salary, wages
sale, dirty
salle (f.), room
  salle à manger, dining room
  salle de bains, bathroom
salon (m.), living room
salut! hi!
samedi (m.), Saturday
sans, without
  sans cesse, constantly
santé (f.), health
satisfaisant(e), satisfactory
satisfait(e), satisfied
sauf(ve), safe, unhurt
sauf, except
sauvage, wild
savoir, to know
savon (m.), soap
schéma (m.), diagram, sketch
sec (sèche), dry, harsh
  être à sec, to be broke
sécher, to dry
  sécher un cours, to cut a class
sécurité (f.), security
sel (m.), salt
selon, according to

semaine (f.), week
la semaine prochaine, next week
semblable, similar
sentiment (m.), feeling, sensation
sentir, to smell, to feel
sentir (se), to feel, as in *je me sens bien,* I feel good
septembre (m.), September
sérieux (se), serious
serviette (f.), napkin, briefcase
servir, to serve
sévère, strict
siège (m.), seat
silicium (m.), silicon
simple, uncomplicated
sirop (m.), syrup
sœur (f.), sister
soif (f.), thirst
avoir soif, to be thirsty
soigner, to care for, to take care of
soir (m.), evening
soleil (m.), sun
sort (m.), fate
sortie (f.), exit (output)
sortir, to go out
souci (m.), worry
soudainement, suddenly
souhaiter, to wish
soulagement (m.), relief
soulager, to relieve
souple, supple
sourcil (m.), eyebrow
sourire (m.), smile
sourire, to smile
sous, under
souvent, often
station (f.), stop, station (subway)
stationner, to park
stylo (m.), pen
succès (m.), success
succursale (f.), branch (of a bank)
sucre (m.), sugar
sud (m.), south
suivre, to follow
superbe, superb
supprimer, to suppress
sur, on, over
sûr(e), sure
surtout, especially, mostly, above all
surveiller, to watch
sympathique, nice, pleasant, likable

ta, ton, tes, your
tableau (m.), blackboard
table trançante (f.), plotter
taie d'oreiller (f.), pillow case
talc (m.), talcum
tante (f.), aunt
tapageur (se), noisy
taper, to hit
taper à la machine, to type
tapis (m.), rug
taquiner, to tease
taux (m.), rate
télévision (f.), television
temps (m.), time, weather
à temps, on time
tenir, to hold, to keep
tenir à, to insist, to cherish
terminer, to finish, to limit
terminer (se), to end
tête (f.), head
tirer, to withdraw, to pull
toilette (f.), restroom
tomber, to fall
tôt, early, soon
toucher, to touch
toucher un cheque, to cash a check
toujours, always, still
tournevis (m.), screwdriver
tousser, to cough
tout(e), all
le tout, everything
tout à fait, quite
tout de suite, right away
toux (f.), cough
train (m.), train
travailler, to work
traverser, to cross
trébucher, to trip over
trésor (m.), treasure
triste, sad
tromper, to cheat
tromper (se), to make a mistake
trop, too much
trottoir (m.), pavement
trouver, to find
trouver (se), to be located, to find oneself
tube (m.), tube

un, une, one, a
uni(e), united

unir, to assemble, to unite
usage (m.), usage, custom
usé(e), used
usine (f.), factory
utile, useful
utiliser, to use

vacances (f.), vacation
vaisselle (f.), dishes
  faire la vaisselle, to do the dishes
valeur (f.), value
valise (f.), suitcase
valoir, to be worth
  valoir la peine, to be worth the trouble
veau (m.), veal
vedette (f.), movie star
vendeur(se), sales clerk
vendre, to sell
vendredi (m.), Friday
venir, to come
  venir de, to have just
ventre (m.), belly, abdomen
vérifier, to verify, to check
vérité (f.), truth
vers, towards, about
versement (m.), payment
verser, to pour
vert(e), green
vetements (m.), clothing
viande (f.), meat
vide, empty
vidéo (f.), video cassette
vider, to empty
vie (f.), life
vinaigre (m.), vinegar
visage (m.), face
vite, quick
vitesse (f.), speed
vive!, long live!
voir, to see
voisin(e), neighbor
voisinage (m.), neighborhood
voiture (f.), car
vol (m.), flight, robbery, theft
volant (m.), steering wheel
voler, to fly, to steal
voleur(se), thief, robber
volonté (f.), will
volontiers, gladly, willingly
vouloir, to want
  vouloir bien, to be willing
  vouloire dire, to mean
voyage (m.), travel, trip
  un chèque de voyage, traveler's check
voyager, to travel
voyageur(se), traveler
voyant(e), fortune teller
voyons!, let's see!
vrai(e), true
vraiment, truly
vue (f.), view, sight
  point de vue, point of view

wagon (m.), wagon, coach
  wagon aux bagages (m.), baggage car
  wagon-lit (m.), sleeping car
  wagon-restaurant (m.), dining car
W.C. (m.), toilet (Water Closet)
week-end (m.), weekend

y, there
  y compris, including
yeux (m., plural), eyes

zèbra (m.), zebra
zéro (m.), zero
zut! darn!

un, una; a

los, le, la, the

250

3 212-427-5133